i love you, but...
i'm not **IN LOVE** with you

ANDREW G. MARSHALL

Seven Steps to Putting the Passion Back into Your Relationship

Health Communications, Inc.
Deerfield Beach, Florida

www.hcibooks.com

Library of Congress Cataloging-in-Publication Data

Marshall, Andrew G.
I love you, but—I'm not in love with you : seven steps to saving
  your relationship / Andrew G. Marshall.
    p. cm.
  ISBN-13: 978-0-7573-0548-1 (trade paper)
  ISBN-10: 0-7573-0548-2 (trade paper)
    1. Man-woman relationships.   2. Interpersonal relations.   3. Love.
  4. Interpersonal communications.   I. Title.
  HQ801.M37183 2007
  646.7'7—dc22
                                                                    2007009287

HCI, its logos and marks are trademarks of Health Communications, Inc.

Publisher: Health Communications, Inc.
          3201 S.W. 15th Street
          Deerfield Beach, FL 33442-8190

Interior design and formatting by Lawna Patterson Oldfield

To Polly Vernon and Ed Jaspers:

Thank you for helping

get this book off the ground.

Contents

Contents

Introduction

$\mathcal{F}ive\ years\ ago$, the occasional couple would present themselves at my therapy office after one partner had confessed, "I love you, but I'm not in love with you." To start off, I was surprised. The phrase seemed to belong to a character in a smart New York TV sitcom. Yet real people were using it to describe something profound that was happening to their relationship. But how could someone love but not be *in* love?

These couples would describe each other as best friends or that their relationship was more like a brother and sister, except most were still having sex. In essence, the partnership had become defined by companionship rather than passion—and that was no longer enough. Over time, more and more couples complained of the same problem—until the number was something approaching one in four. Not everyone spontaneously used the phrase, "I love you, but I'm not in love with you," but all recognized the sentiments. For these couples, the dilemma was especially painful: The ones who had fallen out of love still cared deeply about their partners and certainly did not want to hurt them, but they wanted to end the relationship.

A typical couple would be Nick, a forty-two-year-old sales manager, and Anna, a thirty-nine-year-old teacher. They had been married for fifteen years and despite some difficult patches, like Nick's layoff, their relationship had flourished. So when Nick dropped the, "I love you, but" bombshell, Anna was devastated: "I thought we had a happy relationship, I really did. Not perfect, of course, but then who can claim that? I've tried to get him to explain why he doesn't love me anymore, but he keeps saying he doesn't know. The best he has managed is that I don't listen. Except, he's never told me before he was unhappy." Nick explained that the feeling had been building for several years and that he needed to tell their two teenage children and have a trial separation. "He has no honor, no loyalty," Anna complained. "He is completely selfish. I feel he's leaving me for someone he hasn't even met yet."

Faced with couples like Nick and Anna, I turned to the professional literature but found it dominated by couples who dislike, or even hate, each other—whereas I needed to know about couples who did not love enough. Worse still, I could find no research into how prevalent the problem had become, no theories about why it should be happening now, or any suggested treatment program. There was only one solution; I would have to fill the gap myself.

I initiated a research project in which all couples seeking help were asked to fill out a questionnaire after their first session. They were given a list of common problems that could have brought them into counseling. The results were startling:

+ 47 percent complained that the "passion had gone."
+ 43 percent said, "I love my partner but I'm no longer in love (or my partner no longer loves me)."

Many of the traditional reasons for seeking help polled much lower:

+ Money issues: 24 percent
+ An affair: 21 percent
+ Differing opinions on how to bring up children: 19 percent
+ Fights out of control: 15 percent

When couples were asked to choose the problem causing the most distress, "I love my partner but I'm no longer in love (or my partner no longer loves me)" came third at 24 percent, narrowly behind "difficulty understanding each other's viewpoint" at 26 percent, and "argue too much" at 25 percent.

The research also backed up something that I had observed in my therapy office. People who checked the "I love you, but" option were also less likely to also check "we argue too much" and more likely to pick the neutral, "we find it difficult to understand each other's viewpoints."

Anna certainly did not like arguments: "My parents would scream at each other the whole day long, and I swore I'd never put my kids through the same thing." If worst came to worst, she would simply walk away. Meanwhile, Nick was so considerate and good at seeing her side that he talked himself out of any disagreement: "I wish Anna didn't go up to bed so early. I don't get in 'til late, and I'm left tiptoeing around the house alone, but it's not her fault, really, because after 10:00, she can hardly stay awake." In fact, they were both so thoughtful that the only open source of friction was that both enjoyed and, therefore wanted to do, the ironing! This might sound like heaven, but when someone cannot truly voice his or her feelings—even if only about minor issues—the relationship cools. Slowly, over the years, degree by degree, all the emotions are dulled. Ultimately, it is as harmful to argue only occasionally, just as it is to argue all the time.

My second observation from my "I love you, but" (ILYB) clients was that this lack of arguments exacerbates the tendency for two partners, over time, to grow more like each other. The modern trend to be friends as well as lovers is another pressure—as we normally choose friends who are like us. Once again, this might seem wonderful, but relationships need friction, too. It is the grit in the oyster that makes the pearl and the difference that provides the love interest. More important, when there is so much pressure to be everything to each other—to share friends and even tastes—there is little room to be an individual as well as one half of a couple. "I started to feel that I couldn't be myself," explained Nick. "I was trapped by what people expected of me."

The third key observation was that most partners who had fallen out of love had recently had a life-changing experience. In Nick's case, it was the death of his father: "I remember standing at the foot of his bed and thinking, 'Shouldn't I be doing something with my life?' Worse still, I could see how little time I had." While Nick was struggling with abstract questions about the meaning of life, Anna retreated into herself, too: "I was close to Nick's dad. He'd almost been a second father, but I thought I'd be most helpful by offering support. So I held back my tears and didn't burden him with my grief, too." While she thought she was being strong for Nick, he read her response to his father's death as unfeeling, and he felt very alone. Instead of sharing their different reactions, neither said anything for fear of upsetting the other. It was not until later in counseling that all Nick's resentment came tumbling out. Other events, like a milestone birthday, the birth of a child, or a parent's divorce, can also trigger a crisis of self-examination, which, in turn, tips over into questioning the relationship.

Over an initial twelve-month period, I tried some tentative treatment programs with these early ILYB clients and started to read a wider cross section of literature. I researched business experts, philosophers, social biologists, marketing gurus, and also looked into alternative relationships and found a small amount of research into successful couples. Some of these ideas could be taken directly into my counseling room, while others had to be adapted. Slowly, I found something that not only saved relationships, but also helped ILYB couples achieve a much deeper intimacy and a truly satisfying bond.

I decided to write this book for three reasons. First, I wanted to share a program that works both with people in crisis and with other therapists. Second, a lot of the information that can significantly improve a relationship is difficult to pass on in a therapy session. Counseling is about listening to people's problems—not about teaching. With this book, couples and individuals can digest the ideas at their own rate. Third, and most important, I wanted to spread the message that falling out of love does not mean the end of a relationship.

How Does the Program Work?

This book is not a lecture about trying harder or not expecting too much from love—there are plenty of those books already. My mission is to help people understand love and to point out the everyday habits that we think protect relationships but, in fact, undermine them. The most common question, when people hear about my work, is to sidle up and ask, "Is it really possible to fall back in love?" My answer is always the same: an emphatic yes. What's more, couples can emerge with a better knowledge of themselves, a greater understanding of each other, and a stronger bond. This book explains why and how.

Part 1 introduces the Seven Steps to Saving Your Relationship. These help you communicate better, have more productive arguments, take your sex life to a deeper level of intimacy, and find a balance between being fulfilled as an individual and being one-half of a couple. If your relationship has already reached crisis point, Part 2 provides a strategy for talking through the issues and dealing with the immediate fallout. Part 3 shows how to bond again and rediscover love. Alternatively, if you have already separated, Part 3 helps you understand what happened, recognize your options, and learn how to move on to a more fulfilling future. Throughout this book, you will find illustrations from my casebook and from a questionnaire filled out by people throughout North

America who are not in counseling, but who have fallen out of love. However, I have changed names, altered details, and sometimes merged two or three cases to protect each couple's identity and confidentiality. In addition, at the end of each chapter is a series of exercises. These can be done alone or, if you are working through this book with your partner, together.

Part One

The Seven Steps to Saving Your Relationship

Step One

 UNDERSTAND

"You know we've been having problems."

"I thought things were getting better."

"I've been feeling like this for a long time; I hoped things would change."

"What? You didn't say anything."

"It's just that ... I love you, but I'm not *in* love with you."

When a relationship hits a crisis, the natural response is to try to fix it as quickly as possible. But in the panic, it is very easy to get confused about the true nature of the problems and head off in the wrong direction. So the first step is to truly *understand*.

One

What Is Love, Anyway?

In the past, couples split up because they hated each other; today, it is just as likely to be because they don't love each other enough. Love has been elevated from one of the ingredients for a successful relationship into everything: the glue that binds us together. Previous generations may have stayed together for economic need, because of what the neighbors might say, or for the sake of the children, but we are no longer prepared to live in anything other than a passionate and fulfilling relationship. On the one hand, this is wonderful. Within a society fixated on working longer hours, being more productive, and aiming higher, love remains a small beacon of happiness. But on the other hand, these new demands put a lot of strain on our relationships.

If our relationships are going to live or die by love, we need a pretty good idea of what love is and what sustains it.

When everything is going well, we tend to relax, letting love smooth over everyday problems, and do not ask questions—almost as if letting in too much daylight will destroy the magic. This is fine, until the love disappears and the couple is left wondering what happened. One partner cannot explain why he or she might still care, but is no longer in love, while the other wants to know what he or she has done wrong. Sometimes, the partner with ILYB ("I love you, but") will arrive in my counseling office with a list of complaints: "He is disrespectful," "She shouts at the children," "He's rude to my parents," and similar gripes. But however comprehensive, it never explains what happened to the promise: I will love you, no matter what, until the end of time, for better or worse. What happened to the days when just hearing your beloved's name could quicken your pulse, and what about all that walking on air? What about those feelings that the two of you could take on the world? More than anything else, these couples long to know how their passion turned from something special into just something okay—and finally into something disappointing—because without understanding the causes, how can they fix anything?

A typical example is Michael and Elizabeth, both in their late thirties and together since their late teens. "I no longer feel I'm special to Elizabeth," complained Michael. "I know we have responsibilities, but we used to be everything to each other. Now I seem to come way down on the list. I might joke that I come after the kids' guinea pigs, but it's not really very funny." Michael had been feeling like this for several years and had withdrawn into himself. At first, Elizabeth thought there might have been someone else, but finally, Michael confessed that he loved her but was no longer in love and was considering leaving. "We're not a couple of kids sharing french fries in a bus shelter anymore," she moaned. "It can't be how it used to be. Just think of all the things I do for you—cooking, cleaning, ironing. Do you think I feel special every day? Life isn't like that." Michael and Elizabeth were both talking about love but had very different definitions. With no agreement about what constitutes love, their conversations went around in circles.

ILYB is especially frustrating when there is much to celebrate in the relationship. Irene is sixty-one and has been with her husband for over thirty-five years. She lives in Toronto, Ontario, and is one of the respondents to a questionnaire I circulated throughout North America. "We are good friends and have wonderful conversations about everything, but I can't pretend that I wouldn't be happier if the passionate and affectionate sides of myself could be expressed and received," writes Irene. "But I no longer know how to deal with that. I try to show my love in other ways, but the truth is, at times I still feel bereft." With most problems, when someone has the courage to admit everything, he or she expects to be greeted with sympathy and understanding. Sadly, people who have fallen out of love are often told just to try harder. Naomi is thirty-four and comes from New Jersey: "My soul is lost, and I am almost emotionally dead. I confided in my mother, but she just reminded me that I have a wonderful husband who loves his children. She's right. But I just cannot let love into my heart. I want it so badly but just don't know what to do." Instead of feeling supported, Naomi feels more alone than ever before and is no further forward in finding a solution.

Almost every popular song is about love, as are half of all novels and films; we read about it or see it on TV every day. Surely, we should understand love and, at the very least, be able to define it. But this is where the confusion starts. We can love our mothers, our children, and our friends—even chocolate. When it comes to our partners, love can describe both the crazy, heady days at the beginning of a relationship and ten years later, taking his or her hand, squeezing it, and feeling sure of each other. Can one little word really cover so many different emotions? Dictionaries are not much help. They list almost two dozen synonyms—including affection, fondness, caring, liking, concern, attraction, desire, and infatuation, and we all instinctively agree there is a huge gap between "liking" and complete "infatuation." The problem is that we have one word for three very different emotions: the early days/honeymoon passion; the day-to-day intimacy with a long-term partner; and the protective instinct for a child or bond with a parent. To clarify the differences between these three types, we need a new vocabulary, partly to remove the confusion between two partners with different takes—like Elizabeth and Michael—but mainly because by naming and explaining the differences, we will understand love better.

In the mid 1960s, experimental psychologist Dorothy Tennov set out to understand what happens when someone falls in love; she was surprised how few of the founding fathers of her discipline had examined the phenomenon. Freud dismissed romantic love as merely the sexual urge blocked, while pioneering sexologist Havelock Ellis reduced these complicated emotions down to an equation: love = sex + friendship. Once again, we instinctively know that falling in love is far more complicated. So Tennov interviewed some 500 people in depth and found—despite differences in age, sexuality, and background—a startling similarity in how each respondent described his or her feelings during the early days of love. These are some of the most common descriptions of being in love:

+ Intrusive thinking (you can't stop daydreaming about your beloved)
+ An aching in the heart when the outcome is especially uncertain
+ Buoyancy, as if walking on air, if there is a chance of reciprocation
+ An acute sensitivity to any acts or thoughts that could be interpreted favorably ("She wore that dress because she knows I like it"; "He hung back after the meeting so he could talk to me.")
+ A total inability to be interested in more than one person at a time
+ A fear of rejection and unsettling shyness in the presence of the beloved
+ Intensification of the feelings through adversity (at least up to a point)

- ✦ All other concerns fall into the background (as a respondent told her, "Problems, troubles, inconveniences that normally have occupied my thoughts became unimportant.")
- ✦ A remarkable ability to emphasize what is truly admirable in the beloved and avoid dwelling on the negative—even to respond with a compassion for negative qualities and turn them into another positive attribute ("It doesn't matter that he is shy because I can enjoy bringing him out of his shell"; "She might have a temper but that shows how deeply she feels everything.")
- ✦ Despite all the potential for pain, love is a "supreme delight" and "what makes life worth living."

Not only do people all over the world experience almost exactly the same feelings in this early romantic phase, but both men and women also report the same intensity. To distinguish between these overwhelming emotions and the more settled ones of a long-term couple—who are, after all, only too aware of their partner's failings—Tennov coined a new term to describe this early phase of falling in love: Limerence.

Limerence

The obsessive, intrusive nature of Limerence would be immediately recognized by Joshua, a twenty-eight-year-old, whom I counseled. "I met her at a salsa class, the attraction was instant, and we ended up exchanging telephone numbers—even though I knew she was married. It was against everything I believed in, but I couldn't stop myself. It was impossible to work until we'd had our morning talk. I'd ache if she didn't call and even found myself 'just happening' to walk down her road to stare though the window so I could picture where she made those surreptitious calls." Twelve months later, when the affair had ended, Joshua admitted that they came from totally different backgrounds and had little in common. He put the attraction down to "lust," but most of the time, the affair had been non-sexual. Tennov agrees: "Sexual attraction is not 'enough,' to be sure. Selection standards for Limerence are, according to my informants, not identical to those by which 'mere' sexual partners are evaluated, and sex is seldom the main focus for Limerence. Either the potential for sexual mating is felt to be there, however, or the state described is not Limerence."

Limerence can come, as it did for Joshua, when a sparkle of interest is returned and becomes what the French call a *coup de foudre*—a thunderbolt. Alternatively, it can sneak up and, in retrospect, the moment is recognized as something very special. Anthony, a thirty-nine-year-old web designer, had been dating Tasha for several months. They were enjoying each other's company but Anthony had not seen her as the "one" until a visit to an art exhibition: "She was so wrapped up in the painting that she didn't realize I was watching. In that detached split second, I was overcome with tenderness. The vibrant greens and blues spilled from the painting onto Tasha. She had somehow joined the sun-tanned naked bodies from the canvas, the cool water, and the reflections from the trees and the grass. All the natural colors of the scene had been heightened and exaggerated by the artist, and I found myself being sucked into the painting, too. My feelings were bolder and more colorful, too—could that tenderness really be love?"

For other couples, a friendship can turn into something passionate when one-half finally sees the other in a different light. Juliette and Edward, now in their forties, were at school together and shared an interest in music, but nothing more, until Edward's eighteenth-birthday party: "I don't know how, but all of a sudden, I noticed Juliette as a woman. It sort of sneaked up on me—maybe it was her long, dark hair—but suddenly a light switched on: love at first sight, but several months later. I plucked up my courage and decided to kiss her, but I was very aware that she was a friend and worried about how she would take it. It felt odd, and I remember a quizzical look on Juliette's face as I leaned closer, almost like she was saying, 'do you know what you're doing?' No words were exchanged—it was all in the eyes—but I hoped she understood, 'Yes, I do.'"

As hinted at before, Limerence can be the source of as much unhappiness as pleasure. It is possible for the object of Limerence to remain a complete stranger, or to be someone you know who is unaware of your feelings. Even under these barren circumstances, Limerence can still grow and develop. Samantha was taking a language class and became obsessed with her teacher: "The way his tanned muscles would ripple as he reached up to write on the flip chart; the pattern of the springy black hairs on the back of his arms as he'd lean across my desk to mark an exercise; how he'd push his fingers through his thick, black hair. Even if he lived to be a 100, you knew his hair line would never recede." Samantha began to develop a set of complicated scenarios for how a relationship could develop. "My favorite involved my car breaking down after class and the tow truck unable to come for at least five hours, so he'd offer to take me home. Except his car would break down in the middle of a forest—a strange detail, as I lived in the city—and neither of us would have a cell phone. Our only hope of rescue would be a passing car, but nobody would come along that deserted road. So we'd have to snuggle together for warmth." In reality, Samantha was too shy to express her feelings and, in any case, her lecturer was married. Yet years later, the smell of a school corridor— "a strange combination of bleach, unwashed gym clothes, and chalk"— can bring back vivid memories for Samantha that are just as potent as those associated with real long-term relationships.

Tennov describes five stages of Limerence in her book, *Love and Limerence* (republished by Scarborough House in 1999):

1. **Eyes meet.** Although the sexual attraction is not necessarily immediate, there is some "admiration" of the beloved's physical qualities.

2. **Limerence kicks in.** Someone under Limerence will feel buoyant, elated, and ironically free—not just from gravity but emotionally unburdened, too. All these beautiful feelings are attributed to the beloved's fine qualities. Tennov's respondents identified this as probably the last opportunity to walk away.

3. **Limerence crystallizes.** With evidence of reciprocation, either real or interpreted as such, from the beloved, someone under Limerence experiences extreme pleasure, even euphoria. Tennov writes: "Your thoughts are mainly occupied with considering and reconsidering what you may find attractive in the LO (Limerent Object), replaying events that have transpired between you and LO, *and* appreciating qualities in yourself. It is at this point in *West Side Story* that Maria sings 'I Feel Pretty.'"

4. **Obstacles occur and the degree of involvement increases.** "You reach the stage at which the reaction is almost impossible to dislodge," says Tennov, "either by your own act of will or by further evidence of LO's undesirable qualities. The doubt and increased intensity of Limerence undermine your former satisfaction with yourself. You acquire new clothes, change your hairstyle, and are receptive to any suggestion to increase your own desirability in LO's eyes. You are inordinately fearful of rejection."

5. **Mooning about, either in a joyful or a depressed state.** (Tennov's respondents were surprisingly willing to describe themselves as depressed: 42 percent had been severely depressed about a love affair, and 17 percent had even thought of committing suicide.) "You prefer your fantasies to virtually any other activity," writes Tennov, "unless it is a) acting in ways that you believe will help

you attain your Limerent Object, or b) actually being in the presence of your LO." A third option is talking endlessly about your beloved to friends. As all the popular songs about the broken-hearted attest, even being rejected or ignored does not dampen the madness.

Tennov's respondents mentioned eye contact so often—"the way she looked at me, or rather the way she rarely did"—that she believed the eyes rather than the heart to be the true organ of Limerence. Indeed, research by social psychologists Michael Argyle and Mark Cook confirm the importance of eyes meeting across a crowded room. They found that when humans experience intensely pleasurable emotions, our pupils dilate and become larger, which unconsciously and involuntarily betrays our feelings. What is more, a small increase in the secretion of the tear ducts causes the eyes to glisten, producing what Argyle and Cook call the "shining eyes of love."

So, how long does true Limerence last? At the bottom end of the scale, Tennov found few full-blown cases that calmed down before six months had passed. In my opinion, the most frequent—as well as average—duration for Limerence is between eighteen months and three years. This fits with the findings of social biologist Cindy Hayman of Cornell University, who tracked three brain chemicals (dopamine, phenylothylamine, and oxytocin) in 5,000 subjects in thirty-seven different cultures and also found that the intense phase of attraction lasted somewhere between eighteen months and three years.

But once Limerence has faded, does it have to disappear completely? Certainly the crazy, obsessive, possessed side of Limerence cannot be recaptured, but the intense joy, walking on air, and supreme delight elements can return but more as flashbacks than the sustained, full-on, early stages of Limerence. Often, these flashes come after periods of adversity, for example, being separated from your partner while she was away at a conference or during the reconciliation phase after he had an affair. According to Stendhal, a nineteenth-century French writer famous for his essays on love, "The pleasures of love are always in proportion to the fear." Many couples experience a burst of Limerence after an argument, especially during the "making up" phase. Phil and Kimberly experienced a blast of returning Limerence after Phil crashed Kimberly's laptop, destroying a report she'd been writing. "We both hate arguing," said Phil, "but this fight went around and around; even the next morning, we weren't really talking. I saw things my way, and she saw them her way—and that was that. We were completely stuck. At lunchtime, we each had to meet other people. On the way to the car, she brushed her fingers gently across the back of my arm. It felt electric—a huge surge of joy—because I knew she didn't want to fight either. We could work this out. My heart leapt, and I felt like I floated down the street."

Although resolving a conflict or returning from a long trip is the most effective way of reexperiencing Limerence, there are other, less dramatic ideas in the exercise section at the end of this chapter. However, it is important to remember that neither the intense form of Limerence nor the associated biological attraction lasts forever. Do not castigate yourself if you no longer feel the same as at the beginning of the relationship. And maybe it is just as well. Would it really be practical to be forever thinking about our beloved—to the exclusion of everything else—or to be always shy around him or her and fearful of rejection? When people make serious errors of judgment, for example reckless affairs or inappropriate relationships, and later claim to be "blinded by love," they are nearly always describing the effects of Limerence. In many ways, Limerence can be a curse as well as a pleasure.

So what happens to "love" after Limerence? Once again, the problem is how to define terms. Some books and articles refer to "mature love," which sounds very boring, or to "deeper feelings," which seems to be condescending to Limerence—which, although not deep-rooted, is strongly held. Again, we need another new word to explain this second kind of love; therefore, I have coined the term Loving Attachment. This kind of love is not as flashy as Limerence, but it is just as beautiful: your partner stepping out of the bath on a Sunday morning and suddenly seeing him or her from a new angle; watching your children together in the school play and sharing a look of complete pride; or spontaneously buying a bowl of hyacinths for your partner when you had gone out only for a paper. Understanding Loving Attachment is important because it offers an important clue for ILYB. When someone talks of not being in love, he or she is complaining about a lack of Loving Attachment.

Limerence Versus Loving Attachment

Our culture's romantic myths of "True love conquers all" and "I'll love you no matter what" are all built on poets' and songwriters' experiences of Limerence. Although the magic brings us together and helps us over the first few obstacles, to achieve and sustain a relationship, something more is needed: Loving Attachment. Perhaps one of the easiest ways to understand this type of love is to compare it with Limerence. Someone under the spell of Limerence is bound tightly to his or her beloved, however well or badly he or she behaves. In the case of Samantha and her lecturer, because he was unaware of her feelings, he virtually ignored her, but her attraction to him still stayed strong. In contrast, Loving Attachment needs to be fed, or it will wither and die. While Limerence makes someone turn even their beloved's weaknesses into strengths, long-term couples—Loving Attachment couples—are only too aware of their partner's weaknesses. Finally, a couple under the spell of Limerence does not care about practical matters like earning a living because they have "their love to keep them warm," whereas a Loving Attachment couple tackles the complexities of life and its practical demands together.

Unfortunately, the myths about romantic love—and lack of knowledge about Limerence—make us believe that once we have found our partner, we can then relax, because love will automatically bridge any problems. Even when overworked or preoccupied with children, we imagine our partner will understand if he comes at the bottom of the list of priorities, or she will forgive if we fail to complete that task for her. In the short term, Loving Attachment will survive this kind of neglect. But if consistently abused, a relationship with Loving Attachment will deteriorate. "I feel taken for granted," explained Amy, sitting in my office while her husband, Jerry, shifted in his chair until he'd almost turned his back on her. "As long as the house runs smoothly and the kids don't make too much noise, he ignores me. He comes home and turns on the TV or plays on the Xbox with the boys. He doesn't actually talk to me, not about anything important." This was too much for Jerry; he finally turned around and took her hand: "But I love you. Isn't that enough?" He had assumed that their relationship worked in the same way as when they first met, when Limerence was at its height and their bond could survive no matter what. Most couples end up in my office because one partner feels that his or her love is not returned and has, over time, become detached. This was the case with Amy. It is easy to think that love ends because of some monstrous piece of bad behavior, but more often, it decays gradually through a million minor hurts. In fact, Loving Attachment can never be taken for granted and, like anything precious, it needs to be carefully tended.

What Feeds Loving Attachment?

For most people, the following list will be second nature. However, couples under stress will skimp or disregard these relationship necessities.

- ✦ **Listening:** Giving full attention, nodding, asking questions so the speaker knows he or she is truly being heard
- ✦ **Sharing:** Feelings and snippets from your day, or chores
- ✦ **Generosity:** Giving your time, doing a job for your partner that he or she does not like, or buying a small gift
- ✦ **Body contact:** A cuddle on the sofa, stroking the back of your partner's arms in the car, or full sexual contact
- ✦ **Supporting:** Watching your partner play a sport, giving a compliment, watching the kids while your partner takes an adult education course, buying into his or her dreams
- ✦ **A shared sense of humor:** Private jokes, kidding around, and general silliness
- ✦ **The extra mile:** The gestures that are really tough for your partner, like humoring your difficult mother or agreeing to that joint bank account

If Loving Attachment has been lost, is it possible to reattach? I firmly believe it can be, and at the end of this chapter is an exercise to get you started.

Next we come to the third kind of love and more clues to understanding ILYB. If Loving Attachment has been neglected, and the couple has detached, their "love" turns into Affectionate Regard—which is very similar to what we feel for our parents, children, siblings, and best friends. Affectionate Regard will make us care for people, want the best for them, and certainly not want to hurt them, but a person's destiny does not feel intertwined with ours in the way it does with Loving Attachment. In ILYB, the "I love you" invariably means "I have Affectionate Regard for you."

Loving Attachment Versus Affectionate Regard

Although Loving Attachment needs to be nurtured to thrive, this third kind of love is seldom conditional. I call it Affectionate Regard because affection exists largely independently of how the recipient behaves. This is why the bond between parent and child can survive more dislocation and even neglect than the bond between partners. It is a sad truism that many children who have been abused by their parents still want a relationship with them, and generally even the parents of murderers passionately defend their sons or daughters. Of course, most parent/child relationships do not have to survive such extremes. But within even the happiest families, parents can put their children through grief that would not be acceptable from anybody else. Conversely, no matter how often our children disappoint or exasperate us, our Affectionate Regard for them endures. The love for a close friend is also Affectionate Regard, as once again we "let pass" behavior from a friend that would be difficult to accept from a partner. A petty but telling example would be the friend who slurps his coffee: This behavior is mildly annoying when someone pops over for a visit, but living with a slurper would quickly set your teeth on edge. More serious character defects can be overlooked in friends; our lives are not so intertwined and we can either close our eyes to bad behavior or simply see less of someone. This is why friendships ebb and flow, but the Affectionate Regard remains.

Confusing Affectionate Regard with Loving Attachment can cause a lot of misery. This is what had happened in the case of Nick and Anna, the sales manager and teacher profiled in the introduction. His relationship needs had not been met, and he had detached. "We always go out with other couples," he complained. Almost in despair, he asked his wife, "When was the last time we went out just the two of us?" Anna saw things differently: "But we still had fun, that time we all rented the cottage down in North Carolina—all those endless games of Monopoly. That game of strip Monopoly!" Nick couldn't disagree but, in his eyes, their marriage had become like a warm bath—comfortable but not very exciting. Anna had not realized how bad things had become because she had misread the Affectionate Regard, left over from fifteen years of shared memories, as Loving Attachment. Indeed, Nick described their relationship as one between brother and sister. For him, the loss of the passion from the early Limerence was a particular letdown.

So why can Loving Attachment slip into Affectionate Regard? I will go into this further over the next few chapters, but there are two main culprits: neglecting physical intimacy and not allowing each other to be different enough. "I have a lot of respect for Bobby's opinions," writes Shelley from Athens, Georgia. "But I wish he didn't take it for granted that I will always go along with him." Their sixteen-year-old daughter had been invited to a movie by a school friend. However, the boyfriend arrived in an old wreck, and Shelley's husband put his foot down. "Bobby thought the boy looked reckless—he had on ripped jeans and a ratty T-shirt. So Bobby insisted on driving them and picking them up. Our daughter was rolling her eyes, and I tried to tell Bobby it was okay, as long as they weren't back late, but he cut me off. 'We've always seen eye to eye about the kids—let's not ruin things now,' he said. And although I basically agree, it was like I'm not allowed an opinion." Instead of being two individuals in a relationship, partners become one amorphous couple, and either one or both will complain about losing their identity—a common symptom of ILYB. Here is one of the most difficult paradoxes about sustaining Loving Attachment: for a long-term relationship, instead of Limerence, we need to find enough similarities with our partner—either culturally, socially, or emotionally—to make a connection, yet we need enough difference to keep the relationship from stagnating. Often, it is the friction of rubbing off each other's rough edges that provides the spark of passion. Look at all the great fictional characters we fall in love with at the cinema, at the theater, and in books: Rhett Butler and Scarlett O'Hara, Cathy and Heathcliff, Elizabeth Bennet and Mr. Darcy, Romeo and Juliet. Not only are they all passionate in their relationships, but each half is also very different from the other.

Summary

+ Popular romance feeds us the ideal of unconditional love; during the Limerence phase, something approaching this is often achieved. However, once a couple has moved into Loving Attachment, truly unconditional love becomes a distant memory.

+ Unlike Limerence, Loving Attachment dies if it is not reciprocated—especially sexually. However, Loving Attachment can also last forever.

+ When a relationship has been going happily enough along, it is possible to confuse the warm feeling as Loving Attachment, when in reality it has become Affectionate Regard: caring for and wanting the best for someone but with no underpinning romantic passion.

+ When someone says: "I love you, but I'm not in love with you," he or she probably means, "I have Affectionate Regard for you but I have lost the Loving Attachment." In the worst cases, there is an additional layer: "I miss the Loving Attachment so much that I now feel nostalgic for the excitement of Limerence."

+ We consider falling in love, and sustaining love, as something magical, and we deliberately choose to shroud the process in mystery. Although understanding how a magician saws a lady in half might spoil the illusion, understanding love is the first step in discovering how to revitalize it.

EXERCISES

Limerence Exercise—Eye Contact

To quote the writers of popular songs, in the early days of Limerence "I only have eyes for you" and "I can't take my eyes off you." However, once we have settled down and moved into togetherness, there are countless other distractions from our partner's beautiful eyes: the television, the newspaper, and deadlines. "When my partner looks at me, stops and gives me his full attention, that's when I feel most loved," writes Katie from Montréal, Québec. When asked what made her feel unloved, she replied: "When I am ignored as a person." When Harvard psychologist Zick Rubin conducted an experiment using sophisticated recording apparatus, he discovered that couples whose questionnaires indicated a greater intensity of love looked into each other's eyes for significantly longer than couples less in love. In fact, couples in love spend 75 percent of the time looking at each other when they are talking, rather than the usual 30 to 60 percent.

We could debate forever: Do we stop really looking at our partners and the love fades, or does the love fade and we stop looking? Certainly, Rubin believes that staring into each other's eyes can trick the brain into releasing phenoylothylamine, a natural amphetamine and one of the brain chemicals that makes people fall in love. Try the following eye contact exercise:

1. Attract your partner's attention, either by calling his or her name or putting your hand on his or her shoulder. The second tactic is particularly effective, as you can use gentle pressure to bring her or his head away from the computer screen, for example, to look at you.

2. Wait until you have your partner's full attention and he or she is looking into your eyes and wondering what is happening.

3. Look into your partner's eyes. It does not need to be for more than a second, just long enough so that you really see each other.

4. Give him or her a kiss on the lips.

5. Your partner will be suspicious and probably ask something like, "What do you want?"

6. Just smile and walk away.

7. Repeat the next day.

If your partner asks about the kiss, don't be defensive ("Can't I even ask for a kiss?") or go on the attack ("I have to ask for a kiss because you never give me one"). Just explain how you used to enjoy eye contact when you were first dating. Although at first, this exercise will seem forced, before long, it will be incorporated into your routines and will become second nature.

Limerence Exercise—Connections

In the early stages of Limerence, Tennov noted how people are desperate to make links between themselves and their beloved. "If a certain thought has no previous connection with the Limerent Object," she writes, "you immediately make one. You wonder or imagine what the LO would think of the book in your hand, the scene you are witnessing, the fortune or misfortune that is befalling you. You find yourself visualizing how you will tell about it, how LO will respond, what will be said between you, and what actions will—or might— take place in relation to it." How different this seems from the dull evening routine of many long-term couples: "How was your day?" "Fine." End of conversation.

To reintegrate this element of Limerence back into your relationship, look for events that can be stored up and shared in the evening with your partner. You could even write them down in a notebook, so as not to forget. There are two secrets to making these snippets interesting. First, look for the details that bring a story to life. Second, seek out events, opinions, and characters that play to your partner's particular interests.

Often, with ILYB couples, one partner has been editing his or her daily news. It can be for a variety of reasons: fear of boring the partner; a desire to protect the partner from the unpleasantness of the daily business grind; a way to forget about minor irritations. All these reasons may be valid, but holding back creates a gulf between you and your partner. So make certain not to edit and, instead, just like in the early stages of Limerence, make a full and frank disclosure. A good start is telling your partner something about the day ahead when you say goodbye in the morning and replaying something that happened when you return in the evening.

Ultimately, everyone needs a witness to their lives—without one, we feel invisible, misunderstood, and—in the worst cases—unloved. So listen attentively to your partner's news and ask questions to draw him or her out and show that you are truly interested.

Loving Attachment Exercise

Try auditing everything that happened yesterday between you and your partner.

- Start from when you woke up and make a list down one side of the piece of paper. A typical list would be something like this: breakfast, got ready for work, kissed goodbye, called from work, went on a walk, ate supper together, talked about the day; watched TV. On the weekends, it would be longer and more involved.
- Now look back over the list and ask yourself what, if anything, fed your Loving Attachment.
- Give yourself a checkmark beside anything positive on the list, but be certain the event has truly strengthened your bond. For example, a phone call to chat could be included but not one to ask your partner to pick up something at the grocery store.
- Are there any other items that could be changed so that tomorrow they could be transformed into feeding Loving Attachment? For example, massaging her feet while you watch TV, or leaving some freshly squeezed orange juice on the kitchen counter for when he comes down later.
- Could you add in an act of kindness tomorrow, like running her a bath or sending him a sexy text message?
- Is there anything on the list that you wished you had not done? Often, we conveniently forget our less loving acts, so be sure to write them down, too. This will encourage you to be more patient tomorrow.

Here are some of the questions my clients ask about the Loving Attachment audit:

Q. How long does it take to make a difference?

A. Changes do not happen overnight. Generally, it takes couples three or four weeks to make a significant difference in their feelings about each other.

Q. If I have fallen out of love with my partner, shouldn't it be up to him or her to change?

A. When we're upset with people, our natural instinct is to treat them less well. Guess what? They normally sink down to our level, and relationships become trapped in a negative circle. Why not lead by example and do something nice instead? Your partner might not immediately respond in kind, but before long, she or he will feel better disposed and ready to return the favor. Miracle of miracles, you have set up a positive circle. It just takes somebody to make the first move. Why not you?

Two

The Six Stages of a Relationship

In classic love stories, eyes meet across a crowded room. Two people fall in love, get married, and set up a home together. But what comes after "happily ever after"? Our culture offers a few landmark events—engagement, wedding, christening—but not every couple can or wants to fit into this pattern. Without a proper template of what to expect, how can we tell whether problems are a natural part of a relationship maturing and changing, or are a fundamental flaw? Unfortunately, psychologists and social scientists are not much help. They have put their energy into studying failing relationships and have virtually ignored happy ones. So, most couples are left fumbling in the dark, comparing themselves with friends but with little true understanding.

In the early 1990s, when I started seeing gay couples, there were even fewer ideas about what happened after their first exchanged glances than for heterosexuals. So I started researching the literature and came across a study by Dr. David McWhirter and Andrew Mattison *(The Male Couple: How Relationships Develop)*, which had, for five years, tracked 156 gay couples in California between the ages of twenty and sixty-nine. None of these couples was in therapy, which made the couples representative of the general population. McWhirter and Mattison soon found patterns and went on to identify a series of key stages that gay couples went through, each with specific issues and problems. Using my own experience from counseling, I adapted this model and found it so useful that I presented my findings to colleagues. Before I was even halfway through, it became obvious to all of us that these stages were equally applicable to heterosexual couples. By taking away all society's expectations about how relationships should progress, we had revealed the underlying patterns for how all partnerships actually develop.

My road map, from the first tentative "I love you" to a whole lifetime together, has six stages; each of which has particular hurdles and lessons for keeping love alive. In some cases, couples will interpret issues that arise naturally when crossing from one stage to another as personal failure or even as "falling out of love." In reality, however, the Loving Attachment has moved into another phase and been subtly changed. Other couples are simply stuck at one point on the journey or one partner has moved more quickly into the next stage than the other, opening up a gap of different attitudes and expectations. This chapter explores each stage, discusses when they happen, and looks at the skills to be acquired.

Stage One: Blending

First year to eighteen months into the relationship: The new lovers want nothing more than to be together. Dorothy Tennov, who named this phenomenon (see more in Chapter 1), writes: "The goal for Limerence is not possession, but a kind of merging, a 'oneness' the ecstatic bliss of mutual reciprocation." Every couple has special memories from this time. Katie is thirty-three and comes from Montréal, Québec. She writes: "I remember hanging out at the park, walking, talking, eating. I was sitting on his lap kissing him, when he stole the gum out of my mouth. I thought it was hilarious, so I started laughing, that kind of feel-good laugh." Couples at this stage also report high sexual activity. Paula and Mark had been dating for three months when Paula admitted, "We took to brushing each other's teeth and using the same toothbrush. I know it sounds disgusting but I think it's really sexy and has brought us even closer." All differences are overlooked or ignored as two people blend into one.

Blending provides new experiences and an opportunity for self-improvement. If one half of the couple has a passion, for example, for opera, mountaineering, Egyptology, or dog breeding, even if the new partner has previously had no interest, the new partner will immerse himself or herself into the hobby. It might start as part of the process of sharing everything with the beloved, but it can build into a lifetime of enjoyment. "Dating Paula, I actually felt smarter," explained Mark, a twenty-nine-year-old who works in information technology. "I hadn't gone to college; I just learned on the job. Although Paula had a degree, she was so interested in everything about me that I gained enough confidence to speak up more at work." Mark's experiences are typical; during Blending, partners appropriate desired qualities from each other and integrate them into their own personality.

The intensity of togetherness means that both halves feel that they understand their partner and are completely understood in return. When couples look back at this period, it seems full of magic and madness. In fact, humans need a bit of both; otherwise how could you trust a stranger enough to let her or him into your life?

Most Common Problems

The following issues often come to the fore during Blending:

◆ Each partner is frightened of upsetting the other and of love being withdrawn, so everything possible is done to avoid arguments.

✦ If there is an argument, it feels like the end of the world. Unlike couples who have been together for years, couples in Blending have no experience of getting angry with each other, disagreeing, and making up again. Intellectually, Blending couples know it is possible to survive a fight but with no actual proof of living through one, they worry that any disagreement could be fatal.

✦ One partner holds back for fear of losing his or her identity.

Skill: Letting Go

It is important to surrender to the feelings during Blending. On the one hand, Limerence helps a couple let down its barriers, but at the same time, the rational head is forever warning, "Be careful." Relationships put two fundamental human instincts at war with each other: We all long to be close—to be understood, to hold, or to be held by another person—yet we also want to be in control, to be masters of our own lives. Successful relationships strike a balance between these two needs. However, to start on the journey—especially as we grow older and more cynical—we need to trust and to believe that this time, it will be different.

Stage Two: Nesting

Second and possibly third year: The couple becomes more committed and decide to move in together. Sexual desire moves from perhaps three times a day to a more manageable level. Finally, the couple is aware of things beyond the bedroom and creating a home together becomes the new dimension to express love. This is where Loving Attachment begins. But living together and decreasing levels of Limerence mean that issues suppressed during Blending come up to the surface. Previously, when visiting each other's places, it was easier to avoid arguments over "who does what," but in Nesting, these practical issues become center stage. "It just wasn't the same anymore," said Nina who had been with Juan for just under two years. "I got really frightened that I was falling out of love. In some ways, that wasn't a bad thing. I was concentrating better at work—goodness knows what my colleagues must have thought when I'd spend half the day on the phone to Juan." While the previous stage capitalized on the attraction and minimized the distractions, moving in together can highlight the differences. "I thought Nina also wanted us to buy a place of our own, our own little corner," said Juan, "but she thought paying off her student loan was more important. For the first time, I looked at her and thought, 'Do I really know this woman?'" Fortunately, instead of denying their different opinions or ignoring them, Nina and Juan talked through and resolved their argument. "We've agreed to buy a few pieces of really good furniture that we can take with us," said Juan. "We're just putting a layer of paint over the worst areas of this rented apartment," added Nina. "Nina's got a really good eye," said Juan. "I know it's not much, but when we show our friends, I really feel we've achieved something: This is us," Nina finished his thought off. Unfortunately, some Nesting couples, especially those with ILYB, worry about their emerging differences—"What's wrong with us?" is a typical cry. These couples, in particular, need reassurance that their relationship is not dying but moving into another phase.

Most Common Problems

The following issues often come to the fore during Nesting:

+ Familiarity can breed annoyance—eccentricities have transformed themselves into nasty habits.
+ Often, arguments center around "male" and "female" roles in the

house. No matter how modern a couple might be, moving in together can reawaken old role models from childhood.

✦ Arguments go around in circles without getting resolved.

✦ Long-term tracking by the University of Texas suggests eighteen months to three years of courtship as the optimum period for a happy marriage. But some couples find commitment difficult and find that deciding to live together is a big decision.

✦ Previously, during Blending, the couple only had eyes for each other, but during Nesting, friends and family become important again. The return of these outside forces can cause tensions between the couple.

Skill: Arguing

Often, the arguments seem to be about petty things—like whose responsibility it is to clean the bath or which color to paint the bedroom—and couples, especially ILYB couples, often feel it is pointless to make a scene. However, this type of argument should not be avoided, partly because if they don't argue, the issues will fester, but mainly because arguing provides an opportunity to practice settling disagreements. It is far better to learn on minor issues, where the stakes are low, than wait until something major and unavoidable crops up.

Stage Three: Self-Affirming

Third or fourth year: Up to this point, couples have always stressed their similarities—perhaps encouraging a partner to join in with a favorite hobby or even giving something up to spend more time together. However, during Self-Affirming, a couple has to feel confident enough to enjoy separate activities, to remember that there exists an "I" as well as a "we." After all, it does not take two people to go to the home-improvement superstore and chose a hammer. Not only is it natural for the couple's individual traits, habits, and characteristics to reemerge during the Self-Affirming stage, but the relationship actually *needs* each partner's individuality to ensure growth.

An example of a couple who successfully negotiated the self-actualizing skill of being independent and interdependent are Maya and Ray, who both have children from previous relationships. "At the beginning, we'd only do stuff as a whole family," explains Ray, "but after a while, I missed playing tennis. Because both my son and Maya's boys were interested, too, I started coaching them on Saturday mornings. I felt guilty when I suggested it because I didn't want to exclude Maya, but she was actually happy to take my daughter shopping. And it doesn't stop us all from meeting up for lunch." On the first week of the new arrangement, Maya was not so sure, but she was soon won over: "It was stupid really to expect to be everything to each other. Ray doesn't like going to the theater, and there's really nothing to stop me going at the beginning of the week with one of my friends—and it's cheaper then." Ray and Maya found other benefits, too. "Being apart gave us something to talk about when we met up later," explained Ray.

During this stage, each partner has to balance what is in his or her best interest with those of the relationship. This can come as quite a shock, especially after Blending and Nesting, where the needs of the relationship have always come first. Some couples pretend their personal needs are not important, but this builds up long-term resentment and potential identity issues—a hallmark of ILYB. Another problem during Self-Affirming is one partner asserting his or her individual needs sooner than the other. This is often read as personal criticism—"Why don't you want to spend time with me anymore?"—rather than a natural phenomenon of this relationship stage.

Most Common Problems

The following issues often come to the fore during Self-Affirming:

+ If one half has no clear idea of who he or she is, or has low self-esteem, it can seem more comfortable to hide in a couple identity than to reestablish his or her own parallel, separate identity.
+ With ILYB couples, one partner will often think the other's time alone is a threat to the partnership; or one partner will be unable to voice his or her independent personal needs.
+ One partner tries to stop the other having personal time, for fear it will signal the end of the relationship.
+ Power struggles emerge center stage.

Skill: Compromise

If the squabbles during nesting have been resolved, the couple finds it easier to deal with the bigger issues that have been lurking behind the pettiness. During the first two stages, the basic human need to be close has been at the forefront. Now, with Self-Affirming, the need to be in control of our lives reasserts itself. So the couple remembers its individual needs and begins negotiating how much personal time is permissible. Often, this can take hours and hours of discussion, and particularly with smaller issues, this can be exhausting. Compromise is important; otherwise, the balance will fall too much in one person's favor and ultimately undermine the relationship.

Stage Four: Collaborating

Approximately fifth to fourteenth year: Couples use the security gained from within the relationship, along with a greater sense of themselves gained from Self-Affirming, to launch successful outside projects. It could be a career change, a return to school, or simply new interests. This stage is called Collaborating because of the high degree of support the other partner gives. The excitement and freshness generated is brought back into the relationship and shared. Alternatively, the project can be a joint one—using complementary skills—the most common of which is having children together. Couples who meet later in life may decide to launch a business or travel together. Whatever the joint or individual goal, it brings new things into the relationship and avoids stagnation.

During Collaborating, reliability and dependability replace the insecurity and fear of possible loss from the previous stages. Couples have earned their easy familiarity and have developed complementary skills around the house; they know how the other thinks and feels, but without the illusions of the first year. A shared shorthand, rather than the previous stage's hours of negotiation, is used for sorting out differences. Although this type of communication is time effective, it can cause misunderstandings. If a couple is tired and stressed by children, one partner often needs extra reassurance. "I sort of know that Miranda loves me," said Don, "but it wouldn't have hurt her to show me on a couple of occasions." "When we first met," Miranda responded, "he'd kiss different parts of my body and tell me that he loved them. It seems stupid to ask, but it would be so nice to have that again." If this type of thinking is not dealt with, one half will feel isolated—a housemate rather than a lover—and become a ripe case for ILYB.

Most Common Problems

During Collaborating, couples have to overcome the following obstacles:

+ Taking each other for granted, or one partner growing quicker and therefore risking leaving the other behind; this is especially common for couples who met in their late teens and early twenties.

+ If there is poor communication, one partner can become too wrapped up in an outside project and neglect the other.

+ There is a fine line between separate activities that enrich the relationship and those that cause the couple to grow apart.

+ This is probably the hardest stage of the six stages. It is, therefore, no surprise that the average duration for a failed first marriage in the United States is 8.2 years for a man and 7.9 years for a woman (source: U.S. Census Bureau, 2001).

Skill: Generosity

Previously, compatibility and common goals were the ingredients for a successful relationship. In these later stages, a lack of possessiveness is the key. It can be a difficult transition and especially hard when one partner launches into something new when the other is either not ready or has not found his or her own path. ILYB couples have often found independence within the relationship difficult; this is unfortunate because couples who successfully negotiate the issues of collaborating stop living in each other's pockets. The extra distance helps keep the interest in each other alive and minimizes the potential for boredom. Couples at this stage have to be generous enough to bless each other's projects and believe they will ultimately improve, not undermine, the relationship.

Stage Five: Adapting

Fifteen to twenty-five years: These couples are busy adapting to the changes thrown at them rather than dealing with internal changes within the relationship. These can be everything from children leaving home to aging parents. By now, each partner has given up the fantasy of what the other person might be and tends to think, "He has always been like this and probably always will" or "What's the point of talking about her bad habits; actually, they're quite endearing." Perversely, when someone stops trying to change us and accepts us as we are, this is when we are most likely to bend. Couples at this stage feel contented; friendship and companionship are important. With increased self-confidence and less concern about what other people think, this is often a period of sexual reawakening. The frequency might not be as high as the first stage, but the quality is much better.

An example of how outside pressures can impact a couple is again Nick and Anna, first mentioned in this book's introduction. Nick felt extra responsibility for his mother following his father's death. Meanwhile, Anna talked about what would happen when their two teenage boys went off to college and how empty the house would seem. For Anna and Nick, looking at how their relationship had changed through the first five stages of love provided not only a fresh perspective, but also a breakthrough in their counseling. Previously, Anna had been always upbeat, always focusing on the positives about the relationship. Concentrating on the challenges during the Adapting stage, in her case the boys' leaving home, Anna said: "It's not just their physical presence, because they're always out, but the thought that it will be just the two of us. I feel all empty." She turned to Nick: "Just you and me for Sunday dinner." Now, Nick felt she understood that real changes needed to be made in order to save their relationship.

Although Collaborating might be the hardest stage, Adapting is the one most likely to throw up ILYB. The downside of accepting partners, warts and all, is that it makes change seem impossible. With this viewpoint, "She or he has always been like this" quickly shifts from reassuring to depressing. Both men and women tell me: "I want to feel special again." However, by taking a fresh look and doing a little work, what seems stale and empty soon becomes warm with life again.

Most Common Problems

The following issues often come to the fore during Adapting:

+ Couples can take each other for granted and become less expressive and less likely to show emotion.
+ Although there are advantages to accepting each other's foibles, there is also a darker side. ILYB couples, in particular, often assume that the partner is incapable of change, so ending the relationship seems like the only option.
+ Sometimes during a crisis, one half might wish to retreat back to the safety of an earlier stage. Men who have been laid off are compelled to start home improvements of the Nesting stage, or want a return to the closeness of Blending. Women who previously shouldered the majority of the caring—for children or elderly relatives—can return to Self-Affirming.
+ One partner will assume that the other has enough to worry about and not confide his or her own problems.
+ "Sleeper" problems begin to burst to the surface, reawakened by family events. For example, the death or serious illness of a parent can make someone reassess his or her childhood, and that leads to taking a closer look at the relationship today. A couple's children reach the same age as when they first met, and thereby unwittingly bring back issues long since buried. However, these connections are difficult to spot, so couples need to keep talking rather than retreating into separate corners.

Skill: Listening

By this stage, couples feel they know each other very well. However, major life changes—bereavement, milestone birthdays, and teenagers' traumas—can hit in entirely unpredictable ways. Adapting couples make assumptions about their partners' reactions and needs based on the past, which is not always the best predictor for the future. Therefore, it is important to listen—really listen—both to what is being said and what is being left unsaid. Some people try to solve their partner's problems, but listening is more important, especially when someone is still absorbing the shock of change.

Stage Six: Renewing

Twenty-five years to fifty-plus: Older couples are often the most romantic and the closest. This stage is much more than an echo of the Limerence during Blending. Closeness at Blending was based on the promise of a future together. Now the bond is based on the reality of a lifetime together. Renewing partners stop looking outside the relationship and focus all their attention inside. In effect, they have come full circle and begin reaping the benefits of the investment in their relationship. Shared memories and private jokes are very important for Renewing couples: "Every night before I turn out the light, I tell Martha that I love her," says Tim, "but she has to chip in that she loves me more than I love her. Maybe she's right—we've been through a lot together, but I've always known that I can count on her." This sort of security makes these the couples least likely to have ILYB. However, when it does infect a relationship at this stage, the shame of not being able to solve the problems can be particularly undermining. Irene from Toronto, Ontario, who has been with her husband for thirty-seven years, writes, "It is hard to admit at sixty-one that I can't resolve these issues, and I am embarrassed to talk about them." However, like many people with years of negotiating, letting things ride, and pulling together, Irene remains upbeat. "I suppose every relationship is an ongoing work and can continue to evolve after so many years—maybe even more so with all this experience behind us."

Most Common Problems

Although there are fewer problems at Renewing, in comparison with the early stages, there are still issues for couples to overcome:

+ Sometimes, like the Blending stage, these partners can be afraid to voice differences. In particular, this happens when other people start encroaching on the couple's time together—for example, children expecting too much help watching the grandchildren.
+ Health worries can isolate and turn closeness into claustrophobia. However, these are just minor difficulties for the relationship, and this stage can truly be called the best of times.

Skill: Patience

As we grow older, we seem to become a caricature of ourselves. For example, someone who might previously have worried only about being late starts doing dry runs of journeys to make certain he or she knows exactly how long it will take. Not surprisingly, this can also make a partner more difficult to live with. Therefore, patience and understanding can be useful skills to negotiate a way through idiosyncrasies and keep the worst in check.

What if I Don't Fit These Stages?

Generally, the first three stages work at whatever age someone meets his or her partner, whether it is first love or love number ninety-nine. The fourth and fifth stages are of shorter duration for couples who meet later in life and for second marriages. The sixth stage, however, is another universal experience. Remember that the Six Stages of a Relationship are a guide, not a prescription. So don't worry if you have not done everything in the right order. For an example, some couples have a child together (Stage Four: Collaborating) before moving in together (Stage

Two: Nesting). Although this makes it harder to balance the independence and interdependence of a successful relationship (a crucial skill in Stage Three: Self-Affirming), most couples figure it out. It makes for a bumpier ride, but then the potential for growth is even greater. Alternatively, when times are tough, you might find yourself retreating back to an earlier stage. A classic example is a couple recommitting to the relationship after one of them has had an affair—they will spend several intense months Blending again, although this stage will be much shorter the second time around.

Summary

+ Relationships have a natural rhythm, and each stage has a natural season.

+ Although every partnership is different and subject to its own particular circumstances, following the general pattern makes for an easier journey.

+ During times of stress, couples or one half of the couple will sometimes retreat to an early stage. However, once secure again, they will boomerang back to their natural stage.

+ Problems arise because people assume their partners will always have the same needs as at the start of the relationship, but life changes us and our expectations.

+ Getting stuck at one stage, through not learning the key lessons, can seriously undermine a relationship.

+ ILYB couples often find the Self-Affirming stage hard because they prefer to stress "couple" needs rather than individual needs.

+ Understanding these six stages is the first step to diagnosing some of the problems behind an ILYB crisis. It can also be the first step on the fast track to a fulfilling partnership.

EXERCISES

Although each exercise has been designed for the relevant stage of love, the skills can be useful at any time. So it is worth browsing through all the exercises and finding other ideas for tackling your issues.

Blending: Get in Touch with Your Inner Adult

New love can turn even the most self-assured adults into frightened teenagers again. This exercise aims to help you find the competent adult side of your personality again.

1. Down one side of a notebook, make a list of the things you argued about in the first year of previous relationships.
2. Down the other side, fill in how you solved them. This will get you back in touch with your hard-earned life skills.
3. If you find it difficult to remember problems, here are a few suggested headings: money, household chores, time apart, friends, child care, and how often each of you initiates telephone calls.
4. Finally, think about how you can use these skills to solve today's problems.

Arguments are vital to clear the air and learn about each other's needs. When your head has seen that these issues can be solved, it will be easier to let go and trust your heart.

Nesting: Hot Seating a Decision

Moving in together is a big decision, and some couples try to put it off for as long as possible. If you are having trouble taking the plunge, remember that relationships cannot stand still—they need to develop. The best way to deal with ambivalence is to "hot seat" the feelings.

Normally, we try to talk down our partner's fears. For every potential problem, we have an immediate answer. This might be a practical solution, reassurance ("Don't worry, I would never do that . . .") or dismissal ("Don't be so stupid"). With this exercise, you not only listen to your partner's fears, but also ask him or her to expand them and discuss all the "what ifs." Try questions like this: What will be the consequences of moving in together? What other disadvantages are you worried about? What is the worst that could happen? What else?

Don't be afraid of silence while your partner thinks. As a counselor, I find that nodding my head encourages people to open up further. This actively shows that you are listening but does not interrupt someone's thought patterns. Don't be tempted to talk down the problems, just keep going with a fear until all the possibilities have been exhausted. Next, jot down a heading that encapsulates the fears (for example, "lack of space") and move onto the next area. If the fears come out in a rush, write them all down, and then tackle the "what if" scenarios one by one.

Once all the fears have been given a heading, you will begin to see which are the most important. After a fear has been named and is down on paper, my clients will often say, "Actually I'm not that bothered about that one." So I cross it off the list. After listening to your partner's fears, identify the ones that you share and add any different fears of your own.

Once everything is out in the open and you feel listened to, your fears are much more manageable. Now you are finally ready to look for possible solutions.

Self-Affirming: Relationship Board Meeting

The following exercise will not only help separate the individual from shared responsibilities, but also provide an opportunity for compromise—the main asset for this stage.

1. On separate cards, write down the major tasks and responsibilities that your life together generates. The list could include money, social life, the cars, the yard work, cooking, grocery shopping, decorating, insurance, paying bills, families, making large purchases, vacations, pets, household chores, and laundry. Some couples like to include abstract ideas like fun, spontaneity, and cuddling. The choice is up to you, but the more cards and the more detailed, the better.

2. Each partner divides a piece of paper into three columns: me, you, and us.

3. Next, each of you writes where you feel each task should go; afterward, share your responses and the thinking behind them. Often, you will simply agree on who does what but often, there will be a proviso—for example, one partner looks after the cars but deciding on a replacement will be a joint responsibility. These provisos are opportunities to clarify how far one partner's power extends.

4. Remember that compromises work only when there is something in it for both parties. So go back and check: Does the division feel fair? Did one of you back down too quickly? Was one of you too ready to please? With genuine compromise, there are no winners and losers.

Here is an example of the Relationship Board Meeting in action. Samantha instantly took the card with their social life, but subsequently admitted: "I've never been very good with money and have no idea how to budget. Bob is very good, so I let him take over the bill paying and working out how much we spend in different areas. It was a relief to stop worrying about it." Bob was happy to take the card with these particular responsibilities. It soon became clear where each partner's strengths lay. The problems arose when either Bob or Samantha felt they were not properly consulted in the other's areas of expertise. So we looked for a compromise. Samantha consulted Bob about whether he wanted to go to a particular concert, but she bought the tickets and checked whether other friends wanted to join them. Bob consulted Samantha about budgets but he made the arrangements—like consolidating their loans. The secret is to find a balance that plays to individual strengths without undermining the loving bond.

Collaborating: Finding Your Dream

If you have yet to find a project, either together or separately, this exercise should help. Before starting, it is important to understand the blocks to reaching your potential. Instead of fantasizing about a potential project or interest and properly investigating the possibilities, many people immediately tell themselves:

- "It's not practical." (Forget about the practicalities; anything is possible in dreams.)
- "It won't bring in any money." (Dreams feed your soul, express who you are, and

provide an interest so all-consuming that time just disappears. It could be taking an art course, putting a tennis court in the backyard, or getting down your golf handicap. Money does not come into it.)

- "I'm not talented enough." (First, dreams are about enjoying yourself, so whether you do something well, indifferently, or badly is completely unimportant. If you enjoy it, keep on doing it. Second, researchers have found that anybody can reach professional standards in anything, no matter what their original aptitude. It just takes about 10,000 hours of practice. So who knows?)

Having temporarily silenced your internal critic, you are now ready:

1. Find somewhere quiet so you won't be disturbed.
2. Close your eyes and imagine where you would like to live, and then think about what work, what kind of relationship, what social life, what hobbies.
3. Imagine all the details, so that the fantasy seems as real as possible. Don't rule anything out as impossible until you've finished creating your perfect life.
4. Really fill in the pictures: what colors? what smells? what sounds?
5. Imagine a door in a room in your dream world, open it, and enter into the dream. What more can you learn as you really immerse yourself?
6. Open your eyes and work out the how to start realizing your dream.
7. The next day, make a start: Book the golf lessons, buy a book about watercolor painting, or start measuring your yard for the tennis court.

Adapting: Listening Skills

Couples at this relationship stage think that they know so much about their partners that they can predict what they are going to say—so they may have stopped actually listening.

Everybody thinks that they are good at listening—after all, it just involves a bit of concentration and not saying anything. Simple. Or is it? In 1984, two American professors of medicine, Howard Beckman and Richard Frankel, recorded how long doctors let patients talk without interruption. The average time was just *eighteen seconds.* Remember, these doctors knew they were being studied, so one would imagine they were trying to show off their listening skills. When the doctors were presented with the research, two things happened: First, they insisted that they had let their patient talk for much more than eighteen seconds; second, they claimed that if they listened without interruption they would never get anything done, as the patients would talk endlessly. So Beckman and Frankel did some follow-up research. This time, the patients were allowed to talk for as long as they wished, without interruption. Most talked for only thirty seconds, and no patient talked for more than ninety seconds.

This listening exercise is very simple, but one of the most effective.

1. Flip a coin to decide who goes first.
2. Partner number one can talk for as long as he or she likes about a current issue—without interruption.
3. To make certain that partner number two is really listening, rather than rehearsing an answer, she or he has to summarize the main points when partner number one has finished. Three examples of what your partner talked about will normally suffice.
4. Swap roles. Partner two talks while partner one listens.
5. Partner one summarizes number two's views.
6. Repeat the above as many times as necessary.

Renewing: Sculpting Your Relationship

Couples at this stage have known each other for so long that it is good to have a fresh perspective. This exercise also brings complex feelings to the surface and helps put them into words. It can be done alone but is better if completed with your partner.

1. Take a pile of change and spread it out on a table.
2. If you are doing this with your partner, divide the change up so that you have half each.
3. Without conferring, each person chooses one coin to represent him- or herself, and then one for the partner and each member of the family.
4. Now you are going to create a picture of your family with the coins.

5. Start with you and your partner. How close or how far apart should you put these coins? Don't think too much about where to put the coins; go with your instincts for now.

6. Next, move on to your family. Is your daughter closer to your partner than you? Does she get in between you sometimes and, therefore, should be sculpted in the middle? Does your son seem outside the family? What is the best way to show that?

7. Next, add in hobbies, pets, interests, or jobs that make up part of your world. Where should these coins be placed?

8. When you have finished adding everything, take a second look at your sculpture and check that everything is in the right place.

9. Share your thinking with your partner? Did you choose the coin to represent yourself and your partner for any special reason? Explain what all the coins symbolize and the reasons for placing them where you did.

10. Finally, if you could change one thing in both your own sculpture and your partner's, what would it be? How could you make this happen in reality?

11. Remember that an open mind and new ideas will allow your relationship to continue to grow.

Step Two

 ARGUE

"You never talk to me, not really."

"I do."

"I never know what you're thinking."

"I go along with what you want, don't I? Nobody loses their temper; it's better that way."

"But nothing ever gets worked out."

Most people would rather avoid arguments; they are unpleasant and sometimes make the problems worse. However, having too few arguments is as bad for a relationship as having too many. One or both partners will swallow their opinions and end up feeling resentful, or the couple will just drift apart. Nothing gets the issues out in the open better than starting to *argue*.

Three

Why Arguing Is Good for Your Relationship

When clients facing the "I love you, but" dilemma arrive in my office, they have no idea how to answer the question that most obsesses their partner—why have you fallen out of love with me? My most common diagnosis is that the couple is not arguing enough. Twenty years ago, couples used to arrive at my practice complaining of terrible arguments. These days, they turn up and say: "We can't communicate." It is almost as if arguments have been banned from many modern relationships.

No arguments, no falling out, and no bitterness—it sounds wonderful, but is it really possible to completely transcend the tensions and live blissfully ever after? In reality, arguing is an important part of a healthy partnership; it uncovers the issues that really matter and enables partners to distinguish between minor irritations and serious problems. An argument creates the impetus to speak out, cuts through excuses, and finally creates a sense that "something must be done." Although arguments make us uncomfortable, sometimes, that can be good.

So why are we so afraid to let 'er rip with our loved ones? The first reason for being less confrontational is the trend for couples to be each other's best friends as well as lovers. It's considered bad form for friends to scream at each other. Friends should be supportive, be understanding, and, most important, accept us as we are. "My husband has a terrible habit of interrupting people," says Kate, a thirty-two-year-old market researcher. "His best man even joked about it in his wedding speech. I've tried teasing him, but he says I knew his failings when I married him. So now I have to bite my lip." This "partner as best friend" trend is getting stronger and is probably one of the key reasons for the modern epidemic of falling out of love. Researchers at Duke University in North Carolina have found that we have become too busy to keep up with traditional friends—twenty years ago we had, on average, three-and-a-half people in whom we could confide, but that has dropped to just two intimate friends today. We have also become more detached from our parents and our brothers and sisters—with researchers finding fewer people trusting them with problems or secrets. Meanwhile, our partnerships have been taking up the slack. In 1985, 30 percent regarded their partner as their closest confidant, but today this figure has increased to 39 percent. On the one hand, this added intimacy is great, but on the other, our partnerships have become so important to our emotional welfare that we dare not risk an argument and swallow the discontent that would have traditionally have had an outlet by moaning to friends or family.

Couples with children can be especially nervous of having arguments. "Not in front of the children" is the catchphrase for a generation that is ultra-cautious about undermining their sons' and daughters' confidence or causing other psychological problems. And, with children being allowed to stay up later as they get older, "not in front of the children" is soon transformed into seldom arguing at all. "When we had kids, we made a pact to be civil to each other, with no disrespectful, harsh, or cruel language," says Veronica, thirty-one, from New York

City. "We didn't want our fighting to give them a confusing message. The problem is that my husband seems to think this includes even the mildest criticism of him. He gives me his 'time-out' look, and I have to clench my teeth. It leaves me feeling that my opinions are worthless but by the time we're alone, I've lost all desire to bring up my gripe." This is a pity because when children witness a constructive argument, they learn important lessons about honesty, compromise, and reconciliation.

Another reason is that couples are simply too nice to argue. In many of these partnerships, one or both halves have watched their parents get divorced and are only too aware how apocalyptic an argument can be. "The day we got married, I told Jim: 'I'll discuss, I'll listen, but I won't fight," says Lydia, a fifty-nine-year-old dental technician. "I watched my father and mother fight incessantly, and it's no way to live."

In an insecure world, where work is forever restructured and our extended families live farther apart, our relationships are more important than ever. Therefore, is it any wonder that we play safe and avoid the conflict? Busy work schedules also mean that couples spend less time together. On the most simplistic level, if you hardly see each other, you have fewer opportunities to fight. But it goes deeper. Just as overworked parents stress the importance of "quality time" with their children, couples want what little time they do spend together to be perfect. Not only does this expectation put pressure on a couple to get the most out of their shared leisure time, but it also makes them less inclined to express their dissatisfaction. "Our only concentrated time together is on vacation or weekends away," explains Kate's partner, Robert, a thirty-five-year-old software salesman. "After doling out thousands of dollars to fly to the Maldives, I was not going to let myself get jealous about the way Kate flirted with the staff." It takes sustained time together to feel relaxed enough to let down your barriers and be open about your grievances. When does a two-career couple have that?

The changing nature of the workplace is another culprit in making us less likely to argue. New management techniques have done away with old-fashioned confrontation in favor of finding consensus, and this is making itself felt at home as well as in the office. Michael is a forty-year-old senior manager whose wife, Sue, noticed a marked difference after a particular training course. "He decided we could only make a point if we were holding the talking stick—a wooden spoon from the kitchen," she explains. "I wanted to clock him with it. But every time I lost my temper, he would calmly say things like 'I hear your anger' and 'We won't get closure this way.' I had to keep telling him 'I'm not one of your middle managers.'" As Sue discovered, it takes two to make an argument.

Some younger high-flying couples—particularly those in their twenties—feel an immense pressure to be perfect. These individuals may have excelled in school, attended the best universities and colleges, graduated into exciting or high-paid jobs, and are now buying their own homes. The perfect relationship is another hallmark that perfection and sadly, arguments do not fit into that profile. Michelle, a twenty-seven-year-old TV researcher, speaks for many who strive for perfection: "I would have been mortified if any of our friends had known that Matt and I were having relationship problems." Michelle was very concerned about achieving—and worried if any of her contemporaries were promoted, in case she was falling behind—and her marriage had become part of this competition. Unfortunately, this couple had played the game so well that even Michelle was not aware of any serious difficulties until her husband disappeared for two months and reappeared on the other side of the world.

Other couples do not argue because one half is so eager to help the other grow that they almost become a personal therapist or guru. How can you complain about that? After all, it is done out of the best possible motive: "I just want the best for you." However, these well-intentioned partners can soon be telling their other halves how to feel. Joe, a forty-two-year-old financial consultant, found himself in this position: "My father had died, and I was in shock. I thought he'd always be there for me. How could this have happened? I just wanted to sit quietly in the car and get my head straight. However, all the way through the four-hour car journey home, my wife kept at me: 'You've got to get this out.'" There is a short distance between trying to help someone and controlling him or her.

However, underlying all the above reasons for not arguing is one unifying fear: What will happen if an argument gets out of control? My clients confess: "Often, I'd like to get angry but I'm frightened I'll never stop," or "If I let it out, will I go completely nuts?" or "Will he/she think less of me or reject me?" Of course, these are all perfectly reasonable concerns—especially for someone who has seldom let go before. Other couples have argued in the past but have had bad experiences: "When she loses her temper, she shouts me down, and I hate it" or "If I get angry, he shuts me out for days afterward, and the atmosphere is horrible." For other couples, the fallout is worse than the original disagreement. "My wife complains that I won't argue, but trust me, it's safer to keep your head down," writes Carl, a forty-three-year-old from Albuquerque, New Mexico. "We were going on vacation, and I needed to pick up a prescription on our way to the airport. Before I knew it, we had a three-ring circus and days of silence." So why can some couples have productive arguments, ones that solve issues and ultimately bring them closer together, while others end up with arguments that are nasty and drive them further apart? After twenty years of helping couples dissect their arguments, I have found that the unproductive arguments fall into three traps: blaming, belittling, and going around in circles. Meanwhile, couples who are good at arguing have unconsciously taken on board three ideas that neutralize these problems.

Three Laws of Relationship Disputes

This knowledge is key for keeping arguments constructive.

All Arguments Are "Six of One and Half Dozen of the Other"

This wisdom was always my mother's response when my sister and I got mad at each other and tried to get her to take sides. In twenty years of relationship counseling, I have yet to meet a couple who did not share equal responsibility for their problems. (The exception is violent and abusive relationships or when someone is an addict.) From time to time, I hear such a persuasive story that I've been tempted to believe I've finally found an exception to the first law. However, with a little digging, I always find that the story is not so black and white. Both sides have made an equal, if different, contribution to their unhappiness.

Unfortunately, our culture, and particularly the law, is determined to divide the innocent from the guilty. When we tell our friends, "You'll never believe what he said to me" or "Guess what she's done now?", we edit the story for us to appear in the best possible light. We do not mention that we were two inches from our partner's face screaming at the top of our lungs or conveniently forget our own mean and inconsiderate acts. As we reconstruct the fight, either in our heads or to anyone who will listen, we become more in the right and our partner more in the wrong. This process might make it easier for us to live with ourselves, but harder to live with each other.

What about adultery? Is that also six of one and half dozen of the other? Certainly, after an affair, society likes to label the "guilty" party who cheated and the "innocent" party who was cheated on. Yet in my experience, even here the circumstances are always much murkier. When Donna had an affair at work and her husband, Martin, found out, she was deeply ashamed, and they came into counseling. "What Martin won't listen to is the reasons why I felt tempted," explained Donna. "He had been so busy that it seemed he paid me no attention whatsoever. When this man at work noticed me, it was very tempting. He even seemed interested in what I was saying." Before anything happened, Donna tried to talk to Martin and plan more activities together, but Martin's most important contract was up for renewal. Tied up with his work, Martin did not even notice that she had embarked on an affair. Donna found this particularly upsetting: "I'd make this extra special effort whenever I went out, and of course I was going out more often. My moods were all over the place—excited one minute, horrified that I could do something like that. Yet still Martin didn't guess." Eventually, she confessed to the affair, and it ended. What Donna did was wrong, but Martin's behavior was a contributing factor. Innocent? Guilty? Can anyone truly apportion blame? And, ultimately, does it matter?

When all the "buts," "ifs," and "extenuating circumstances" have been stripped away, the responsibility in every relationship dispute is pretty much fifty-fifty. Maybe someone could claim forty-eight-fifty-two, but a generosity of spirit—a very good asset in a relationship—would suggest that it is pointless to quibble about.

Once "six of one and half dozen of the other" has been taken on board, couples are much less likely to fall into the trap of blaming during a nasty argument. After all, both halves have contributed to the problem.

Emotional Equals Attract Each Other

When I studied to be a relationship counselor, I had found this idea of "emotional equals attract each other" hard to accept. Surely, in every relationship, one person is better at talking about his or her feelings—doesn't that make the person potentially better skilled with emotions? It is certainly a widespread belief that one-half of a partnership—normally a woman—is better at relationships. On many occasions, one partner will bring the other with the implicit message—one sometimes spelled out in the counseling session—that "I'm fine; it's him/her who needs sorting out." However, twenty years of counseling has taught me to know better. I smile, as it soon becomes obvious that both partners need the sessions—equally.

To explain the second law, it is important to understand what makes up an emotionally healthy individual. The first factor is an ability to be honest about and engage with feelings. Every family has its own problem topics handed down from one generation to the next—subjects that the family are so uncomfortable about that each family member pretends do not exist. Common examples would be sex, anger, money, competitiveness, sibling rivalry, and jealousy, but the list is endless. "When I was growing up, my mother would get all flustered whenever there was kissing on the TV," said Terry, a twenty-nine-year-old plumber, "and although I'd tease her about it, I've never really felt comfortable talking about sex. Unlike the guys at work, I would never brag about conquests or make dirty jokes. It just doesn't feel right." Obviously, being human, it is impossible to cut ourselves from complicated emotions, so we ignore them. I think of it as like putting blinds on a window to hide an unpleasant view. As a general rule, the fewer emotions hidden behind the blinds, the more emotionally healthy the individual. Some people have low blinds and find it easier to look behind at the difficult emotions; others have such high and thick blinds that they are totally unaware of the off-limits subjects.

The second factor for emotional health is well-balanced boundaries. In some families, everybody is so in and out of each other's business that it becomes hard to know what problems or emotions belong to which family member. These soft boundaries can be a problem as these children can grow into adults who do not respect their partner's need for privacy or grasp that he or she might have different viewpoints. Conversely, there are some families where the boundaries are so high that the members share virtually nothing; and these children grow into adults who shut their partners out.

On many occasions, someone who appears very good at talking about relationships turns out to be happy with only a narrow range of emotions. Meanwhile, the partner—who talks less but thinks deeper— could find it easier to delve into the difficult topics hidden behind the blinds. Alternatively, the silent partner might be better at listening. Whatever the different skills, blinds, and boundaries each half of the couple brings to the relationship, each has a matching level of emotional maturity. Often the skills are complementary, and the secret of relation- ship counseling is to get a couple pulling in the same direction.

An example of a relationship that seemed, on the surface, to be emotionally unbalanced is Carrie and Jay—in their fifties with two grown-up children. Carrie did most of the talking and whenever I asked Jay a question, he would either shrug or tell me, "I don't know." That would be Carrie's cue for a long discussion of Jay's mother, his child- hood, and what he was feeling. Jay would sit there, nodding. Carrie was certainly fluent in the language of feelings but became increasingly uncomfortable when the spotlight was turned on her. Out of her mouth would come a barrage of words, but afterward, when I looked at my notes, it seemed she had said nothing concrete. So instead, I asked Jay to talk about Carrie's background and, slowly, a few facts emerged. "Carrie's mother was ill for much of her childhood and used to lie on a sofa in the living room," he explained. "I became her eyes and ears," Carrie chipped in. Slowly, they painted a picture of a little girl who would listen for hours to her mother's complaints and be her permanently on-call agony outlet. Carrie would also bring snippets of news from the family and neighborhood, and they would pore over the details together. "It made me feel important, okay," explained a more subdued Carrie. Conversely,

Jay came from a family where nobody ever talked about feelings. No wonder Carrie and Jay were attracted to each other. Jay found someone to discuss those forbidden feelings and Carrie found a partner for her ventriloquism act. This relationship had worked well at the beginning but Carrie had become more expressive and Jay quieter until both started hating the other—as often is the case—for the very quality that first attracted them to each other. Finally, it was a question from Jay that proved the breakthrough: "Did you and your mother ever talk about your relationship?" Carrie blustered; I kept quiet. "It can't have been fun stuck inside with your mother when the other girls were out playing," Jay added, thoughtfully. Carrie had often analyzed the family, but there were unspoken limits. Her own relationship with her mother, and the restraints it placed on Carrie, were completely taboo. Although Jay might have been more detached from his family, the distance had sharpened his perception. Both Carrie and Jay had their emotional strengths and weaknesses; in effect, equals had attracted.

"Emotional equals attract each other" is a very difficult philosophy to accept. I remember explaining it to a journalist who became very thoughtful. "So what does it say about me that I've just had a short relationship with someone needy and paranoid?" she asked. That made me wish I had kept quiet. However, she decided to answer her own question: "After my divorce, I suppose needy and paranoid just about summed me up." Many other people would have found it easier to blame the ex-partner than look at themselves. Yet blaming our partner makes us disrespectful and cruel toward them, and it ultimately produces destructive belittling arguments.

Understanding that emotional equals attract each other makes people less likely to fall into the second argument trap—belittling. After all, each partner has just as many failings—and strengths—as the other.

The 80/20 Rule

The stubborn issues, those that are really hard to resolve, are nearly always 80 percent about the past and only 20 percent about today. Patterns set up in our childhood seep into our adult relationships, but often we are completely unaware. When Cindi passed her driving test in her mid-twenties, she could not understand why her partner's inability to drive became such a big issue. "It had never bothered me before," she said. However, when introduced to the idea that arguments can have roots back to childhood, Cindi began to make connections. "My dad started losing his sight when I was about three; in fact, my earliest memory was of his car being towed away after a nasty accident. From then onward, my mother did all the driving, and there were times when naturally she resented being the one always drinking soft drinks at parties." For Cindi, her partner automatically leaping into the passenger seat had triggered past associations. Once she understood her feelings and explained them to her partner, driving became less of a flash point.

Another example of the 80/20 rule are Brian and Andrew—a gay couple for whom taste and design caused rifts. They were most likely to fight over purchasing something for their house. The 20 percent was about a natural fiber rug for the living room, but the 80 percent was about their backgrounds and their families' attitudes about money. Andrew had been brought up in a middle-class family where money was always plentiful until his father's drinking habits got out of control and the business failed. From this experience, Andrew learned to enjoy money while it was around. Meanwhile, Brian had come from a working class family—with six brothers and sisters—where, although his father had a steady job, money was always tight. One of his strongest childhood memories was of finding a $20 bill on the beach—and of the pleasure of being able to give it to his mother and the extra food it brought that week. Brian's lesson from his childhood was that money is scarce and should be hoarded. Although understanding the 80/20 rule did not settle whether Brian and Andrew should have bought the rug, it did stop the dispute getting out of control or going endlessly around in circles.

Understanding the 80/20 rule will prevent the same issues from repeatedly coming up and keep arguments from going around in circles. To learn more about the three laws of relationship disputes, and how they can become a safety net that will keep your arguments constructive, look at the exercises at the end of this chapter.

Summary

+ Arguments are necessary for solving the inevitable conflicts between two people in a loving relationship.

+ Many couples are frightened of having arguments in case they spin out of control.

+ Misunderstandings, problems, and arguments are "six of one and half dozen of the other"; by taking this responsibility, couples will stop blaming each other.

+ The second law of relationship disputes—emotional equals attract each other—shows that not only do both halves of a couple have equal skills with which to solve an argument, but also that these skills are usually complementary. This knowledge stops couples from belittling each other.

+ If a dispute seems insolvable, look at how the 80 percent from the past is driving the 20 percent from today. This helps couples understand what a dispute is really about and stops the argument from going around in circles.

EXERCISES

Six of One and Half Dozen of the Other

Naturally, it is easier to spot when other couples are equally to blame than it is to accept equal responsibility in our own relationships. So while getting the hang of this idea, take a break from examining your life and look at a couple from a favorite TV show, book, or movie.

For example, Jane Austen created a timeless couple with Mr. Darcy and Elizabeth Bennet. She even helps us spot their respective weaknesses, by calling the book *Pride and Prejudice.* Austen carefully balances her characters so that the misunderstandings and the obstacles to their happiness can be equally laid at both their feet. What about Jane Eyre and Mr. Rochester, or Rhett Butler and Scarlett O'Hara? From the sitcom *Friends,* examine the responsibility of Rachel and Ross, or Chandler and Monica.

After a while, spotting the "six of one and half dozen of the other" for famous couples becomes easy. When this is the case, start applying the same test to your own relationship.

Emotional Equals Attract Each Other

When something is hard to accept on faith, it is a good idea to find evidence from your life experience. This exercise helps you explore the concept and provides a launching pad for thinking about your own relationship.

- Choose a couple whom you know very well and have a chance to watch regularly. If your parents are still together, they would be ideal, but your partner's parents, a sibling and his or her partner, or a pair of friends will work equally well.
- Take a piece of paper, divide it in half, and at the top of each half write the name of one of the partners.
- Think of all the qualities that make for good relationships: expressive of feelings, keeps things in proportion, good listener, open to change, well-maintained boundaries, insightful, brave, forgiving, thoughtful, assertive, willing to compromise, affectionate, curious, good with compliments, self-aware, kind, ambitious, outgoing, and reliable in a crisis.

- Allocate each quality above—and any more you come up with—under each partner's name. If both partners demonstrate the quality, put it down for both of them.
- If you wish, you can add character defects, too, but this is not essential.

Compare both halves. How well balanced is the couple? Does the partner who seems to have less on his or her list have any hidden qualities that are harder to spot?

The 80/20 Rule

This concept is easier to come to grips with than the other exercises, so we will start closer to home.

- Make a list of the petty things about your partner that irritate you. Here are some examples: hanging around the house without getting dressed on his or her day off; winding up the dog or kids; or leaving clothes laying in the hallway.
- Now turn Sherlock Holmes on yourself and discover why these issues get your goat. What does each bad habit mean to you? What memories does each bring back? What would your mother or father say about these things? What would your previous boyfriends, girlfriends, or partners have said?
- Next, think back to your childhood and come up with your earliest memory. How many details can you remember: Where were you standing? Who else was there? What colors did you see? What smells and what tastes do you remember? Were you touching anything? How did you feel? Once the memory is as vivid as possible, look for other childhood moments that might link in.
- Still playing detective, start to put together a case. Remember how detectives first try out a theory, mentally exploring the possibilities, and then looking for evidence to either support the theory or knock it down. Take the same approach with the influences of parents on your personality and your relationship issues. For example, Cindi—whose father lost his sight—could discover how frightening her first memory had been. At three, we are very dependent on our parents. She could then ask what impact this had on her choice of partners. Does she play safe with a very reliable man? Conversely, she might need to keep confronting her fears and chose the excite-

ment of a dangerous man. Do not close down any line of questioning without thinking it through and testing your gut reaction. This is hard, because we are naturally loyal to our parents, but the aim is to understand ourselves, not to blame them.

- Finally, think back to your parents' favorite sayings. They might be philosophical, for example, "Life's not fair," "Do as you would be done by," and "There's no such word as 'can't.'" Conversely, they might be personal, "Why can't you be more like your brother?", "Big boys don't cry," and "Don't worry, you're the _____ _____ one (pretty, clever, etc.)." Look at how much the drip, drip, drip of these sayings has marked your personality or view of the world. How many of the contentious issues with your partner are built on these opinions? Are they still true?

These questions will help you pinpoint the hidden 80 percent of a current issue with your partner to which you might previously have been oblivious.

Four

How to Have the
Right Type of Arguments

The post-1960s generation no longer considers sex to be dirty, bad, or something embarrassing to be hidden away. Today's forbidden feeling is anger. Except, like sex, anger is a part of being a human and cannot be wished away. Whether we like to admit it or not, everybody gets angry at some time. ILYB couples tend to be particularly uncomfortable or frightened by anger and, therefore, develop strategies for keeping conflict at bay. However, all the avoidance strategies not only fail to deal with the underlying anger, but also ultimately cause more pain than dealing with the anger head-on would have. "We don't argue, because my husband won't argue," writes Irene from Toronto, Ontario. "If I get frustrated because nothing is changing, I say how I feel, and he remains silent. I get more upset, and he continues to be silent. I usually end up crying, and he becomes depressed."

Anger-Avoidance Strategies

The four most common avoidance strategies are detachment, rationalizing, skipping, and blocking. After examining the pitfalls and dead ends of each of them, I will show what happens to the unresolved anger. Finally, with our safety net from the previous chapter in place, we are ready to look at the nuts and bolts of productive arguments: what to say, what not to say, and when to stop.

Detachment

Couples tell themselves, "It doesn't matter," "We'll agree to differ," and "Ultimately, who cares?" While putting anger in cold storage can work in the short term, this strategy risks freezing over every feeling—even the positive ones. The effect is devastating. Jennifer is a forty-year-old lawyer: "There were things I didn't agree with—important things—but I didn't want to rock the boat. So I didn't say anything, I just shut down, and gradually all my emotions became dulled." Jennifer woke up one day in a passionless marriage and drifting toward divorce without knowing what was wrong. "The whole focus of our counseling was on teaching us how to argue productively," Jennifer explains. "Although nothing was solved when we were shouting at each other, later when we'd calmed down and had a civilized conversation, we always found a compromise." The round-table discussions were productive because they had been through a cathartic conflict first. However, this is tough, and many couples find themselves trapped in a vicious circle. By not arguing and processing anger, partners will become withdrawn and less likely to communicate—until the only strategy left is to detach.

Rationalizing

While feelings are generally located in the body—for example, love seems an ache in the chest and fear is a sinking sensation in the stomach—rationalizing keeps everything logical, plausible, and in the head. Nick and Anna (see the introduction to this book) had originally preferred to describe their arguments as "heated discussions." Instead of letting the anger out, they tried to neutralize the arguments by keeping everything very logical. A typical example would be the time Nick elbowed Anna in bed during the night. "He attacked me," she complained. "I hardly think 'attacked' is the right word," countered Nick. "That suggests an element of premeditation." Anna was straight back with, "I'm not allowed to have an opinion now?" The underlying issues were not being addressed as the argument quickly became about language, all conducted in the most reasonable voices. By Nick and Anna's standards, it was a nasty fight, but they were both still unsatisfied and quietly seething. So we started to unpack the real issues. The elbow in the back, during a restless night, symbolized what Anna saw as Nick's uncaring attitude. But because she wanted him to stay, she was determined to be "sweetness and light." The feeling still had to come out somehow, and this "heated discussion" was a subconscious attempt by Anna to deal with some of the frustration. If they had both lost their tempers, Anna would probably have blurted out the truth about holding back her feelings. By keeping everything very rational, Nick and Anna were protecting themselves from not only raised voices, but also a proper understanding of their relationship's dynamics and a lasting solution.

Skipping

Couples accept that they will get angry, but because they also feel guilty or uncomfortable, they push it away as quickly as possible. Anger is normally a wake-up call that something is wrong, but instead of listening to the message hidden beneath the pain, these couples skip straight to solving the dispute. Amanda would get home later than her partner, Peter, and immediately start preparing the evening meal. If she were late, she would ask him to help chop up vegetables or cube meat. Although Peter was willing to help, it nearly always ended up with one or the other of them getting angry. Sometimes, she would skip the argument by try-ing to second-guess what his problem might be. "No wonder you're so slow—that knife needs sharpening," she would tell him, or "You're fed up because your favorite chopping board is still in the dishwasher." Alternatively, he would try to solve the problem on the spot: "You've had a hard time at work; go and put your feet up." Immediately, anger appeared on the scene, and Peter and Amanda tried to avoid the argu-ment by heading for the exit sign. These suggestions might have been made with love but by skipping over the anger, they had found only superficial answers. In counseling, we unpacked the layers beneath chop-ping boards and tiredness. Amanda felt that a good wife should have a hot meal prepared by a certain time; Peter was able to reassure her that he was more flexible. However, there was more to their arguments than this—ultimately, the couple had very rigid ideas of what men and women did in a relationship. Nonetheless, Amanda felt that she was doing the lion's share of the household chores and wanted more help, while Peter feared that she wanted to order him around—something like a site supervisor. By no longer skipping the anger, Amanda and Peter dis-covered all the layers of the argument and a workable solution.

Blocking

This anger avoidance technique is fairly rare with ILYB couples, but quite common among the rest of my clientele: One half gets angry, but the other half simply refuses to engage with that anger. In these relation-ships, the conflict is upfront and sometimes bitter. Generally, Tara and Steven could solve their differences, but there was one topic that com-pletely overwhelmed their coping skills. Steven had two large dogs, which had been specially bred to retrieve objects from water, and on the weekends, he would be off at competitions. Tara was not a dog person and certainly not a large, wet, hairy dog person, so the dogs lived in a kennel outside. However, the potential for disagreements about Steven's hobby were endless. If Tara ever tried to tackle him about one of them, Steven would either be silent and let her rant or would walk out of the room. Tara would be left fuming, brimming over with anger. Although Steven would get angry, and perhaps slam a door, none of it would be expressed directly to Tara.

Unprocessed Anger

Some people are so determined to mask their anger—because "good people don't get mad"—that it has nowhere to go but inward. Ultimately, the anger turns into headaches, ulcers, nervous conditions, depression, or self-harm. The other costs of masked anger are not getting what you want and low self-respect. At the other end of the scale is sudden anger. These people deny anger—because they do not like it in themselves or other people—until the pressure builds to an intolerable level, and then they explode. For example, Virginia would—as her partner George described it—go ballistic. She would yell, swear, and even throw things—like the cereal bowl he'd put in the sink rather than the dishwasher. Privately, George would dismiss his partner as "a moody cow." But because Virginia had denied all the previous irritations, George was not aware of the thousand other things that had broken down her composure—only the final straw. From his viewpoint, her anger had no rhyme or reason: "I'd forgotten to put my bowl away hundreds of times before and she hadn't reacted like that, totally out of all proportion to the crime."

ILYB couples, in general, find a less dramatic way to cope with unresolved anger. I think of this as *sneaky anger*, because rather than directly confronting the issue, a person either consciously or unconsciously plays games. In cases of sneaky anger, people may seem cooperative on the surface but actually never do what they are asked. They forget to make phone calls, put off home-improvement projects, or deliberately load the dishwasher incorrectly—so their partner does not ask again. Psychologists call this *passive-aggressive behavior.* While positive anger explodes and clears the air, passive aggression hangs around, poisoning a relationship. As children, these people were often told not to yell, talk back, lose their temper, argue, or rebel. In effect, their parents were saying, "Let's pretend these feelings and impulses don't exist in me, and I'll pretend they don't exist in you." Passive-aggressive adults always have a million excuses that make the real issues become harder and harder to tackle.

Mark, a thirty-seven-year-old local government officer, would agree to do something for his partner but actually felt anything but cooperative: "I'd smile to her face and agree that 'of course it was my turn to empty the laundry basket.' But I'd never quite get around to doing it. I'd be damned if she was going to boss me about." Eventually, his partner retaliated and stopped doing things for him, too. Having reached stalemate, they started counseling, where Mark learned to be honest about his feelings, rather than sneakily hiding his anger away. Finally, they could properly negotiate who did what, rather than bicker at each other. Other games played by the passive aggressive include "oops, I forgot," "yes but _____ (add your own excuse)," acting dumb, being helpless, and sulking. In the meantime, their partner's patience snaps, and he or she loses his or her temper. The passive-aggressive person will then turn self-righteous and blame the partner for the upset. Although someone passive aggressive can seem powerful, their only control is in frustrating others; they lose track of their own wants and needs, and ultimately have unsatisfactory relationships. There is more on dealing with passive aggression in the exercise section at the end of this chapter.

The alternative type of sneaky anger is low-grade resentment. These people do not make direct criticism, just comments with a distinct edge. Jill, a forty-five-year-old animal behaviorist, found low-grade resentment was ruining her life: "He'd make sarcastic comments like 'wonderful' and 'of course, Princess,' when I wanted, for example, to go out with my girl-friends. But if I challenged him, he'd just say something like, 'Can't I even have an opinion now?' It was impossible to pin him down. Did he object to my night on the town, did he have a problem with what I was wearing, or was he just jealous? Who knows? We'd just end up bickering all the time." Behind each sarcastic comment are several unspoken feelings and many different layers of meaning. Is it any wonder neither party knows what they are really discussing or where they truly stand?

Having looked at the pain and problems caused by denying arguments, it is time to turn to look at constructive arguments. When I explain this concept to my clients, one partner will often say, "This is all very well, but I don't want to just pick a fight." The other will chip in with, "It all seems so artificial." So let's be clear. I am not suggesting becoming needlessly confrontational or arguments for the sake of arguments. Every day, we are given invitations to get angry: Someone cuts in front of the car, our call is not returned, we are given unfair criticism. Next time an argument is brewing, however, try not to sidestep it. Some clients who are very uncomfortable with conflict start gently, either with strangers or work colleagues. Amanda, who avoided arguments over preparing the evening meal, could feel herself getting angry with a shop assistant who was too busy talking to a coworker to serve her. "Normally, I would stand there and fume inside," she explained, "but this time, I could feel my teeth clenching and I thought, *Go for it*. I was surprised how calm I sounded when I said: 'Excuse me, could you help me?'" The second surprise for Amanda was that there was no smart comment or comeback from the assistant. "It turned out to be no big deal," she told me. After practicing on strangers, she was ready to be honest with Peter, too. Amanda might have recognized her invitation to get angry, but many couples have become so adept at avoiding issues that they forget the signs, which are discussed in the following section.

The Seven Signs That You Need an Argument

Couples who argue regularly would probably not be too worried about the first few signs, but ILYB couples—many of whom hate even disagreements—should use even one of these signs as an invitation to discover what is annoying their partner.

1. One partner is more silent than usual.
2. Body language: One partner is not looking the other in the eye; has hunched shoulders or crossed arms; shows a tense jaw; or is tapping his or her foot or pacing around.
3. Changes in voice pitch: Tension in the vocal chords makes them tighter and sound more brittle.
4. Taking offense easily, asking, "Why did you do that?"
5. One partner repeatedly checks with the other—with comments like, "Are you okay?" and "Is everything all right?"—but receives a sharp or irritated response.
6. Pointless contradicting, like, "No, I don't agree" and "Are you sure?"
7. Things that you have put up with for ages, without complaint, suddenly start grating on your nerves.

The only way to properly release this anger is to express it. This can range from the pointed comment—like Amanda's icy request for assistance in the shop—through to being angry, shouting, and even giving an exasperated scream. I call this *venting*. Venting not only releases anger safely, but also stops it from building up to the uncontrollable levels that give anger such a bad name. Venting does not include throwing things, using abusive language, or getting physical. These extreme forms of release happen only because all previous provocation has been ignored.

A note of caution: Venting works only if addressed to the rightful target. Indiscriminate venting—for example, shouting at an innocent member of your staff after getting criticism from your boss—will just pump up the anger.

Three Steps for Conflict Resolution

Each of the following steps is crucial, so resist the temptation to skip or move on to the next too quickly.

Explore ("I need to say . . .")

Exploring is all about venting anger, explaining grievances, and expressing frustrations. With any hope, this will come naturally out of an argument. However, for more information about letting go of bottled up feelings, see How to Be Emotionally Honest in this chapter's exercise section.

Sometimes, one partner will need to do more venting than the other. Don't try to reason: Someone gripped by emotions will not have access to his or her rational mind. Acknowledge the feelings: "I can see you are upset." Make sure all the feelings have been vented before moving on to the second step. Check with each other: Do you need to say anything more?

Tip: Don't get personal. Rather than criticizing the person, complain about the behavior. Instead of "You're so sloppy," try, "Please do not leave your coffee cup on my nightstand."

Comprehend

Really hear each other out. Don't use the time your partner is talking to rehearse your defense; instead, listen. Ask questions so that you are clear what is meant and ensure that there are no misunderstandings. If you pay your partner the compliment of active listening, he or she will return the favor. If you are unable to listen, it probably means that you are still angry and need to vent some more.

Part One: What Is My Responsibility?

Remembering that arguments are "six of one and half dozen of the other," think about your contribution. How has your behavior extended or deepened the problem? When you have a clear idea of your own failings, find something—however small—and apologize for it.

For example, Nick and Anna fought after their son's poor exam results. Anna had been away on a training course and blamed Nick for not supervising his studies properly in her absence. The argument went around and around in circles. Anna still felt annoyed, but apologized for her contribution to the friction: "I'm sorry that I gave you the silent treatment." A few hours later, and after more reflection, Anna had another apology: "I was angry with our son, too, and I'm sorry I took some of it out on you."

Part Two: "I Comprehend Your Problems"

Try to look at matters from your partner's viewpoint. Are there any mitigating circumstances? What problems could she or he have been facing at the time? Is there anything from your partner's past that makes this a blind spot? For example, Anna told Nick: "It must have been hard taking on both parental roles while I was away."

Tip: Sometimes, when couples find it difficult to apologize for their contribution or find any mitigation for their partner, I ask them to change seats and literally imagine themselves in their partner's shoes. Five minutes' arguing the other side is normally enough, but this is an effective trick for understanding your partner's case better. Some couples change chairs at home, some cross over and argue from different corners of the room, and some make the switch just in their heads. If you find it impossible to step into your partner's shoes, you are probably still too angry. In this case, return to exploring.

Action

Until you have both vented your feelings and both tried to comprehend each other's viewpoint, it is impossible to find a solution that will stick. Unfortunately, some couples—particularly ILYB ones who hate arguments—will try to move straight to action. As previously discussed, these short-cut solutions can work, but they generally leave one partner feeling resentful and can, therefore, sow the seeds for future disputes.

When Nick and Anna truly understood each other's side of the argument, Nick agreed to make supervising their son's schoolwork a greater priority, while Anna agreed that next time work took her away, she'd try to get ahead of the laundry so Nick had more time to devote to their son. Ask yourself, "What have we learned from this fight?" "Would we do anything different if these circumstances come up again?" "How will we do things differently next time?" and "What should we do about this problem now?"

Tip: Don't be obsessed with winning. Either try to find a compromise, one that pleases both parties, or aim for a trade-off: "I won't read in bed if you give up the disgusting habit of dunking bagels in your coffee." However, being aware of the sensitive areas, along with an agreement to tread lightly, is often enough of an outcome.

What if the Argument Turns Destructive?

Even with the best will in the world, sometimes a productive argument can go off the rails, but don't panic.

Remember that it is better to have a bad argument than none at all.

+ When the temperature rises, this is usually a sign that the real feelings are beginning to come to the surface and offers a sign of hope. In counseling, the arguments get worse before they get better.

+ Resist the temptation to say "and another thing" and throw in additional gripes. These examples might strengthen your case, but they also prolong and complicate the argument. Instead, try to solve one issue at a time.

+ Have you been criticizing rather than complaining? In general, complaints use "I" while criticism uses "you." For example, a complaint would be, "I wanted us to go to bed at the same time," while a criticism sounds like, "You didn't come to bed on time." The first invites a discussion about bedtimes; the second will make your partner defensive and prolong an argument.

+ Shouting and getting passionate are acceptable. But if the language gets abusive or there is even a threat of pushing or slapping, you should separate for ten to fifteen minutes and return when both of you have cooled down. Whoever feels threatened should call "time out." This means separating to different rooms or allowing one another to go out for a short walk/drive. The exact length of time apart is up to each couple, but should be negotiated beforehand. It is vital that discussion resumes—some couples have a quick postmortem, while others enter round two—otherwise, the person in the middle of a vent will be unwilling to let the partner have a time-out for fear of not getting an opportunity to properly release.

✦ Remember the 80/20 rule (see Chapter 3) and look at what might be underneath the arguments that keep returning and returning and returning. One couple in counseling fought about defrosting the fridge. Louise felt that Charlie bought too many frozen products without using up what was already there. He did the cooking and felt it was up to him to plan the meals. It got very nasty, especially as her parents had given them lots of chicken, which he claimed took up most of the space. This battle kept on reoccurring, with variations, for several weeks, and still the freezer had not been defrosted. Finally, we looked deeper and found the core issue. Louise had bought the freezer before Charlie moved in and felt that he did not respect her property. In her opinion, if the freezer was not properly maintained, it would break down, and they could ill afford a new one. He had a more "come what may" approach to money and generally felt that they would muddle through. When he truly understood his partner's fears, the issue disappeared, and the freezer was finally defrosted.

✦ Use the Three Steps to Conflict Resolution section earlier in this chapter to postmortem your argument. A good opening approach would be to apologize for your half of the argument. Next, look at what went wrong. A good way to achieve this, without reigniting the argument, would be to say something like, "I don't want to bring up the issues again, but why do you think it got out of hand?" "How could we have approached it differently?" or "What can we learn?"

Sometimes, my female clients claim that their husbands are so bad at communicating feelings, and anger in particular, that it is impossible to argue effectively. I tend to shy away from gender stereotypes, partly because I have met plenty of emotionally articulate men and women who are not in touch with their feelings, but also because of the "six of one and half dozen" rule. Nearly every woman who complains about her partner using one of the anger avoidance strategies turns out to be using a complementary one herself. Sometimes, it is easier to criticize your partner than it is to understand your own contribution.

Summary

+ Trying to avoid anger can cause more problems that just letting 'er rip.

+ Destructive strategies for keeping anger at bay include detachment, rationalizing, skipping, and blocking.

+ Only after a couple has vented their feelings will they be ready for a productive, rather than negative, argument.

+ Although arguments are never nice at the time, they do provide an opportunity to solve long-standing issues.

+ If arguments solve nothing, it is often because one of the three stages of conflict resolution—explore, understand, action—has been skipped.

+ Arguing and properly making up again is the most intense form of bonding you can have. Isn't it about time to prove how much you love your partner by having a really good argument?

EXERCISES

How to Be Emotionally Honest

Couples like to think that they have integrity and generally tell each other the truth. One partner might pretend that the new big-screen TV cost a little less, and the other forgets to mention the stripper at her best friend's bachelorette party, but there are few serious transgressions. Yet when it comes to our feelings, the rules change. We constantly tell white lies to preserve the peace or avoid upsetting our partner: How often have you said, "No problem," "Of course, I don't mind," or "It's nothing" when actually you meant the exact opposite? Often a couple will boast that, "We can tell each other anything," but in reality, they tell each other close to nothing. Although both saying and hearing the truth can be scary, emotional honesty will set your relationship free and save it from becoming dull. So follow these simple steps.

Learn to Name Your Feelings

Many clients claim not to have many feelings, but the reality is that they are not always aware of their full range. At first, some clients look blank when I ask them to write down as many "feelings" as possible. But I bring in a flip chart and, before long, we have filled a complete sheet.

- **How many feelings can you list?** Write as many as you can on a piece of paper, and then try to think of some more.
- **Look at the range of your feelings.** Feelings belong in families, so circle and connect ones that you think belong together. In my opinion there are probably seven main groups: **shock** (which includes surprise, confusion, amazement); **anger** (which includes rage, resentment, frustration, annoyance, irritation, impatience); **sadness** (including grief, disappointment, hurt, despair); **fear** (including anxiety, worry, insecurity, panic, jealousy, guilt, shame); **love** (which includes acceptance, admiration, appreciation, gratitude, relief, empathy, compassion); **disgust** (including contempt, disdain, aversion, scorn, revulsion); **happiness** (including joy, fulfillment, satisfaction, pleasure, contentment, amusement). However, you might find more families or decide

some emotions belong in different places. There are no right or wrong choices.

- **Understand the complexity of your feelings.** So many of these feelings seem negative—four whole families in fact—and the "love" and "happiness" families are often overlooked during our original brainstorm. On closer inspection, though, some of them are neutral, especially in the shock family. The negative ones can have positive sides; for example, there is always passion along with jealousy. Meanwhile, the positive ones have a down side: admiration, for example, can become hero worship.

- **Keep a feelings diary.** For a week, whenever you have a spare few minutes, jot down any feeling that you have experienced. It could be when on the train, when your next appointment is running late, or while watching your kids playing. Write all your feelings down, even the ones that feel uncomfortable—in fact, especially those. This is a private diary, so be emotionally honest with yourself. You don't have to do anything with these feelings, just be aware of them and practice naming them.

- **Be bold.** Within each group, the feelings range from the mild to the wild. When unsure of our emotions, we try to keep them down at the mild end of the spectrum for fear of being overwhelmed. Yet most people feel something a notch or two up from what they first report. So next time you write down, for example, that you are upset, try to be more honest and move farther up the scale to the hidden emotions, like anxiety, disappointment, or frustration.

Looking back at the families of emotion, ask yourself whether you are experiencing feelings from every category. If one family is particularly under-represented, it is important to understand why. Did your parents have trouble experiencing these feelings? Why should you be inhibited? Next, deliberately look out for these emotions—even if they all come from the mild end. For example, if you feel very little from the "love" or "happiness" family, make certain you record the small pleasures. If you see a beautiful flower or smile at a cartoon in the newspaper, write down "pleasure" or "contentment."

Distinguish Between Feelings and Thoughts

Just writing "I feel" at the beginning of a sentence—for example, "I feel you were wrong" or, "I feel you were out of order"—does not make someone emotionally honest.

Both sentences tell us nothing about the emotions of the person talking. We could guess disappointment, perhaps, but maybe frustration or even contempt. What the speaker has expressed is an opinion.

- If you find yourself slipping into this habit, go back to your list of feelings and find the most appropriate word.
- Another useful strategy is to write a letter to yourself explaining everything. Go back and underline all the feeling words in one color. Next look for the thoughts. These are normally examples of the behavior that is driving your feelings—underline these in another color. Finally ask yourself: what is the most important feeling expressed in the letter?

Communicate the Feelings

Once you have become fluent in identifying and naming feelings in your diary, move on to expressing them with your partner.

- **Own the feeling.** "I feel" rather than "you make me feel." For example, "I feel angry (infuriated, frustrated, or whatever) when you keep leaving plastic bottles by the back door for me to put into the recycling box," instead of, "You make me angry with your thoughtlessness." The more specific the complaint, the less it seems like an attack on someone's personality. After all, it is much easier to change your behavior—putting out the plastic bottles—than your personality.
- **Often just acknowledging the feeling to yourself will put you less on edge.** In some cases, you will no longer even feel the need to tell your partner, but if you do decide to tackle the issue, make certain to follow the next bullet point.
- **Be responsible when handling negatives.** There is nothing wrong with being angry, frightened, or even disgusted—it is part of being human. These emotions get bad press because we do not handle them well. So think what you want to say beforehand and weed out any "you make me" statements. Try to start every sentence with "I feel . . ." and after telling your partner about your feelings, be prepared to listen to what he or she has to say, too.

Listen Attentively

In the same way that you expect your partner to be attentive to your feelings, be prepared to offer the same respect back.

- **Do not interrupt, try to minimize your partner's feelings,** and don't tell him or her not to feel that way.
- **Acknowledge what has been said, even if it has been hard to hear.** A responsible way to handle this, without taking all the blame would be, "I feel sad that you say that I . . ."

Remember: A greater awareness of feelings leads to a richer life with not only a better understanding of yourself but better empathy with your partner and improved people skills.

Working Through the Three Steps to Conflict Resolution

ILYB couples want to either minimize disagreements or get over them as quickly as possible. Therefore, this exercise is designed to slow down your journey through the three steps.

1. Take three pieces of paper and mark one of these EXPLORE, another COMPREHEND, and the third one ACTION.
2. Take either a current dispute or an argument that you had recently.
3. Exploring is all about feelings, so each time one of you comes up with a feeling, write it down on the EXPLORE page.
4. Exploring is also about opinions and beliefs: "A good father would look after his kids; a good wife would not go out in the evening." Write all this down, too.
5. Exploring is also about facts: "I can't get home before 7:15; our household generates ten loads of washing and someone needs to do it." Write the most important ones down.
6. Check back over your EXPLORE page. Make certain that along with the facts there are plenty of feeling words and beliefs. Can you think of anything more from either of these two categories?

7. Sometimes, a potential solution (for the ACTION sheet) might come up early in the conversation. Write the discovery on the relevant sheet, so it is not lost, but return to filling up the EXPLORE sheet.

8. Next, take the COMPREHEND sheet. Comprehending is about why things happen. For example: "I get angry because I'm stressed from work" or "I don't feel like sex when I'm ignored." Write these down.

9. Beliefs always come from somewhere: our upbringing, religion, the general culture, or the media. The particularly powerful ones are from our childhood, so how might your upbringing affect your beliefs? Write down your findings.

10. Looking at the EXPLORE and COMPREHEND pages, how can you use these insights to find a solution?

11. Solutions work best when there is a benefit for each party. For example, Partner A agrees to give Partner B five minutes of peace and quiet after arriving home, but in exchange, Partner B agrees to give the children a bath later in the evening so Partner A can rest. Make the tasks something that can be checked—as above—rather than general and hard to verify like, "I'll try harder." Write the agreement on the ACTION page. You could even write it like a contract: "I agree to _____ _____ if you agree to _____ _____." Both parties can then sign it.

12. Bring out the ACTION sheet a week later and see whether both of you have kept your sides of the bargain. If you haven't, take three new pieces of paper, write out the headings and go through the exercise again, exploring how both of you feel, comprehending what went wrong, and setting a better action plan.

How to Deal with a Passive Aggressor

1. Ask yourself, "Why can't my partner assert himself or herself directly?" Passive aggression is normally the choice of people who feel powerless. Is your partner allowed to say no?

2. Bring your partner's hidden hostility up to the surface. Often passive-aggressive people will agree to do something—for example, decorate the spare room—even

though both of you know that this is unlikely to happen (or at least not in the near future). Instead of hoping for the best, challenge your partner's "too easy" agreeable nature: "I don't think that you want to . . ." or "I think you have mixed feelings about that." Keep asking more questions, but keep them neutral—for example: "Have you any idea what stopped you from saying that?" Once you have a better understanding of your partner's true feelings, the two of you are ready to properly negotiate.

3. Avoid misunderstandings. Repeat back instructions, set precise deadlines, and, at work, establish penalties for procrastination.

4. Once you've made a stand, follow through. If someone is always late, and you've told him or her you'll leave after ten minutes and they haven't called, make sure you wait for those ten minutes, and then go. Failure to carry out the penalties will severely weaken your position.

How to Stop Being Passively Aggressive

1. Accept that anger is normal.

2. Accept that you can still be a good person even when you feel angry.

3. Look at the benefits of using anger well. It gets things done and rights wrongs.

4. Understand your fears about being angry. What is the worst that could happen? What strategies could you use that will allow you to be angry but circumnavigate these fears?

5. Old behaviors, even if they worked for you as a child, will need updating. Unlike a kid who has to go to school whether he likes it or not, you have choices.

6. Practice saying no. It cuts through a lot of passive-aggressive behavior. If there is an argument, at least both of you know what you are fighting about, instead of having your anger being masked by sneaky behavior.

7. Tell your partner when you feel pushed around.

Step Three

 TARGET

"How do you think things are going between us?"

"Fine. Look, I don't know."

"I'm trying to make things better. I love you, and I'll do any-thing to make everything better."

"I know."

"We talk, but it just goes around in circles. What do you want from me?"

In most long-term relationships, there is no shortage of love floating around but, somehow, it just doesn't seem to get through. No wonder one half ends up feeling unloved. Better loving com-munication comes from better *targeting*.

Five

Do You Both Speak the Same Language of Love?

If you wanted to communicate with somebody from Japan, you might hire an interpreter or study that person's language and culture. However, when you fall in love, you may assume your partner has exactly the same take on romance as you do. During the early days of a relationship—when Limerence is at its height—these differences do not matter. Your whole focus is on your beloved and, given this level of attention, you are almost guaranteed to hit his or her love language. The problem comes after the honeymoon phase, when realities such as earning a living begin to intrude on the romance. At this point, you may retreat into your main language, with perhaps a little bit of a second language thrown in. There is no problem if your partner's take on love is the same as yours, but here is the catch: there are several different languages, in fact, and I have identified five different languages of love. While researching this book, I was fascinated to find that someone else had come up with similar conclusions. I discovered a book called *The Five Love Languages* (Northfield, 1992) by Gary Chapman, who directs marriage seminars. He has different names for the languages, but essentially it is the same concept. If you would like more information on the subject, I recommend Chapman's book. It is particularly good at stressing the importance of giving love, while many self-help books concentrate only on receiving it.

So what happens if you speak one language, and your partner mainly speaks another?

Kathleen and Philip, a couple who sought my professional help, are a good example of this kind of miscommunication. Beneath some terrible arguments, it was clear they had a very special bond, but neither of them felt loved. When I asked how they showed they cared, Kathleen explained about spending the months before a birthday or Christmas scouring the shops for just the right gift, hiding it in a secret place, and finally decorating the parcel with fancy ribbons. By contrast, Philip demonstrated his caring side with compliments about Kathleen's looks and by every day saying, "I love you." Both are equally good ways of expressing love. Except that here, each partner secretly wanted the other to speak his or her own very particular love language. In consequence, she felt devastated when he gave her just a card and money to buy her own present; he was upset because she never whispered sweet nothings. No wonder they were in trouble.

Often, our love language will be set by our upbringing. "My husband grew up in a family that did not show physical affection. However, my family, especially my mother, was exactly the opposite," explains Irene from Toronto, Ontario. Although Irene has come to appreciate her husband's loving gestures like buying flowers and holding doors open, she still does not feel truly loved. "He feels he is showing affection, but all his advances are stiff and uncomfortable. I long for a hug that isn't self-conscious. My grandchildren show their love in spontaneous ways that are wonderful—like leaning up against me or touching my face."

Different love languages would certainly explain the dilemma that many ILYB couples bring to my office. While one partner has fallen out of love, the other is still very much in love and devastated about what has happened. The in-love partner is probably getting his or her needs met, but unwittingly is not talking in his or her partner's love language often enough for the partner to feel loved. Why should this happen? Sadly, we assume that our partner's love needs are exactly the same as ours. It is a natural assumption, but a deadly one. With other couples, one partner will be trying a multitude of ways to express love but still fail to get through. Alice, a forty-two-year-old wildlife conservation manager, was no longer in love with Jasper, her partner of seventeen years. Originally, Jasper had pledged to do anything to rescue their relationship: He had started helping out more around the house; paid her more compliments; and generally tried to be more attentive. "I didn't know love had to be such hard work," he complained when he started counseling. To make matters worse, Alice was still not certain whether she loved him. "I think she wants me to be somebody else," said Jasper, "and I don't know if I can be—or even want to be." Not only was he failing to communicate his Loving Attachment, but the effort involved was driving the couple further apart. The answer was not for Jasper to try harder—a scattergun approach—but to do less and target better.

The Love Languages

Over the past twenty years, I have observed many different ways of expressing love, but they seem to fall into five broad categories, as follows.

Creating Quality Time Together

This can range from lying in each other arms while watching TV to taking exotic foreign vacations. People who speak in this language can become fed up if their partners spend too much time on friends, hobbies, or at work. Their most likely complaint would be, "We never have any fun together" or "You've got time for everybody but me." The worst thing a partner can do is to put off a "date" or "family day out" to catch up on chores, or cancel because a friend needs him or her.

If this is your partner:

The event is less important than spending time together, but a generous partner would choose an activity that gives the partner pleasure, too. Even if the date involves something that you do not particularly enjoy, go along with good grace—as this will earn you even more points. During time together, make certain that you are truly focused on your partner and not just sharing your time but your thoughts, too. This could be a comment on the shared activity or something personal that has come up during the week.

Caring Actions

Sometimes, these actions can be basic partnership tasks like earning a good salary or keeping a nice house but normally, they are more intimate: cooking a three-course meal, helping your partner clean out the garage, or taking his sister to the airport at 3 AM. People who show their love through caring actions are most likely to say that "Actions speak louder than words." The worst thing a partner can do is not finishing that little job he or she promised.

If this is your partner:

The stakes have increased since the days when salary earning and housekeeping truly counted as caring actions, especially as work tends to be invisible to your partner and, sadly, a smooth running house can be taken for granted. So look for the extra special things that your partner might not have even thought about: taking the car in for maintenance, installing some new anti-virus software on the home computer, or baking a cake. These actions are especially appreciated if they are something you would not regularly do. If you are uncertain what might constitute a caring action in your partner's eyes, listen to what she or he complains about. At the moment, this will feel like being nagged but look for a twist to turn it into a demonstration of your love. For example, the complaint might be a messy bathroom. Don't just tidy up, but buy small votive candles and run him or her a hot bath as well.

Affectionate Physical Contact

Sex immediately springs to mind, but often the hugs and spontaneous kisses are more important. These people adore back rubs and massages and are most likely to say: "Come here and give me a kiss." Naturally, they can be devastated if their partners push them off because they're too busy doing something else.

If this is your partner:

Affectionate Physical Contact works best when it is taken out of the sexual arena, as the power of an orgasm can overwhelm everything else. The hand in the small of your partner's back as you guide her through the door, stroking the back of his hand as you watch a movie together, or a kiss on the nape of the neck as you pass in the hall; all these are simple non-sexual ways of showing love. Feedback is particularly important for this language, so don't be afraid to ask which contacts were appreciated and which felt uncomfortable or ill-timed.

Appreciative Words

If anybody is likely to write romantic poetry, it is this group. They want the whole world to know their partner is special by dedicating "You Light Up My Life" to "the love of my life" at the local karaoke bar and placing sloppy advertisements in the paper on Valentine's Day. Not everybody who uses Appreciative Words is as outgoing; some are more introverted and consider love a more private affair. But even if the words do not trip easily off the tongue, they are very heartfelt. Whether extrovert or not these people are most likely to say, "I love you"—and really mean it. Therefore, they will be upset by their partner brushing them off with "You're just saying that."

If this is your partner:

Compliments are very important to these people, and they want their partners to be cheerleaders urging them on to even higher achievements. It is not just work that needs praise but chores about the house and arranging a social event: "Thank you for choosing such an interesting play" or "You got a really smooth finish on the paint work." As well as the appreciative words, make certain that your body language matches. When you tell your partner "I love you," make certain that you are looking directly in her or his eyes. These partners may also enjoy giving compliments, so make certain that you accept them graciously. It might be tempting to try to brush them away with, "It was nothing" or "Isn't that what anybody would have done?" Instead, go for the simplest and most effective response: "Thank you."

Present Giving

From an expensive piece of jewelry to a chocolate bar bought on the way home, present givers love to surprise their partners and will go to great lengths to pull off a stunt. These people are the most likely to say, "I saw this and thought of you." The worst thing a partner can do is not appreciate the gift or dismiss it: "I don't need one of those." Mike from Oakland, California, is certainly a Present Giver. That's why he was quick to spot an opportunity to please his partner, who collects teddy bears. "She saw a bear in a Halloween costume, and she said she doesn't have one like that. So I grabbed it and went straight to the checkout. Price wasn't a factor—I wanted her to have what she wanted." He has also run bubble baths with candles around the tub, reserved a cabin for Valentine's Day, and they even got snowed in together. However, Mike is worried: "I feel as though I'm losing my touch, because she is doing less and less. Not that she doesn't do anything for me, but I definitely do more in the romance department."

If this is your partner:

Gifts are an integral part of love and central to our marriage rituals. However, today's culture is obsessed with the value of presents and has forgotten their true message: "This is something to say that I've been thinking about you." Cutting an appropriate picture out of a magazine and making your own card can be a hundred times more effective than automatically buying the same old perfume. Don't wait for a special occasion either; lots of little presents will make these partners feel especially loved. What if you are not a natural present giver? First, get advice—either from people who know your partner's tastes or from a store clerk. Second, look at the type of gifts she or he gives. This will provide clues for what makes an acceptable present.

Love Languages in Action

Daniel and Elaine had been together for two years. They both knew that something was not right but had been unwilling to confront the issues for fear of what they might discover. Finally, after a tense Christmas, Elaine complained that she did not feel loved. It all hinged on Daniel's previous marriage—his wife had died five years earlier—and Elaine felt that although she didn't want to compete, she still played second fiddle. Daniel kept on insisting that he loved her, but she complained "actions speak louder than words; show me." The more she talked, the more obvious it became that her love language was Caring Actions. So I explained the concept to Daniel and he went away, thinking. The couple returned the next week wreathed in smiles. "I looked at my house afresh, through the eyes of someone who might feel excluded, and saw just how many photos of my first wife are up. At least one in every room, sometimes more, even in the bedroom," said Daniel. "I don't need to see her face all the time, it's up here." He pointed to his head. Daniel had taken the photos from beside the bed and reduced the others until one remained in his study and one in the living room. This Caring Action had really spoken to Elaine, who not only felt loved when she discovered his decision, but replied in his love language: Appreciative Words. "I know it must have been hard for you," she told him, "but I really felt that you had understood me."

Alice and Jasper, whom we met earlier, found love languages a breakthrough after several difficult weeks of counseling. During arguing—the previous step in the Seven Steps to Saving Your Relationship—Alice had repeatedly complained how little time they spent together. Jasper had countered that his job was very demanding and listed their recent trip to the movies, a meal out, and a summer vacation. When I brought up love languages, Jasper quickly spotted that Creating Quality Time Together was Alice's language. So he turned up at her office, on a day when he was less busy, and took her out for lunch. When bringing work home was unavoidable, Jasper took breaks with Alice in front of the TV, whereas previously, he would have played computer games in his home office. Alice began to feel truly loved: "Emptying the washing machine and the other things he'd done were nice, but I really appreciated lunch. You should have seen the look on the other girls' faces when he walked me back to my desk." Jasper had targeted his energy into Alice's most effective love language.

Kathleen and Philip, the other couple from the beginning of this chapter, also began to speak each other's love language. He started bringing home flowers and she finally started saying "I love you" without being prompted. In fact, it was Kathleen and Philip who introduced me to the concept of love languages. Twenty years ago, I had just started working as a couples' therapist and was making little headway with this couple until my supervisor—who seemed to have an intuitive grasp of my clients' problems—suggested asking about present giving. My next session with Kathleen and Philip produced the breakthrough; I started using the idea with other couples and found other ways of expressing love.

How to Find Your Relationship's Love Language

Many people will immediately recognize their main love language. If you are unsure, ask yourself to complete these two statements: "I feel most loved when . . ." and "I am most likely to complain that my partner never . . ." The second statement is particularly revealing, as what we complain about most is what we long for the most. To discover your partner's love language, imagine how he or she would complete those statements. It is also useful to look at how your parents showed their love when you were growing up. Some people speak one love language because that is what they heard as children, while others long for what they never had. There is more about finding each other's love language and learning to speak it in the Love Cards exercise at the end of this chapter.

Love Languages in Reverse

If your partner's love language is a fast track to rebuilding Loving Attachment, what happens if you slip up? Zach's love language was Caring Actions. When his partner, Pam, forgot to pick up the dry-cleaning, it became a big deal. He told her, "This just shows that you don't care." Pam, whose language was Creating Quality Time Together, thought that he had got everything out of proportion. By not understanding Zach's love language, she had unintentionally insulted him—just like someone with no knowledge of Japanese culture would be considered impolite if he put a business card away without looking at it properly. These simple misunderstandings turn a potentially positive moment between a couple into a negative.

Dr. John Gottman, a professor of psychology at Washington University, set up a special apartment as a laboratory to study couples. As his volunteers went through their "natural" interactions, he would observe them and monitor biological changes as the couples discussed areas of conflict. He claims to be able to predict with 94 percent accuracy who would be happily married, miserable, or even divorced within four years. He found that with happy couples, positive attention outweighs negative by a factor of five to one. In other words, for every criticism there should be five compliments; for every time we let our partner down, there should be five times that we come through. Sadly, we imagine that one good deed will cancel out one bad, but Gottman shows that our natural instincts are way off the mark. This is why it is vital to target your partner's love language. First, it will help maximize the positive interaction and build Loving Attachment. Second, it will avoid unintentional negatives. Third, when you do need to "make up" with your partner, paying attention to each other's love language can often clue you in to the most appropriate approach.

What Keeps People
from Communicating Effectively

It is not just love that is hard to communicate; some clients reach a point where almost everything is misinterpreted. These partners don't mean to cause offense. They even start choosing their words very carefully—but somehow still end up miscommunicating. So what is going wrong and how can targeting help here?

Andy and Jackie had a flare-up over Jackie's not filling the car up with gas after she had used it. "What did I do?" asked Andy. "I just had a simple request." But Jackie had a very different take on the incident: "He came at me, accusing, all guns blazing," she explained at their next counseling session. They had sniped at each other and spent an unpleasant evening, each at their end of the sofa, nursing very different interpretations of events. Jackie was convinced that he had been aggressive; Andy was convinced that she had taken offense over nothing at all.

A neutral observer would have been surprised that something so trivial could be so divisive. But the first thing to understand is that neither Andy nor Jackie is neutral. Each of them is viewing the argument through their shared history, their past individual experiences—which stretch back to their childhood—and, most crucially, a million and one assumptions. It is these assumptions that undermine good communication.

So when Andy and Jackie brought the incident to counseling, I asked them to replay the conversation but this time I would intervene and help them uncover their hidden assumptions.

Andy started: "What I said was, 'Why didn't you fill up the car after you used it?'"

Jackie was about to jump in but I stopped her. She would get her chance in a minute.

"Why was that important?" I asked.

"Filling it up in the morning takes time, and there can often be a line at the pump. Those ten or fifteen minutes can make all the difference between being on time for work and getting stuck in rush hour," explained Andy.

"Did you know this, Jackie?" I asked.

"I knew that if he gets going too late, he gets caught in traffic," said Jackie, "but not about the lines at the pump."

"I thought you knew how fine the timing can be. Five minutes can make all the difference," replied Andy.

I had found assumption number one.

"It wouldn't matter so much," continued Andy, "if you'd have told me when you got back, 'Oh by the way, the car is low on gas,' because I'd have left earlier the next morning."

"Have you ever told her that?" I asked.

Andy had to admit that he hadn't. He had sort of assumed that Jackie would know this alternative approach.

Assumption number two.

Next, I asked Jackie to rewind and replay her answer to Andy's question about the empty tank.

"I told him, 'There's no need for you to get mad at me,'" she said.

"You sounded quite upset—in what way do you think he was getting upset?" I asked.

"He was accusing me of being lazy—not bothering to fill it up," Jackie replied.

"Did you think Jackie was being lazy?" I asked Andy.

He shook his head. Jackie had just assumed this accusation—assumption number three.

After a short discussion about her childhood, Jackie admitted that her father had been very critical and often complained about her not trying hard enough. He would start with a seemingly innocent question about what she'd been up to at school but soon veer off into a lecture about applying herself.

Jackie acknowledged that her childhood makes her sensitive to criticism: "Andy didn't ask about the car in the calm way he did just now in your office."

"How did he say it?"

"It came out all aggressively."

In fact, 90 percent of communication happens without words—and this is particularly the case when we are under stress. Andy's tone, hand gestures, and delivery had given the words much more punch than he had intended.

Looking at how many assumptions underlie even a simple conversation and how our unconscious body language complicates matters further, it is a miracle that any couple communicates well. Normally, love and goodwill smooth over any misunderstandings. With this mindset, the assumptions are all positive: She was probably rushing back to watch her favorite TV show; he must have had a hard day at work. By contrast, all Jackie and Andy's assumptions had been negative. In fact, a partner becoming prickly over seemingly unimportant matters is often an early warning sign of falling out of love. For ILYB couples, previously easygoing communication is quickly bogged down by negative assumptions that further exacerbate one partner's desire to leave. So how can you stop hidden assumptions from clouding your communication?

The Three-Part Statement

Assumptions happen because we fail to give our partners enough information. This is why the Three-Part Statement is so powerful.

I feel (x) when you (y) because (z).

In Andy's case it would have been:

I feel (annoyed) when you (don't fill up the car) because (I don't have time in the morning and can be late for work).

The beauty of the Three-Part Statement is that it is so tightly targeted that there is no room for assumptions. Jackie knows exactly what Andy feels because he has told her. She has stopped relying on reading his body language and no longer *assumes* something worse than annoyance—like anger—because he has told her what he is feeling. The "when you" in the Three-Part Statement keeps things specific. Jackie knows that it is only a particular behavior that makes Andy feel this way—not her as a person. Third, she knows the exact reason and can see that there are no hidden moral judgments. Although the Three-Part Statement will seem artificial at the beginning, like all these relationship skills, it will quickly become second nature. The exercise section has advice on incorporating it into your everyday life.

Summary

+ There are five main ways of expressing love: Creating Quality Time Together, Caring Actions, Affectionate Physical Contact, Appreciative Words, and Present Giving.

+ The power of Limerence means couples use all five languages simultaneously. They want to spend not just quality time but every moment together; each partner searches for small gestures to show they care; they cannot keep their hands off each other; compliments come naturally; and they send cards or pick out spontaneous presents for the fun of it.

+ When Limerence wears off, each partner will retreat into one major love language—or possibly two—and expect the other to speak the same one.

+ When a partner does not seem to respond, try expressing love in a different way.

+ Careful targeting prevents misunderstandings and unintended slights, and channels energy into the most productive ways of communicating.

EXERCISES

Love Cards

Get a packet of index cards or blank post cards and write the title of one of the five languages onto one of the cards. Keep going until you have a complete set: Appreciative Words, Present Giving, Affectionate Physical Contact, Caring Actions, and Creating Quality Time Together. If you have another way of expressing love that doesn't fit under these categories, make up another card. Next, create an identical set for your partner. A good tip is to use a different colored paper or ink in case they get mixed up.

1. **Find a good time.** It's best not to introduce this exercise when there is a tense atmosphere, as it requires a certain amount of good faith.
2. **Make it sound fun.** Everyone dreads the phrase, "We need to talk." All too often, we interpret that as, "You need to listen while I complain." Introduce the cards as a game or a puzzle "to help us understand each other better." You can also explain that it won't have to take long. I've had couples complete the love cards in a few minutes; others have taken the whole session to talk through the implications. It's up to you.
3. **Give your partner the cards.** Ask him or her to spread the cards out on a table, and then put them in order from the most important way of showing love to the least. While your partner is doing this, you can be putting your love cards in order, too. It can be off-putting if someone is watching you.
4. **Ask for examples.** It may be tempting to comment on your partner's choices right away, but first make certain you understand them. For example, if her or his number one is Creating Quality Time Together, ask which times she or he particularly enjoyed. You could also share one of your favorite quality times and double check that you both mean the same things. Go through each card and ask for more examples. Your partner might have problems thinking of an example for the bottom few; it can be hard for something we consider unimportant.
5. **Share your examples.** Now it is your turn to give examples for your love cards. Keep

it positive. Remember it's about what you like doing, not what you don't want. Children respond best to compliments—so will your partner.

6. **Compare your responses.** Discuss the order in which you have each placed the love languages. What are the differences and what are the similarities? If you have any ideas why one is particularly important to you, share them—for example, "I came from a family where nobody ever hugged so . . ." Don't worry if your priorities are very different; the next step will help tackle this.

7. **Learn to speak each other's language.** Remember, the way we show love is also the way we like to receive it. So try to increase the number of times you speak your partner's favorite love language. This is particularly important if your partner has fallen out of love with you. Ask him or her, "What one change could I make that you would particularly appreciate?" These tasks should be small and easily checked. For example, if your partner's top priority is Creating Quality Time Together, set a contract for one meal out together a month. Don't leave any loose ends—decide who books the table and the baby sitter. For any changes to stick, there have to be benefits for both of you. So ask for something small in your language, too.

If your relationship has been going through a rough patch, a helpful twist on this exercise is to rearrange the love cards into the order you would like in the future. One couple I helped started with Present Giving as their first choice. They explained that this was the only love language that felt safe. When we looked at their ambitions for the future, Present Giving dropped down, and Affectionate Physical Contact came up in the rankings.

The Love Language Audit

Ask yourself the following questions and pinpoint the last time you used each of the five love languages.

- When did I last give my partner a compliment?
- When did I last buy my partner a present without it being a special occasion?
- When did I last take my partner out on a date with just the two of us?
- When did I last touch my partner in a tender way without it being a prelude to sex?
- When did I last do some chore for my partner without having to be asked?

Looking back over the five questions above, if your answer was in the last few days, give yourself a pat on the back; last week is good and last month is also fine. Or, if you cannot remember, try incorporating that love language into your repertoire. It could provide a breakthrough in communicating your feelings to your partner.

Three-Part Statement

In times of potential conflict, ambiguous remarks can become so loaded with hidden assumptions—from both the speaker and listener—that clear communication is almost impossible. The three-part statement is designed to get as much information as possible out in the open as quickly as possible, and to limit the potential for pointless arguments.

Don't skip any of the parts or improvise, as the recipe works best when followed to the letter:

1) I feel _____ 2) When you _____ 3) Because _____

Very few people can automatically put their thoughts into three-part formula. It takes practice.

- Think back to the last time you wanted to say something and it came out all wrong.
- Write down the framework above and fill in each part. For example: "I feel *humiliated* when you *ignore me* because *I'm trying my best to change.*"
- Try to come up with four more examples from the past.
- Now think of something current that you need to communicate. It does not necessarily need to be to your partner—the Three-Part Statement works well with sensitive teenagers and work colleagues, too.
- Write down the framework and again finish off each part.
- Ask yourself, "Is this statement clear, is it accurate, and do I need to add anything?" If so, make the necessary changes.
- Practice the finished statement a couple of times. This will help it flow naturally when you approach the other person.

Step Four

 PLAY

"We don't seem to do anything together, just you and me."

"When I offer a cuddle, you push me away."

"I'm not talking about sex."

"Why do I bother?"

"At least we agree on something."

When a relationship hits the skids, fun is the first thing to go. But to be truly close—rather than just colleagues running a house or raising children together—you need to reconnect with *play*.

Six

How to Boost Real Intimacy

$\mathcal{E}$*verybody favors* intimacy—much like peace, vacations, and bargains, we all want more. So why does intimacy slip so easily out of our grip, with the result that many couples find themselves friends rather than lovers? The usual excuse is that modern lifestyles are stressful and eating into quality time with our partners, but this is only part of the story. Intimacy has been made to equal sex—and nothing else. Much in the way that everybody has become obsessed with league tables, performance, and delivery, we've shoehorned loving intimacy into targets, too. Sex might be reducible to the statistics of "how often" and "how long," but intimacy is not so obliging. Plus, in all the sweaty passion of lovemaking, it is easy to imagine that we are genuinely close. Men are particularly guilty of confusing sex and intimacy, and they may consider their marriages good even if the lovemaking is routine and unfulfilled. Yet even physically satisfying sex can leave both partners feeling isolated, lonely, and secretly wondering whether things can ever improve.

Most of my ILYB couples don't complain about their love lives. They normally brush away questions with, "It's fine." Further questions reveal polite sex rather than intimate lovemaking. Patrick is a twenty-nine-year-old teacher who says, "My pleasure is giving Cathy pleasure." There is nothing wrong with this, but Patrick had become so considerate he was not being honest about his own needs. "I occasionally think of trying something slightly different—like making love in the shower—but I don't say anything. What might Cathy think?" They were so worried about upsetting each other—and, therefore, so self-censoring of their needs—that their sex routine had become boring. Worse still, they were unable to talk about the problems, which were pushing them further and further apart.

So what is intimacy and how do we recapture it? Intimacy is made up of three main components: vulnerability, good verbal communication, and physical closeness (of which sex is probably only 30 percent). Get these key ingredients in the right balance, and you will always feel both loved and desired.

Vulnerability

Vulnerability is all about being open and risking revealing something about yourself. Not surprisingly, it is also the hardest intimate quality to achieve. This is because our fear of getting hurt may be almost as strong as our desire for intimacy. So we hold back and build up our defenses as an insurance policy against pain. In the early days of a relationship, this "one foot in, one foot out" approach makes sense. We imagine that it will get easier after marriage, but often, we become even more scared. Our partners learn so much about our failings as well as our strengths from our new domestic, financial, and child-rearing life together that sharing too much more can feel like being swallowed up. Also, if you know somebody well, rejection feels more personal, so we step up our defenses.

Good Verbal Communication

Even couples who were good at communicating at the beginning of a relationship can find their skills evaporating. In the heady early days of love, we never stop talking; we share our opinions on everything from shellfish to Shakespeare. Contrast this with the stress of everyday life, when communication is cut down to the bare essentials—what time you're back, kids needing money for school—as we cross in the kitchen. Although this shorthand is very efficient, there is no space for the rich details that taught us so much during courtship. In the gaps, we start to make assumptions. We fail to notice that our partner's tastes have changed and that our opinions need updating. Worse still, we can swallow our irritations for the sake of avoiding an argument and the smooth running of the household. The feelings do not disappear but turn to resentment and further distort good communication. For Dionne, a thirty-two-year-old from Fort Lauderdale, Florida, the problems started on her wedding day: "I felt overwhelmed and sad about the fact that my father wasn't there. My emotions got the best of me and, at the end of the night, I began to cry for about 30 minutes. When we got to our hotel room, I was exhausted and just wanted to go to sleep. He couldn't understand this. Instead of being there for me, he became angry and went to bed mad." The couple has been suffering from ILYB for twelve months, and communication in the bedroom is still a problem. "He makes sex feel like an obligation. It doesn't feel sexy or fun. It feels like a chore that is part of my responsibility to him," explains Dionne.

Physical Closeness

What about physical closeness? The casual touch on the arm as you make a point, stroking your neck as you watch TV, smooching, long cuddles. Sound wonderful? These little gestures are just as important as sexual intercourse. But why do they disappear from so many marriages after the first flush of passion? Sadly, casual physical closeness is often seen as an overture to lovemaking, rather than a joy in its own right. So if one half is not in the mood—even though he or she might be enjoying the sensations of the moment—that partner turns away. After all, both people know where it will lead. Very soon, these couples get locked in the "all or nothing" syndrome, where everything beyond a quick peck on the cheek is off-limits—unless, of course, you want full intercourse. These problems are exacerbated for men and women over forty, who find themselves at very different stages with their sexuality. Women whose children are more independent are no longer so exhausted. They feel better, have more time for themselves, and feel that their confidence is boosted. Men, on the other hand, are moving in the opposite direction. They are less confident about achieving arousal and will often stay over on their side of the bed unless 100 percent certain of delivering. When one partner is always responsible for initiating lovemaking, he or she can be left wondering whether their partner is still attracted. "Although when we make love, it is good," writes Rob, thirty-one and from Los Angeles, California, "my wife rarely feels horny. I understand that we both lead busy lives—jobs, kids, and so on—but I make the effort. I know she cares, but does she still want me?" The intricacies of initiating lovemaking often need updating in long-term relationships. What seemed comfortable and safe ten years ago—the hand snaking across the bed—can now seem like you're being taken for granted.

Sexual activity—like love—changes as a couple moves through the Six Stages of a Relationship (see Chapter 2). While Limerence is at its height during Blending, couples report intense sexual excitement, high frequency, and often lengthy lovemaking. One of the great pleasures is slowly exploring every inch of each other's bodies—almost as if each partner is claiming the other as his or her own. "I almost wanted to climb into him," explains Jackie, "and we still joke that when we cuddle, I will burrow into his armpit." This intense sharing diminishes any potential sexual obstacles to almost the point of insignificance and is remembered as a golden period. For most couples, this stage lays the foundation for a lifetime of emotional and physical intimacy.

During Nesting, there is a gradual decline in lovemaking. However, the increased knowledge of each other's likes and dislikes can act as compensation, and there is generally plenty of non-genital caressing and stimulation. During Self-Affirming, sex is most likely to become an issue, especially for couples who have been unable to handle conflict. At this stage, different needs for affection begin to emerge, but some couples find it easier to switch off the light and turn over than talk. The unresolved anger does not disappear but instead builds a wall between the couple and shuts down the sexual libido. (If this is you, see the exercise called How to Be Emotionally Honest at the end of Chapter 4.) However, for couples who allow each other to be individuals, as well as half of a relationship, during the Self-Affirming stage, the changes in the relationship create new interest. Each partner learns to both give and take in lovemaking and thereby avoids one party feeling permanently in debt to the other.

Collaborating, stage four, is a time of new activities, and many couples start experimenting with their lovemaking, too. However, this can also be a time when one or both parties feel exhausted—especially if the couple has children. "I thought Sue never had time for me," complained Cliff. "Although I know it's not easy having a four-year-old and an eighteen-month-old, I feel I'm being constantly pushed away." Over time, Cliff felt that he had been turned down so many times that he seldom risked asking, and their lovemaking had dwindled to just a few times a year. A good tip for overcoming this problem is that instead of saying no, make an alternative suggestion. It worked for Cliff and Sue. "I might not have wanted intercourse, but often I could really do with a back rub," said Sue, "afterward, I would return the favor." Alternatively, Sue learned to ask for a "rain check" and the offer of making love on the weekends.

With Adapting, after fifteen to twenty-five years, couples report a decline in the frequency of lovemaking but say, conversely, that the quality is better. However, some people have issues about the changes to their body, and their partner's, and about feeling desirable. I would recommend two approaches for this—hiding the offending body parts or, conversely, emphasizing them. A sex therapist friend of mine gets women who feel very conscious of stretch marks or men sensitive about post-operative scars to actually color them in. She finds that not only does this bring fun and play back into the relationship—always useful—but that afterward, when the color has been washed off (maybe together in the shower) the couples report that the marks were not so noticeable after all. For the opposite approach, the person with the body parts that he or she feels are undesirable is given the opportunity to cover them up. This partner starts with the fabric of their choice—normally something quite thick—and, over time, replaces it with something thinner. Often, the couple moves in stages until they end up with just a scarf as they make love; eventually, the person with the issue will be ready to go naked again. However, the choice and timings are always up to him or her. This program was designed to help women after a mastectomy but it works well for anything that makes someone self-conscious.

The final relationship stage is Renewing. The urgency of orgasmic release is replaced by an increase in cuddling, holding, and caressing. Older couples often have the highest level of peace and contentment.

Boredom can be an issue at any stage in a relationship—possibly with the exception of the first year—and is generally an early warning of intimacy problems. And if a lack of intimacy is the problem, the answer is to play—the fourth step to saving your relationship. When we were children, play was at the center of our lives and acted as a gateway to learning, a chance for team building, and an opportunity to let off steam. After we grow up, we forget the simple joys of playing and many people even drop out of sports—the adult-approved form of play—and become spectators rather than participants.

But why is play so important? First, play tackles the three ingredients for intimacy at the same time. Good verbal communication and physical closeness are obvious byproducts of play; and in the excitement of the moment, there is also vulnerability—as lovers don't stop to think how they might look or whether they are being ridiculous. Second, play reconnects us to our childlike sense of creativity, and that is useful for combating boredom.

How to Fancy Your Partner Again

At the movies and on TV, couples are always having passionate and exciting sex, but reality can be very different. In the landmark Sex in America study, one in three women and one in seven men reported that they have little interest in lovemaking. When married couples were asked to look back over the whole of their relationship, 50 percent reported that one partner had lost interest at some point in sexual intercourse. So how do you re-light the fires of passion?

The first step is to understand that this is not an uncommon problem. In sex therapy, a low sex relationship is defined as making love only every other week and affects 35 percent of married couples in the United States. A no sex marriage (which does not mean total abstinence but intercourse less than ten times a year) affects 20 percent of North American married couples. A typical couple is Maddy and Scott, in their late thirties, who have been married for ten years and have two small children. "We used to have such a great love life. I'd pick him up from the station on a Friday night, and I'd almost be tingling with anticipation," Maddy reminisces. "We'd make long slow love on Sunday mornings and even be known to go back to bed in the afternoon for a cuddle. I loved the way the sun would stream through the curtains onto his naked torso."

She expected it to be even better when they lived together, but first their lovemaking dropped in frequency and then became boring. "It now seems to be the last thing on our minds. We're either too tired or I think, *Okay, let's get it over with.*"

Sex is easy at the beginning of a relationship. Pure lust helps us over any general inhibitions and hang-ups—like messages from the church or our parents that "sex is dirty." During Blending, two separate individuals become a couple, but to achieve this they have to lower their defenses, and what better way than sex? Maddy felt the urge to blend particularly strongly: "I wanted to be so close to Scott that I wished I could unzip him and climb inside." Add the blindness of Limerence, our need to get to know our new lover, and pure lust, it is not surprising that new couples report having great sex. The problem is that lust wears off after a year, and Limerence generally lasts somewhere between eighteen months and three years.

Unfortunately, the ease of early lovemaking and the Hollywood myth of being swept away by our feelings stop us from understanding how we move from the mundane reality of being a couple—diapers, laundry, bills—into the bliss of sex. That's why it is so important to be aware of the four phases of good lovemaking: **desire** (positive anticipation and feeling that you deserve sexual pleasure), **arousal** (being receptive and responsive to touching and intimate stimulation), **orgasm** (letting go and allowing arousal to naturally culminate in pleasure), and **satisfaction** (feeling emotionally and physically bonded after a sexual experience). At the beginning of the relationship, lust almost hardwires us into arousal stage, so we don't need to be aware of desire and how to feed it. We just magically fall into each others' arms. By the time the honeymoon period finishes, most couples have found other bridges from day-to-day life into the desire stage. But the couples who depend on just lust and limerence are left stranded, frustrated, and blaming each other.

The most important bridge to desire is casual touching, for example, holding hands in the street, a neck massage while watching TV, a hand in the small of the back to guide you through a door, or nibbling your ear. This is the bedrock for a healthy love life. Sadly, Maddy and Scott had stopped everything beyond a quick peck on the cheek for hello or good-bye. "The only time Scott tried to touch me was when he wanted sex. I needed to be nurtured not propositioned," Maddy explained. Scott might have seen his casual touching as an invitation to get close, but Mandy read it as demanding sex: "I'd go all cold inside and push him off because I felt taken for granted." They had fallen into the classic low-sex trap: all or nothing. They either had full intercourse or did not touch at all. To unlink the idea that a cuddle on the sofa was agreeing to making love, I set up a series of tasks where Maddy and Scott would spend time kissing and fondling, but other more intimate touching and intercourse were banned. A week later, they came back all smiles. "I really enjoyed having the pressure taken off," said Mandy. "I could just enjoy the cuddle without worrying about where it was leading." Previously, Maddy would have had to decide if she was aroused the moment Scott first touched her—which seldom happened unless she had had a few drinks—now they had a proper bridge to desire. They could either enjoy the non-demanding touching, which is pleasurable in its own right, or decide to have sex.

While every couple enjoys the first bridge from everyday life into lovemaking, the next one is always more controversial. When I tried to convince Adam and Hannah, in their late twenties, that sex needs to be planned ahead—like any activity—Hannah sighed, and said, "It's better when it's spontaneous and natural." I agree, but those qualities alone cannot sustain desire. Adam was more pragmatic: "Remember when I got those tickets for the U2 concert? We looked forward to that for ages and somehow it made the evening even better."

Indeed, anticipation is important for building desire. After probing further into Hannah's worries about a "sex date," she asked me: "But what if I'm not in the mood?" This is important because feeling obliged is a barrier, rather than a bridge to desire. Fortunately, they had started non-demanding touching, and Adam agreed that this would be enough intimacy if Hannah did not want to go further. Ultimately, planning ahead was a success.

"We stayed in and I cooked us a nice meal. Adam bought some new CDs and we danced in the living room and one thing led to another. Actually, it felt quite natural," explained Hannah.

For couples who feel self-conscious about planning ahead, I often use play as another bridge. So I've had couples building dams across streams, having food fights, and playing on children's swings together. These games break down barriers between couples, they see their partners in a new light, and this is ultimately very sexy.

The next bridge from the practical into the passionate is a surprise to most couples: good lovemaking needs distance as much as closeness. Charlotte and Edward, in their fifties, had not made love for over six months and described themselves as best friends.

"I always know what Edward is thinking," claimed Charlotte. "She's right; she does," Edward agreed. They did lots of things as a couple—fine dining, a busy social life—but very little apart. "We hold hands when we go shopping, and he's very considerate—opening doors—but I wish . . . " Charlotte drifted into a sad silence. "There are more important things in a marriage," Edward chimed in.

I doubt that's what Charlotte meant, but she smiled in agreement. Instead of being two individuals, albeit in a relationship, they had become one amorphous couple, frightened of allowing each other to be different. The first step was to encourage them to argue more: the quickest and most effective way to release submerged passion. Next, I asked them to witness each other's separate lives. Edward went to a conference where Charlotte was speaking, while Charlotte watched Edward play tennis (an interest he'd given up when their children were young).

"I really admired how he really went for each shot and he looked quite sexy in his shorts too," Charlotte laughed. "And I saw the respect of Charlotte's colleagues," explained Edward. "It was like looking through fresh eyes." Soon after these visits, Charlotte and Edward reported passionate lovemaking again. It is when we see the distance between us and our partner and recognize them as a separate person who is independent of us that there is enough space for desire to return.

Another important bridge to desire is fantasy. Some people feel guilty about daydreaming about a gorgeous stranger or a famous face from TV; however, 75 percent of men and 50 percent of women use fantasy to build anticipation. Next time you see a handsome stranger in the supermarket, for example, allow the daydream to simmer and bring the fantasy home to act as a bridge into lovemaking with your partner. When the fantasy is about settings or situations, don't be shy about making requests for a particular turn-on. However, be wary of making a full disclosure about fantasy figures, especially if it will cause jealousy. You are entitled to private space in your head, as this promotes the distance necessary for good lovemaking. If you find yourself consistently fantasizing about someone at work or a friend, this is probably a warning that you should see less of that person.

Although not every bridge to desire appeals to everybody (see the exercise section for more ideas), try to incorporate as many as possible into your relationship. This is the best guarantee for keeping lovemaking fresh. If all the bridges leave you cold, there are probably some obstacles to desire that need to be discussed with your partner. These include unvoiced anger, one half pushing for sex, overscheduling, not enough time away from the kids, and worrying about sexual performance.

Five Top Tips for Communicating About Sex

If you find sex a difficult subject, the following points will help you overcome your embarrassment:

+ **Don't talk about problems in the bedroom.** An immediate post-mortem seems like a comment on performance rather than an invitation to find out what is wrong.
+ **Turn it into a positive.** Tell him: "I love it when you're gentle," rather than, "Why do you have to be so rough?"
+ **Use touch as well as words.** Guide her hands to where you like to be touched; telling her can seem like an order rather than a request.
+ **Work as an intimate team.** A turned-on partner is the best aphrodisiac of all.
+ **Take responsibility for your own pleasure.** Don't expect your partner to second guess what turns you on; help him out. If you are unsure, experiment on your own.

Creating Your Own Sex Therapy Program

The traditional approach to solving sex problems has been to buy a book, but even the best ones—which recognize the importance of good communication and maintaining passion—are largely devoted to new positions for intercourse and improving technique. Not only does this approach put physical contact at the heart of intimacy, but it also assumes an easiness with sex that many couples lack—especially when the bedroom has become an emotional battlefield. It also overlooks the importance of fun and play in lovemaking. The final problem with sex manuals is their one-size-fits-all approach. My experience with ILYB tells me that couples fall into roughly three categories:

- **Low sex or no sex:** Intimacy is a very loaded subject, is the source of arguments, and has been reduced to just sex. For these couples, I have created the Twelve Stops on the Road to Intimacy (see the exercises at the end of this chapter), which aim to place intimacy in the context of the whole relationship—in fact, the first four steps are about talking rather than touching.
- **Routine sex life:** Lovemaking happens on a regular basis but has become a box to check off a list rather than a source of true intimacy and joy. For these couples, I have consulted a colleague who specializes in sex therapy and has a reputation for creative and playful solutions. She believes that pleasure is at the heart of intimacy and that many couples, in the hustle and bustle of life and the pressure of bringing up children, have lost sight of this. For her program, see the Pleasure Principle exercise at the end of this chapter.
- **Good sex:** Although intercourse is enjoyable, and in some cases extremely enjoyable, the intimacy from lovemaking does not reach the rest of the relationship and one or both partners still feel alone. For these couples, I have created Intimacy Repair (see the exercises at the end of this chapter).

All three exercises have "play" at the core. So if you are uncertain which of the exercises will be most beneficial, try taking elements from one or more and blending them together. If you get stuck, or start drifting back into old patterns a few weeks later, I would suggest following each of the Twelve Stops on the Road to Intimacy—even if one or two of them seem too basic.

Summary

✦ Intimacy is crucial for preventing a couple from drifting into a brother/sister relationship.

✦ Little by little, without either partner intending it, sex can sink to the lowest common denominator: what is easy or what both do not mind.

✦ Intimacy and sexuality change as couples move through the Six Stages of a Relationship. The challenge is to keep rediscovering what both partners truly enjoy.

✦ The most common cause of boredom in bed is a lack of intimacy.

✦ No matter how long a couple has been together, "play" is the key to unlocking a more fulfilling intimacy.

EXERCISES

Twelve Stops on the Road to Intimacy

These are designed to be done one per week, but stay at each stop until you feel comfortable. If you wish to move more quickly that's fine, too. However, just as intimacy normally bleeds slowly out of a relationship it is best reintroduced gradually. I hope the earlier stops will become second nature, so they are continued—without thinking—even while you are focusing on the later ones.

This program is easier shared with your partner, but don't worry if he or she takes any discussion as an attack; you can instigate the Twelve Stops on the Road to Intimacy on your own. Your changed behavior will lead by example.

1. **Validate each other.** Compliment or congratulate your partner on a job well done. He or she will probably think you are after something, but just smile and repeat the praise.

2. **Take opportunities to talk.** Think back to how detailed your stories were when you were courting. Everything was in the detail, for that brought the story to life. Ask your partner to explain something from his or her life, too.

3. **Set aside quality talking time.** Every couple should take stock about what they want from life from time to time. Where are we heading? What are our unfilled aspirations? Be vulnerable and really open up about your hopes and fears, too. However, the main aim is setting aside enough time for the two of you. We cannot be intimate if our relationship is nothing more than scraps left over from work, family, and friends. Guard this time jealously.

4. **Confide a secret.** You might tell friends everything, but are you as candid with your partner? Choose something revealing about yourself to tell her or him. Don't worry if you seem to be doing all the confessing. Like sitting on a seesaw, your actions mean your partner will move, too, and, over time, become more candid.

5. **Touch your partner.** Reintroduce casual touching into your relationship. Stroke the back of your partner's hand when he is driving the car, hold hands while she is

watching TV, give him a kiss on the back of his neck when he is on the computer. Sometimes, a touch is worth a thousand words.

6. **Share.** Take one bowl of ice cream and two spoons into a warm bath. Couples normally laugh when I suggest this one, but they love it. Use only one bowl—after all, this is about sharing. Try feeding each other, as this can be very sensual. Feel free to make love, but remember this is also about being naked together without being obliged to have intercourse.

7. **Set the scene.** Take a long hard look at your bedroom. Is it a passion killer? When I've asked couples to describe where they make love, I've heard about everything from stacks of bills beside the bed to animals sleeping under the duvet. Clear it out—the bedroom should be a stage for your passion, not a dumping ground. Make certain the room is warm enough, the lighting kind (candles are a good idea), and that there is a lock on the door. Finally, add a sound system to set the mood and to prevent worries about being overheard.

8. **Slow down your lovemaking.** Intimacy needs time. Men often head straight for the genitals while women sometimes want to get things over as quickly as possible, so as we hurtle down the highway, intimacy is left on the hard shoulder. Avoid the temptation to say anything about this during lovemaking. However nicely put, such comments will still be heard as criticism. Instead, slide his or her hands to somewhere else you would like to be touched. Add a positive affirmation: "I love it when you . . ." Another way of slowing down is to change position. For example, the woman being on top allows her to decide the moment of penetration.

9. **Find new erogenous zones.** Where are our erogenous zones? Anywhere where the skin is thin and the nerves are, therefore, near the surface: the middle of your back, the underside of your wrist, elbows, the nape of your neck, the outer part of your lips—this is why nibbling can be more passionate than plain kissing.

10. **Skip intercourse.** Sexual intimacy is a whole-body experience, and intercourse should be an optional extra. Once you can be close without full penetration, the stakes are nowhere near so high. Although you might not be in the mood for penetrating or penetration, you are seldom too tired to cuddle or be stroked.

11. **Make initiation a shared responsibility.** The person who always asks or sets the ball rolling for lovemaking risks feeling taken for granted or, worse, being rejected and feeling undesirable. If you seldom take charge, now is your opportunity. If it is normally your responsibility, hold back and give your partner space to initiate.

12. **Experiment.** Try bringing something new into your relationship. It might be somewhere new to make love—the backseat of your car, down lover's lane—or something different like one of you keeping your clothes on while the other is totally naked. These don't need to be big changes, just something to show each other that you've made intimacy a continuing priority.

Pleasure Principle

Many couples who find lovemaking a chore rather than a joy have lost sight of the full range of possibilities for pleasure. In the worst cases, life has become very serious business that almost excludes playfulness. For many others, pleasure is concentrated in one or two areas, but the effectiveness is blunted by repetition. The best way to explain is to launch into the first stage of the exercise:

1. Think about everything that gives you a warm buzz/real pleasure and write it down. Keep adding to the list—nothing is too trivial. In the movie *Manhattan,* Woody Allen's character lists the things that make life worth living as, "Groucho Marx, Willie Mays, Second Movement of *Jupiter Symphony,* Louis Armstrong's recording of "Potato Head Blues," Swedish movies, Frank Sinatra, Marlon Brando, the crabs at Sam Wo's, and Tracy's face." What would be on yours?

2. Look at your list and decide which of the following categories of pleasure, in your opinion, each item falls under. I have listed a few examples to get you going, but they are not definitive. For one person, a vacation will be an escape; for another, it would be a source of tranquility; for a third person, who might kayak white-water rapids, it would be a source of achievement.

   • **Achievement:** Passing an exam, negotiating a discount, finding the perfect pair of shoes, closing a deal at work

- **Tranquility:** A beautiful view, watching the water lap at the side of a boat, lying in a warm bed on a cold morning, rain falling on a metal roof
- **Irresponsibility:** Putting your feet up for five minutes and reading a magazine, a quick round of golf, using finger puppets at the movies
- **Excitement:** Driving a fast car, horseback riding on the beach, scoring a goal
- **Sensuality:** Roast spring lamb with mint sauce and new potatoes, listening to Leonard Cohen, the smell of freshly roasted coffee
- **Escapism:** Having a couple of drinks, meditation, dancing, buying a lottery ticket
- **Nurturing:** Watching a child sleep, doing some volunteer work, introducing a friend to a really good book

3. The great thing about lovemaking/intimacy is that this provides one of the few forums that can provide all these pleasures at the same time. But how balanced is your list? Do all your pleasures cluster together under one of two headings? How many of the pleasures are shared with your partner?

4. Generally, couples without enough intimacy in their lives have both lost sight of the *irresponsible,* and although each individually may have *excitement* and *tranquility,* they no longer share these pleasures together.

5. Here are some ideas, under each heading, that are a pleasure to share together— away from the bedroom. What other ideas can you come up with?

- **Achievement:** Go on a five-mile walk together or landscape the garden.
- **Tranquility:** Go to the beach and skim stones across the waves together; find somewhere to play Pooh-sticks (dropping sticks in a river or stream and seeing whose stick wins).
- **Irresponsibility:** Rediscover any forgotten childhood pleasures like pushing each other on the park swings or running down a hill singing "Jack and Jill."
- **Excitement:** Visit a theme park and go on a white-knuckle ride together, go to the races.
- **Sensuality:** Go to a concert together, fill the house with fragrant flowers.
- **Escapism:** Spend a weekend away, learn to salsa together.
- **Nurturing:** Plan a special day out for your partner, cook a favorite meal.

What Have I Got in My Hand?

Sharing different pleasures will rebalance your intimacy away from the sexual arena; now it's time to bring the fun into the bedroom. This next game can be as sexy as you wish to make it—I call it, What Have I Got in My Hand?

- Each partner finds an ordinary household item that has the possibility of being sensuous: a small paintbrush, a silk scarf, a pot of strawberry yogurt, skin cream, or an ice cube. Do not tell each other what you've found—in fact, you might like to tease about the possibilities, as anticipation is part of the fun.
- In the bedroom, each partner strips down to underwear and flips a coin to decide who goes first.
- One partner closes her or his eyes, while the other gets out the secret item.
- Slowly, gently, the person with the secret item moves it across the partner's exposed skin.
- The partner with the closed eyes takes a few minutes to become accustomed to the sensations; meanwhile, the other person finds different ways to caress them. Really get into the possibilities and find new places and new ways to touch. (The only thing off-limits is playing in a sadistic way.) How could you confuse? How could you give pleasure? Please avoid the obvious erogenous zones at this stage.
- After at least five minutes have passed, the person with the secret item asks, "What have I got in my hand?" The person being touched can either guess or ask questions— "Is it something found in the kitchen?"—but the partner cannot open his or her eyes.
- After the touched partner has guessed correctly or given in, he or she can choose to continue to be touched or ask to switch, and the game starts again.

Intimacy Repair

When sex is good, but more of a physical release than an emotional connection, try staying awake for five minutes after having an orgasm. I know this is tough for men: drifting off to sleep after making love would be near the top of my list of pleasures. However, pillow talk is a wonderful opportunity to connect. Some couples use the warmth and security of post-lovemaking to give a few compliments, but others talk in ways that would be impossible at any other time. I had one client who was locked in a bathroom as a kid and subsequently suffered from mild claustrophobia. She told her husband that the missionary position brought flashbacks of being shut in—especially when he collapsed onto her at the end of their lovemaking. He, of course, had no idea and promptly suggested trying different positions. Subsequently, their intimacy went from strong to even stronger but without the post-lovemaking closeness, this conversation would have been impossible.

Five Types of Bridges to Desire

Relying on the same old comfortable bridge will eventually turn even the most passionate lovemaking into functional but unappealing sex. How many more bridges could you add to your love life?

- **Romantic:** Dressing up and going out, dancing, satin sheets.
- **Erotic:** Watching yourself making love in a mirror, sharing sexy videos together, lingerie.
- **Location:** In the shower, four poster bed, cheap motel, blanket on the ground.
- **Sensual:** Massages, cuddling on the sofa semi-clothed, long lingering kisses.
- **External:** Sharing gourmet snacks in the bedroom, adult toys, fantasy.

Step Five

 ## TAKE RESPONSIBILITY

"If only you wouldn't keep putting me down."

"What about you?"

"Have you ever thought if you were a bit nicer, I might be, too?"

"You don't give me much encouragement."

"Why is it always my fault?"

It is always easier to take the plank out of someone else's eye than deal with the speck in our own. Nowhere is this truer than in relationships. Although our partner's behavior will have a huge impact on us, we are often quicker to blame than to accept our own part in the unhappiness. This traps us into waiting for our partner to change rather than to *take responsibility*.

Seven

Identity—Does Loving You Stop Me from Being Myself?

$\mathcal{C}ouples,\ over\ time,$ begin to become more and more like each other. It is only natural that one partner's tastes will influence the other and that living together will file away the rough edges of each other's personality. This gradual fitting together generally makes for a more peaceful coexistence. However, some couples take this a stage too far and become too alike. Why should this be a problem? First, as discussed previously, difference provides the spark that keeps love alive. Second, too alike can become suffocating. Indeed, many ILYB couples grow as similar as two peas in a pod and, frequently, one half complains that she or he has lost his or her identity. Worse still, for the health of the relationship, this partner ends up believing that the other is stifling that personality. When this happens, there seems only one solution: separation. This seems terribly unfair, because what is actually happening is far more complicated than it appears. Both parties are playing a part in this merging of identity, and for this reason, the next step in saving your relationship is taking personal responsibility.

Stacey arrived in my counseling office in tears. She was only twenty-five, but she had been with her partner from the age of eighteen and was now finding the relationship so claustrophobic that she spent as much time away from home as possible. Out came the familiar incantation: a) She loved him but was not in love with him, and b) They had no arguments, even though she had run up a large credit card debt during her many "escapes." Her main complaint was that the relationship stopped her from being herself: "I don't know who I am. I've lost myself," and she started crying again. "That's why I've just got to leave him," she explained. From Stacey's account, I expected to meet a controlling partner. Carl joined us for the next session, and he could not have been more accommodating: "Did I say anything about your going out? In fact, I'm not stopping you doing anything." Stacey did not answer but seemed to retreat into herself. She had turned into an entirely different woman from the one I had met before. "What is it that you want?" Carl asked. There was a long silence. Finally Stacey said: "I can't be the person that you want me to be." It was Carl's turn to close up. "Now I've hurt him," Stacey started crying again. "I didn't want to do that." Under all the pain, there seemed to be an unspoken question: Does loving you stop me from being myself?

Stacey is not alone in finding that her relationship robbed her of her personal identity. "The rooms of my house seem so crowded. Pets, children's toys, my husband's files when he works at home," said Barbara, thirty-four and married for fifteen years, "nothing seems to belong to me. Even the kitchen, which is sort of my space, is constantly being invaded by kids raiding the fridge. If I walk down the street at dusk and look into other people's rooms, they all seem so cool and spacious, like lighted stages where the owners are someone in control, autonomous. I find myself listening to friends who've got divorced and envying their talk of a door of their own." Lucy, in her late twenties with an eight-year-old daughter and a five-year-old son, would understand these feelings, too: "There are so many demands on my time. I've had to bottle up the needy part of myself while I've attended to the children. I don't have time for books, so I've put them away and the prospectus from the local college, too. But try as I might—because I love my children and my husband—the needy part hasn't shrunk. It wants to lash out and destroy everything."

Both Barbara and Lucy's partners were willing to help. Barbara's husband promised to keep his work things tidy and talked about creating an extra room in the loft. Lucy's husband agreed to take the children swimming on Saturday afternoons, so that Lucy could read in peace. But somehow, these well-intentioned plans were sabotaged, and nothing really changed. So what was keeping these couples stuck in the same patterns? We needed to look much deeper than the symptoms: no room for Barbara and no time for reading for Lucy. Both couples told me that they got along well and enjoyed the same things; however, when I asked Lucy for more information, she listed only eating out, movies, and mutual friends, and then petered out. All of these were fine, but they did not invoke any passion from Lucy. In fact, Lucy and her partner, David, had not been to the movies for six months. When I asked about personal passions, I was met with a blank face. I had to remind Lucy about reading and finally discovered that David used to play golf but had abandoned it when their son was born. Barbara enjoyed interior design—but felt she could not really indulge herself, as she needed to take her husband's tastes into consideration. Although compromise is fine—and an essential component for building a relationship—there can be too much of it. Both these couples had been so intent on having a happy partnership that they had lost sight of themselves as individuals. No wonder I could not put my finger on their individual interests because they had been sacrificed—a little here, a little there—to create amorphous couple tastes. So why do some couples become too alike?

The Six Stages of a Relationship Revisited

One of the key ways that a relationship will change, over time, is the attitude to "difference." When a couple first starts dating, they look for similarities and shared interests. One partner will watch the other's softball game in the pouring rain; the other attends both the dress rehearsal and the performance of his or her beloved's community theater group. In the first stage, Blending, all the *differences* are subsumed into becoming a couple. During Nesting, the differences start to reappear—perhaps over which shade of paint—and couples no longer pretend that they adore each other's favorite pastimes. However, *similarity* is still more important as a couple builds a home together. During Self-Affirming, the couple should begin to look at their differences, because two people will have different tastes, standards, rhythms of getting up and going to bed—the list is endless. Most couples argue and end up finding an accommodation for their differences. However, some couples, particularly those who will go on to develop ILYB, avoid an open confrontation and pretend the differences do not exist. One-half will drop a hobby—rationalizing that there is no time—the other half will stop seeing a particular friend whom the partner does not like. Instead of resenting the decision, this partner will make up an excuse—for example, "I don't have much in common with my friend anymore." The other tactic for avoiding Self-Affirming arguments is for a couple to stress similarities and to concentrate all the energy on what the couple does have in common. Without tackling difference, it is hard to move on to the next stage, Collaborating, where each partner develops individual projects and brings the new energy back to reinvigorate the relationship. The fifth stage, Adapting, is also tough if a couple pressures each other into similar opinions and approaches to the multitude of challenges that life throws out. The final stage, Renewing, is a mirror of the first one. Once again, the couple becomes everything to each other, and difference is less of an issue.

The following diagram shows what happens to difference from the first date onward, and how it can undermine a relationship if not properly addressed during Self-Affirming:

Aware of similarity → Aware of difference → Ignore difference → Resent difference → Attack and defend difference → Hate difference → Relationship breakdown

Ignoring Difference

Being "best friends" as opposed to partners can put a strain on a relationship. We choose friends who are like us and share similar interests. However, we do not have to live with our friends 24/7, so we can ignore the differences and concentrate on the similarities. What's more, we often have different friends at different life stages as our interests and needs change. The friends that do stay go through cycles of being very close, and then seeing us less often. So instead of confronting differences, it is easy to let the relationship drift. Partnerships do not have the same luxury. When a couple describes each other as "best friends," it always sounds an alarm bell that tells me to check out how they handle differences.

Resenting Difference

Here are the first warnings of identity and indeed more general relationship problems. A bit like a hairline crack in the living room wall, it may not need immediate attention and might not develop into something serious. Conversely, the crack could mean that half the house is collapsing. Replying to my questionnaire about ILYB, Hector, from Fort Worth, Texas, wrote: "My girl doesn't like me hanging with some of the guys; she thinks they're a bad influence and that it's time to grow up.

Maybe she's right, but we've been friends forever. So to stop her going all frosty, I don't mention certain things like dropping by the bar for a beer." This could be just a minor problem in the transition from being single to being half of a couple, with the inevitable change in priorities. Yet if Hector continues to edit his life, he could start believing that only some parts of his personality are truly loveable. The result would be a store of grudges and, finally, an identity crisis.

So what are the signs that someone is resenting difference? The following would alert my attention: even little plans or decisions have become contentious; one or both partners are keeping an imaginary score card on past disputes; and couples tiptoeing around each other. The best way out of this trap is to stop ducking the issues and have an argument. Becoming angry releases all the pent-up resentment, and the real issues can finally be faced. Often, these issues are different, and frequently less scary, than the ones imagined.

Attacking and Defending Difference

We all want the best for our partners, don't we? We are happy for them to grow and fulfill their potential. Meanwhile, our partners will do everything to back our ambitions. This is the public face of many relationships—especially among ILYB couples, who usually have a warm and mutually supportive partnership. Yet underneath, everything is much murkier. Returning to the couples we met at the beginning of the chapter, David understood Lucy's desire to return to full-time education. They had met at college, but she had dropped out when she became pregnant. He was happy to pay lip service to her returning "one day." But in reality, he was attacking her desire to do something different and be someone other than a wife and mother. He used a classic technique: practical objections. "I'm really behind Lucy's ambitions, but how are we going to take care of looking after the kids? Of course I can help out, but it's more than that," he explained. "There's all those hours writing essays, and her money from that part-time job isn't just for luxuries." Every time Lucy would solve one problem, he was ready with another. But this was more than just a case of a husband trying to keep his wife back. Although David might have been attacking Lucy's attempts to be different, she, too, was busy defending the status quo. In counseling, we had negotiated Saturday mornings as Lucy's time for some serious reading while David took their children swimming. But week after week, Lucy would find something else that needed doing that prevented her from sitting down to even this small amount of studying. No wonder they were stuck: both of them were frightened of change. David was frightened that new studies, new friends, and new opportunities could mean that Lucy might no longer want him. Meanwhile, Lucy was worried, not only about upsetting David, but also about whether she was up to the challenge of being a mature student. Unfortunately, because neither wanted to "hurt" the other, they had suppressed and failed to confess these feelings. Lucy might have been unhappy, but David was not getting much out of the relationship either. He had been so busy defending the status quo that he had little idea what he wanted from the future. Unable to deal with difference, Lucy and David's relationship was stuck in the stalemate position of attacking and defending, and both were prevented from reaching Collaborating and achieving their ambitions.

The Paradox of Love

We all need to be loved. The more we love someone, the more important his or her love becomes and the more frightened we are of losing it. So we worry that if we do not do what our partner wants, he or she will reject us. But how do we deal with different tastes, standards, and attitudes? Every relationship faces this problem, partly because no two people are alike but mainly because we are programmed to choose a partner who makes up the qualities we lack. In the best-case scenario, these differences are catalysts for growth rather than estrangement. However, difference can become so threatening that a couple uses strategies, normally unconsciously, to protect themselves from the pain. These strategies include attempting to control your partner, fitting in with your partner and subsuming your personality into his or hers, and pretending to be indifferent to the difference. Nobody sets out to be either controlling or a doormat—they just get frightened. Here comes the central paradox: Almost everything we do is to protect us from pain, but most of the pain we feel comes from this protective behavior.

With ILYB couples, these strategies for protecting us from differences come together into three major combinations.

Control/Compliance

One partner is in charge, and the other falls in with his or her wishes. From traditional sitcoms, we would immediately recognize the overbearing wife and the timid husband. However, in real relationships, it is often more complex, with couples swapping control and capitulating over different issues. For example, with Mike, a thirty-two-year-old truck driver, and his partner, Lori, a twenty-eight-year-old office manager, he was in charge of their social life. Mike would hold court with their group of friends, decide how long they stayed, and generally make decisions about where and with whom they spent their leisure time. Lori would go along with his wishes. However, Lori controlled almost everything in the home—the budget, where everything was kept, what they ate, when and how they cleaned up—and Mike would fall in with these dictates. Some couples can rub along with these tight demarcations for years, until something breaks down the walls. In the case of Mike and Lori, it was the arrival of a baby. She found herself over-

whelmed at home, and he found the restrictions on their social life impossible.

Control is also more complex than just ordering somebody about or physically intimidating them. Sometimes, to the outside world, the half that seems the weaker is actually very controlling. Some of the techniques to take charge, without seeming to, include angry tears, "poor me" tears, illness, threats of leaving, guilt-inducing body language (like sighing, raised eyebrows, shrugging shoulders), blame, accusations, and lectures. Although this list makes control/compliance seem exhausting, in most cases, the behavior can provide a superficial peaceful coexistence. However, the compliant partner will feel more relaxed and spontaneous when the controlling partner is not around. Certainly, Mike felt he could only truly relax at home when Lori was not in. While Lori felt more herself—and certainly not watching every word for fear of upstaging Mike—on the rare occasions that she went out with her girlfriends.

Indifference/Indifference

These relationships are deceptively calm with few lows or highs. The two lives run side by side, in parallel, but the couple has given up wanting much from each other. These relationships were common in the first half of the twentieth century when the emphasis was on survival of the marriage, and personal happiness was considered less important. The modern equivalent of indifference—withdrawing both emotionally and physically—is the workaholic relationship. Here, one partner might claim to want more couple time, but always has an excuse for a few more hours on the home computer. Rather than challenging this behavior, their partner gets on with his or her life. Other distancing behavior includes watching television, getting drunk, and burying oneself in sports or hobbies.

Generally, with Indifference/Indifference, there is little talk, no intimacy, and plenty of boredom. These couples tell me, "We have little in

common but the kids." Peter and Nancy had been married for twenty years, but Nancy complained, "I don't feel I really know Peter; he seems withdrawn all the time." Peter countered with, "What's the point in talking, as all we ever discuss is work and other people?" By avoiding conflict, they had never really opened up on the issues that would let them explore and understand each other. Although both "indifference" partners will have strong separate identities, there is no couple identity. Especially after the children become less central in their lives, one half of these couples will find the loneliness unbearable. Remember, deep down, nobody is truly indifferent. Someone might pretend, or give the appearance of not caring, but everybody wants to be loved.

Compliance/Compliance

These are the relationships where both partners are so intent on making each other happy that they both give up their individuality for a couple identity. Kate and Davis not only worked for the same company, but also sat beside each other in the staff lunch room. When I asked if they ever thought of sitting with their individual work colleagues for a change, they both admitted being bored with the current arrangement. "It would be so nice to talk with other people," said Kate, "and then I'd have something to tell Davis in the evening." Davis put it slightly differently but came to the same conclusions. So why hadn't he said anything? "I thought it was what Kate wanted," Davis explained, and Kate nodded.

Compliance might seem like the best way to run a relationship; after all, the ability to compromise is essential for a happy partnership. But these couples are so frightened of difference, and therefore so defensive, they ignore any painful feelings. In other relationships, the pain would turn to anger and, yes you've guessed it, an argument. If Kate and Davis had argued, one of them would have blurted out, "Don't crowd in on me at lunchtime." Compliance/Compliance will ultimately cause major

identity issues, as nobody gets what they truly want.

Although rare among ILYB couples, there are two other strategies for dealing with difference: Control/Control and Control/Rebellion. For the first, each half of the couple wants to change the other and even small issues become a power struggle. For the second, one half is valiantly trying to change the other; the other is valiantly trying to resist. In small doses, there is nothing wrong with any of these patterns for dealing with difference. Sometimes it is necessary for one half to make a decision and the other to go along with it (Control/Compliance) or to argue about important issues (Control/Control). Likewise, there are times when neither partner has the energy or inclination to get worked up over something (Indifference/Indifference) and digging heels in is more effective than a direct challenge (Control/Rebellion). The problem is when a couple becomes stuck in one particular pattern or, worse yet, retreats into more and more extreme versions of these patterns. In the long term, avoiding and attacking differences drain all the connection, all the understanding, and ultimately all the love out of a relationship. One day, one partner will wake up, look at his or her partner, and think, "He's holding me back" or "She's a stranger."

Dealing with Identity Issues

Grand gestures, like moving abroad or ending a relationship, often just take the compliant or controlling behavior to another country or another relationship. Identity is accumulated through a series of small victories: standing up for yourself, doing something different from what other people expect, understanding your fears and your partner's fears. Here are some pointers on the way:

✦ **Look at your internal dialogue.** Do you spend more time second-guessing your partner's reaction than examining your own feelings? Do you find yourself trying to "hold the line," frightened that if you give in over one thing that it will have a domino effect and change everything?

✦ **Identify which of the unhelpful patterns that you and your partner fall into.** Understanding a behavior goes a long way toward changing it. Even if next time you find yourself falling into the old patterns, keep one eye on observing yourself. This will make you doubly aware of the pitfalls and less likely to fall into the same traps next time around.

✦ **Take responsibility.** Don't cast yourself as the victim; look at your contribution to the pattern. As the old saying goes, "You can't change anybody but yourself."

✦ **Try to understand, instead of trying to convince/cajole/control each other.** Without understanding, it is impossible to build a proper compromise. (For more on this see Break Out of Controlling Behavior in the exercise section.)

✦ **Look at the expectations that underpin your view of the world and yourself.** Where does each expectation come from? How much of your identity has come from your parents? How much from your friends? How much from our wider culture, religion, or the media? How much of this belongs to you? (See the Unpacking Expectations exercise at the end of this chapter.)

✦ **Aim for a compromise.** Is there a middle way that would balance individual and couple identity?

This process helped Stacey and Carl find a way through Stacey's identity crisis. Her internal dialogue was full of questions like, *Is it okay to want to go out this often?* and *Will Carl be upset with me for wanting to go?* Carl's internal dialogue had gone along similar lines: *Should I say something about her going out so much?* and *What will she think about me if I ask her to stay in?* From the beginning of their relationship, Carl and Stacey had both been so eager to please each other that their relationship had been Compliance/Compliance. More recently, Stacey had run up large credit card bills, and Carl had tried to keep spending down: Rebellion/Control. Next, with Taking Responsibility, Stacey admitted that her shopping had been like a reckless teenager and Carl that he had been a critical parent; this allowed them to have an adult-to-adult discussion that created a budget and money set aside for entertainment. During Understanding, Carl learned that nights in front of the TV made Stacey feel old before her time; Stacey learned that Carl thought they should be saving to start a family. We had finally reached the unspoken expectations that had been driving them apart. Where had these expectations come from? Carl's parents had had children in their mid-twenties and as he said, "It just feels like the right time." However, Stacey's mother had regretted having children early and had always advised her daughter to "see something of the world first." Finally, the couple was ready for a compromise. Carl started joining Stacey for some of her nights out and saving for a trip to Europe. Stacey agreed that she would like to have children before she turned thirty.

Meanwhile, Lucy and David just needed a frank discussion about both of their fears. Lucy was able to reassure David that she was not planning to leave, and he was able to be more supportive. Lucy decided to start carving her own individual identity by taking a class part time at her local adult education center. "I wanted to check that motherhood had not completely destroyed all my brain cells," she explained, "but also to be sure I really want this before we lay out a lot of money." David was happy to care for the kids on her college nights.

Summary

- Too much compromise is as bad as too little.

- Try to find a balance between being one-half of a couple and being yourself.

- Do not ignore identity pains; these are normally an indication of a deeper problem in the relationship.

- Secure partners encourage each other to have their own identity because they know this will not undermine the relationship.

- Doing what we want and need for ourselves, while continuing to care deeply for our partner, is not always easy. However, it can be done by understanding each other's differences rather than ignoring or protecting against them.

EXERCISES

I'm in Charge/You're in Charge

Endlessly compromising and trying to second-guess what your partner might enjoy can become boring after a while. A friend had a novel idea for vacations where he would be in total charge for one day and his partner for another. "I really used to look forward to it," says James. "It gave me a chance to get to know Cheryl better. I could almost hear the tone of her voice in what she chose." Even the children would have their allocated day, "although that sometimes got a little hairy." The rest of the vacation would be the usual family compromise. The rules are as follows:

- During your day, you choose all the activities. Except for something that would completely terrify your partner, the choice is entirely up to you; follow your heart's desire.
- It starts at breakfast and ends at bedtime—what food, where you eat, where to visit, or whether to lay about doing nothing are all up to you.
- Your partner agrees to enter into the spirit of your day and try, with good grace, to enjoy your choices as much as possible.
- On another day, you swap, and your partner chooses.
- Afterward, discuss what you have learned about yourself and each other. Ask yourselves, "What could we incorporate into our normal routines?"
- Before agreeing to this exercise, it is worth having a side discussion about any additional personal rules. A few issues to discuss are whether the person in charge has the right to ask for sex and whether there is anything that would be totally unacceptable to either one of you.

The exercise can also work at home, too, with each partner "in charge" for one weekend day or on alternate weekends. The same rules as above apply; the only proviso is that the day is devoted to pleasure—a mini-break at home—rather than catching up on errands and chores.

Break Out of Controlling Behavior

The object of this exercise is to understand both your partner's behavior and your own. Take an issue that causes a lot of tension between the two of you—something that you have argued about frequently in the past (or need to argue about!).

- The partner who is having an identity crisis or who wants change begins. If this is both of you, flip a coin. That person talks about how he or she sees the problem, what the person wants, and how the person feels. The other person just listens.
- The listener can ask for amplification or clarification but nothing else. No defending, no answering back, no comforting or reassuring. Just listening and understanding.
- If the person who is listening feels tempted to speak, he or she should first ask themselves, "Am I trying to convince or defend?" If the answer is yes, bite your tongue. If the question aims to clarify or to dig deeper, feel free to speak.
- When there is a lull in the conversation, check that you have properly understood your partner. "What you are saying is . . ." and "Have I understood properly that you feel . . .?"
- If an argument starts, stop and look at the protecting patterns: Control/Compliance Control/Control, Indifference/Indifference, Compliance/Compliance, Control/Rebellion. Have you fallen into one of these traps? Alternatively, look for expectations that have turned into dictates (see the following exercise).
- The object of the exercise is not to find a solution to the difference but to understand.
- On many occasions, the problems disappear without any action plan. This is because understanding the reasons behind our partner's contentious behavior makes it easier to tolerate. Often, our tolerance makes our partner soften the behavior, which in turn increases our tolerance and sets up a virtuous circle.

If you are working through this book alone, put yourself in the listening position. Ask your partner why he or she feels so strongly about a point of dispute and follow the exercise from there. If your partner refuses with, "You know only too well," explain that you want to double check that you understand—this will take him or her off the defensive. When you've finished hearing and truly understand all of your partner's viewpoints ask,

"Could I explain where I am coming from?" If your partner feels understood, he or she may be open to offering the same courtesy to you. So, if your partner refuses to listen, keep trying to understand before seeking to be understood.

Unpacking Expectations

The following is a list of potential conflicts: Write down beside each one what it means to you and/or what you believe is the approach of a right-thinking person. For example, beside "debt," you could write a necessary evil, shame, a personal failure, good money management, or a fact of life.

Sex, money, Sunday morning, debt, television, role of a man in a relationship, role of a woman in a relationship, flowers, being late, paying bills, play, Christmas or other holidays, credit, experimenting in bed, health, marriage, how time is spent, Saturday night, friends outside the relationship, affection, entertaining at home, the past, communication, hobbies, bringing up children, tidiness, meal times, housekeeping, wardrobe, work, alcohol, disciplining children, promptness, birthdays, interests, presents, behavior at social functions around other people, sports, the bathroom, cuddling, education.

1. Go through them as quickly as possible, so that you record your first spontaneous thought.
2. Afterward, return and ask where these expectations come from: mother, father, friends, media, priest/pastor/rabbi, wider culture, politicians.
3. How do these expectations feed your arguments? Are any of your expectations out of date? Do you need to change any of them? Which are particularly important to your identity?

Want to Change but Can't Change?

Forging a new identity is tough. Below, the journey is broken down into six more manageable chunks:

1. **Ask yourself whether you really want it.** Sometimes, we try to change something—like getting fit, giving up smoking, or going back to school—because we feel we ought to, someone else is putting pressure on us, society expects it, or we like the picture of us doing these things. However, deep down inside, we do not really want to change.

2. **What are the benefits of staying where you are?** If you are stuck, there is probably some hidden benefit to not changing. Once you have truly understood the obstacles to change, you will be better placed to climb over them.

3. **Break the change up into smaller parts.** Getting from today to the future can seem an impossibly long journey. For example, moving to a new house involves a million and one choices and plenty of opportunities for disaster. However, when broken down into smaller chunks—like researching schools in the new area or finding a real estate agent—everything seems more manageable. Once those tasks are achieved, you can move onto the next ones and, pretty soon, you have arrived at your final destination.

4. **Sell the benefits of change to your partner.** If you know your partner will have doubts about a project, you may be tentative about asking. "I don't suppose you'll like it but . . ." This immediately makes it easier to say no. Alternatively, we can even provide ammunition for their side: "I know we're short of time but . . ." Worse still, we fail to convey the importance of the project so that our partner does not understand the consequence of a refusal. So look for all the benefits to you, your family, and your partner. What could make him or her support the change? Finally, find out as much detail as possible and be ready to answer questions. Everybody fears the unknown, and the more information you have, the less likely the change will be overwhelming.

5. **How can you make the first step?** It is very easy to put off change until tomorrow, and then the day after, and then forever. So choose one small job that will get the ball rolling today.

6. **Keep going.** There are always setbacks. But remember, nothing lasts forever, and these difficult times will pass, too. Even the most successful people face dead ends and, sometimes, failure. What makes them different from everybody else is that they are not discouraged.

Frightened of Change?

If your partner is seeking a new identity, the changes involved can feel pretty scary. If you want to change, but are worried how your partner will react, that can also be a scary place. Either way, here are the three keys to coping with change.

1. **Understand.** Because you fear change, you see it as something bad. However, change is actually neither intrinsically good nor bad; it all comes down to how you look at it. For example, we think of rain as bad but in a desert, rain would be wonderful. It's all about attitude. So the first step is always to look for the upside of something new. If you can't see one immediately, try looking a bit farther into the future. How might it look in three months' time, a year, two years? Second, ask what would happen if you didn't change. What is the downside of staying where you are?

2. **Relax.** Scientists have discovered that when we're under stress—like at times of change—our brain operates differently. With our very survival under threat, we use the less sophisticated parts of our brain inherited from our reptilian ancestors. Yet this is the very time that we need to think something through rather than just act instinctively. So next time you're stressed by change, find a way to relax and calm down. For example, take deep breaths, go for a long walk, work in the garden, or clean the house. Later, think back to times when you successfully dealt with change—there will be plenty of examples because you're better at coping than you think. Look at what worked last time and what skills can be used today.

3. **Name your fears.** When you are relaxed, close your eyes and picture the proposed future. Where will it be? What will it be like? What will your partner be doing? Make the picture as detailed as possible. Next, try to analyze what is particularly worrying. Write each of these fears down in a sentence. Go back to the picture and try to imagine other things that could be unsettling you. Write these down, too. It is better to have a list of fears on a piece of paper—however long—than a large, amorphous terror in your head. Go back to the list and cross off anything that, on reflection, is a molehill rather than a mountain. Finally, discuss your fears with your partner. He or she might be able to offer reassurance or provide more information to take the edge off your anxiety. Even if some fears remain, you will have a clearer grasp of the most important.

Eight

Is It the Relationship or Something Else?

Life is complicated, but we like to keep our problems as simple as possible. We worry that if we continue to unpack our unhappiness, we will be completely overwhelmed. One problem, therefore, feels much more manageable that a whole stack. However, in our desire to keep things simple, we can sometimes end up tackling the wrong cause or blaming our partner for something that is not his or her fault. So how do we sort out which issues belong in our relationship and which belong elsewhere?

Deflection

In many cases, the unhappiness has been simply deflected from one part of someone's life onto their relationship. Paul was unhappy at work: "I found the city increasingly stressful, and I hated commuting." He really wanted to write thriller novels. "I could escape into a world of my own, and time flew. However, I had a family and a lifestyle to maintain, and how could I find time to write?" Paul had started to resent his partner, Debbie, but never really talked to her about it. After he had the

ILYB conversation, they had a general talk, and Paul discovered he'd been making assumptions. It turned out that Debbie preferred a happy husband to a new car and exotic vacations. So they restructured their lives, and Paul went part time. However, his novel still did not flow and eventually, in counseling, Paul discovered he was frightened of failing in his new career. It had been easier to blame Debbie for holding him back rather than looking inside and taking personal responsibility.

Recurring Issues from the Past

In other ILYB cases, what originally seemed a relationship problem turned out to be one partner's unresolved childhood problems. For example, George, forty-five and working for a large insurance broker, complained: "I truly feel that nobody understands me. I talk until I'm blue in the face and nobody takes any notice. Then, I shut myself away in my study, but she keeps knocking on the door." Relations between George and Tracy, a stay-at-home mom, had gone from bad to worse, and George was questioning whether he still loved Tracy. "I can't understand it," said Tracy, "I do listen. In fact, I've heard so much about his blessed office, if he were ill, I could probably walk in and take over. But still, he says I don't . . ." and she made quote marks with her hand, "really listen." My gut instinct was that George sounded rather like a rebellious teenager—and he did have a fourteen-year-old son. I knew George's parents had divorced when he was young and, as it turned out, he had also been fourteen. "How did you feel?" I asked. "Nobody listened to what I thought or what I wanted," George replied. His son's reaching the same age as he had been during the trauma of his parents' divorce had reawakened long-buried emotions. It was a personal, not a relationship, problem. With this knowledge, Tracy stopped taking George's mood so personally. They talked and averted an ILYB crisis.

Depression

Alternatively, the general feelings of dissatisfaction and unhappiness with the relationship could be a mild form of depression. Unfortunately, depression is hard to diagnose, because everybody gets the blues from time to time. Answering yes to five or more of the following can indicate a serious depression:

✦ Are you eating too much or too little?

✦ Are you finding it hard to sleep or sleeping too much?

✦ Do you feel tired all the time or generally lacking energy?

✦ Do you feel inadequate?

✦ Are you less productive at home or at work?

✦ Do you have trouble concentrating or making decisions?

✦ Do you have a tendency to brood over things, feeling sorry for yourself or getting pessimistic about the future?

✦ Does the world seem gray?

✦ Are you easily irritated?

✦ Do you rarely enjoy or feel interested in pleasurable activities?

✦ Are you prone to crying?

Anyone recognizing two or more symptoms should also speak to a doctor, especially if the symptoms have existed more or less constantly, with no more than a couple of months' relief, for two or more years. Other suggestions for dealing with depression include consulting a nutritionist to check on diet, cutting down on alcohol consumption, and exercising more—given that an aerobic-style workout releases endorphins, the body's natural feel-good hormone.

Emotional Infidelity

Sometimes, the "something else" behind ILYB can be *someone* else. Although couples with ILYB seldom arrive at my counseling office complaining about an affair, I often find their long-term problems have come to a head because one partner is having an "inappropriate" friendship. These friendships start innocently enough, as very few people go out looking for an affair. First, there are the tingly feelings from just talking together about something mundane, like the first-quarter sales figures. Next, come the longer conversations, and each half opens up first about their true attitudes to work or colleagues, and then about life in general and sometimes their own relationships. These "friendly chats" turn into long lunches—supposedly about work, but the office is barely mentioned. Before too long comes the first touch, normally something innocent like simultaneously reaching for the bill. Both "friends" feel the charge of electricity. The "friendship" begins to become more and more important. He's a good listener; she's really able to open up. He tells himself, *She helps me deal with my stress;* she thinks: *What's wrong with having friends?* The "friends" share their real feelings and discuss how they should not be getting this close. They start having long, clandestine phone calls and sharing sexy texts and intimate e-mails. Anybody eavesdropping or reading these messages would immediately recognize that this pair is flirting. For the "friends," this relationship is becoming increasingly significant to their day-to-day happiness. They might even agree to stop calling but their resolve weakens after a few days. This is the point that the "friendship" can tip over into a full-blown affair with either prolonged kissing or intercourse. Or maybe, it became an affair—in all but name—a few steps back. That is the problem with inappropriate friendships: No individual step along the journey is actually that bad, but before long, the steps have added up to a genuine betrayal.

Inappropriate friendships can not only lead to an affair, and all the resulting pain, but also make it impossible to work on the central relationship because all the emotional energy is diverted into the friendship. Oliver and Tina, married for twenty years, had all the classic signs of an ILYB relationship: Neither shared their true feelings for fear of rocking the relationship; until recently, they had had a superficially happy relationship. However, beneath Oliver and Tina's politeness was a testiness that could barely be concealed. It only took a few neutral questions and Oliver erupted about Tina's friendship with a work colleague. "Yes, we're friends. What's wrong with that?" she countered. Oliver was determined not to lose his temper and calmly as possible produced a telephone bill that showed seven phone calls to one number, totaling three-and-a-half hours, on just one day. Tina was furious, but kept a tight control on her feelings. "He listens to me," she finally said. "I'd listen to you," said Oliver, "but if I added up all our conversations from the last month, from the last three months, I doubt they would add up to three-and-a-half hours." With the truth finally out in the open, we could begin to work on their relationship.

Fortunately for this couple, Tina's inappropriate friendship had not tipped into Limerence (see Chapter 1)—always a risk—and she was still able to focus on her marriage. Other couples are not so lucky. "It started when we were working together," explained Rachel, twenty-nine years old and from Akron, Ohio. "We'd smile across the office divider and send each other e-mails. I'd mention that I liked a song, and he'd buy it for me. Just crazy fun stuff. But on many occasions, I felt we were so close to kissing—the connection was incredible." Unfortunately, Rachel's relationship at home seemed to be going nowhere. "My friend would do all this casual physical contact thing. You know, he'd come up behind me and massage my neck. If we were standing next to each other, I'd put my hand on his shoulder." It was only a matter of time before it became physical, and Rachel temporarily left her partner for her work colleague.

So when does a friendship become inappropriate? Of course it is possible for members of the opposite sex (and same sex with gays and lesbians) to be friends. The acid test is how much the friends are telling their partners and how much is omitted. True friendship is open to public scrutiny; inappropriate friendship is concealed.

So far in this chapter, I have discussed the more obvious "other causes" for ILYB: deflection, recurring issues from the past, depression, and emotional infidelity. The next group is harder to pinpoint as they are buried deeper under the relationship.

Unmet Needs

One of the most useful perspectives comes not from psychology but from marketing guru Abraham Maslow (*Motivation and Personality*, published by Harper in 1954). His Hierarchy of Needs shows that when basic requirements have been satisfied, we move on to higher aspirations. For example, once someone has a full belly, he or she can worry about finding somewhere safe to live, and then about a relationship and being loved. In 1952, he felt the average consumers were satisfied 80 percent of the time in their physiological needs, 70 percent in their safety needs, 50 percent of the time in belonging and love needs, 40 percent in self-esteem/prestige/status, but satisfied only for 10 percent of the time for the top need, which he called *self-actualization:* personal fulfillment and self realization of potential.

Looking at commercials today, products like soft drinks are no longer aimed at quenching our thirst, a basic physiological need, but at offering the illusion of satisfying our higher needs—like identity. Marriage seems to have been climbing the same ladder. Our grandparents placed more emphasis on being a good provider/housekeeper. Twenty years ago, when I first saw couples professionally, they were asking for more love and companionship. Today, people with ILYB are asking their partners for the highest need of all: "Help me become the best that I can be." Although many social commentators complain that we expect too much from relationships, I think this only becomes a problem when it collides with another twenty-first century phenomenon: denying aging.

Turning forty, and the mid-life crisis, is normally treated as the butt of a joke: "What's the best way to cover a bald spot?" Answer: a Porsche. We are encouraged, in particular, to laugh at men sucking in their paunches and reliving their glory days by buying fast bikes and cars, or dating much younger women. For some reason, society has no equivalent stereotype for women, yet I counsel many who are dealing with similar mid-life problems. In fact, a third of all clients, both men and women, and probably 90 percent of all ILYB cases, are facing something akin to a mid-life crisis. All of them have woken up one day and thought, *Life is too short to* _____. Everybody comes up with a different example, but everybody is facing the same ticking clock.

I do not use the term "mid-life crisis" in my counseling, however, as men are quick to disassociate themselves from it even though their wives might agree. Often, when I ask both male and female clients when their problems started, as part of my standard assessment, he or she will immediately protest, "It has nothing to do with turning forty." The second reason I avoid the term is because the problems can strike at any time. In fact, books have been written about the "quarter-life crisis"— twenty-five-year-olds who feel time is running out. My final objection to "mid-life crisis" is that it does not have to be a "crisis," with all the drama that implies.

So what is going on, and why does it have such an impact on relationships? Forgive me for stating the obvious: we are not going to live forever. Although everybody knows this fact, it does not stop us from believing, deep down, that we are immortal. For some men, the wake-up call is the traditional hair in the comb or worrying about declining sexual prowess: at twenty, they managed three orgasms in a night, and now they are pushed to come up with one. For some women, it is the awareness that fewer men are noticing them on the street. They begin to compare themselves unfavorably with younger women, envying their slim bodies, their energy, and how easy everything seems.

The death of a loved one, often a parent, can also be a wake-up call. There is no more concrete proof that we are not immortal than sitting at your mother or father's hospital or hospice bedside, witnessing their decline. Even more startling is the death of a contemporary—perhaps in a car accident or, worse still, some illness—as the illusion that mortality belongs to the generation above is stripped away. Finally, everybody faces the truth that their time on Earth is finite. At this point, some people will ask, "What is the meaning of life?" or "How can I make sense of my own life?" Others will decide that life is too short to be unhappy or in an unhappy relationship and search for remedies. Unfortunately, there is a third reaction: denial. These people will take refuge from an unpalatable reality by drinking too much, burying themselves at work, having affairs, or opting for cosmetic surgery. People in this third category risk turning a natural reaction and readjustment to aging into a crisis.

During this existential questioning, many people reach for self-actualization, the highest level of Maslow's Hierarchy of Needs. According to Maslow, "discontent and restlessness will soon develop, unless the individual is doing what he is fitted for. A musician must make music, an artist must paint, and a poet must write if he is to be ultimately with himself. What a man can be, he must be." At first sight, this seems a perfectly feasible goal, except that most professions today are not as clear-cut as musician, artist, or poet. What about the people whose work is made up of hundreds of different tasks with no clear-cut core? What about the others who don't particularly like their work and have no desire to be the best-ever accounting clerk? Maslow tried to study what self-actualization might be like but found it extremely difficult to find subjects who met his criteria. In the end, he had to settle for just forty-five people: a strange combination of personal friends and acquaintances; twenty students who seemed to be developing in the direction of self-actualization; plus historical and contemporary figures. Even then, he could only find two "fairly sure" historical figures to study—Thomas Jefferson and Abraham Lincoln—but then only Lincoln's last years; six "highly probable public and historical figures," and seven "who probably fall short but who can yet be used for study."

Maslow detailed his subjects' psychological health but had trouble reconciling their strong individuality with the ability to love and be loved: "These people cannot in the ordinary sense of the word be said to need each other as do ordinary lovers. They can be extremely close together and yet go apart quite easily. They do not cling to each other or have hooks or anchors of any kind. One has the definite feeling that they enjoy each other tremendously but would take philosophically a long separation or death. Throughout the most intense and ecstatic love affairs these people remain ultimately masters of themselves as well, living by their own standards even though enjoying each other intensely." In my opinion, these self-actualizers sound rather cold.

Becoming everything that one is capable of becoming seems to run the risk of destroying other people on route. Even a cursory reading of the biographies of the famous suggests that, although we might enjoy their music, books, films, and so on, we would probably not wish to be married to them. Even Maslow warns that the road to self-actualization could be a blind alley: "Higher needs are less perceptible, less unmistakable, more easily confused with other needs by suggestion, imitation, mistaken belief, or habit." He was writing in the 1950s, before advertising, marketing, and public relations became as sophisticated and all-pervasive. Today, we have to be very watchful or, instead of truly discovering ourselves, we are sold, for example, a vacation, a bottle of beer, or a new car.

Unfortunately, all this general resentment and bitterness—from growing older and our desire for self-actualization—gets aimed at our relationship and, in the process, turns something perfectly serviceable into something broken. One of the main reasons our relationship bears the brunt is the "at least we're doing something" factor. However painful and disruptive separation or divorce can be, at least these couples feel that they are moving out of their current situation toward a different script. When it comes to big questions like, "What is the meaning of life?" or "How can I ever fall back in love with my partner?" the temptation is to do something, *anything*. Soap operas reinforce the "something must be done" mentality. Good drama needs plenty of action and in soaps, people tend to confront first and think later. Secrets always come out, and characters always choose the most dramatic option. However, what makes for good soap operas does not always make for happy relationships. As compelling as it may be to act for the sake of action, this is not always the best way forward.

The Search for Spirituality

Ultimately, underneath the so-called mid-life crisis and self-actualization, there is probably a search for spirituality: making sense of the world beyond the self-centered and materialistic. For some people, this can also include a search for some greater power, either mystical or religious. However, when listening to my ILYB clients, especially those who want to leave their relationship, talk about their life in the future—their expected bliss, fulfillment, contentment, and even completeness—I am often reminded of a spiritual quest.

A good example would be José, a thirty-eight-year-old salesman: "Some mornings, while I stand at the train station, waiting for the 7:50, I start thinking, *What's it all about?* Surely, there is something more than daily reports and targets. I want my time to count—rather than just hours that are filled until the next day and I'm standing watching the same discarded newspaper supplements blow across the rails. If I started again, there would not only be space and time to think but the possibility of meeting someone that would make even the seconds count." For José, love had become the passport out of his mundane existence into a better tomorrow. While Jody, from Portland, Oregon, says, "What happened to the lingering kisses, the whispered confidences that made me feel truly alive?" Although Limerence might, temporarily, have the power to transform, it cannot last forever, and while Loving Attachment makes for a more complete life, on its own it cannot make an empty life meaningful.

So if not love alone, how can we make life more purposeful? Why are we here? What is the meaning of life? How do I fill this void at the center of my life? These are profound questions, and, unfortunately, all the books and potential answers are either full of platitudes or they leave one thinking, *Yes, but so what?* I believe the problem is that each of us has to find our own answer: something that fits our world view; deals with the issues from our particular upbringing; and ultimately confront our unique doubts, questions, and personality. My answer is not going to be your answer, but at risk of adding to the pile of platitudes, I will share my thoughts about creating a fulfilled life in the hope they might kick-start yours:

+ **Create rather than just consume.** Instead of watching sports on TV, go out and play. Instead of grabbing a convenience meal, take the time to cook something from scratch. Alternatively, take an adult education class in pottery, music, creative writing—the list is endless. Sadly, we live in an age that values something only if it earns money; don't let this common misconception stop you. If a hobby brings you pleasure, do it.

✦ **The journey is more important than the destination.** Traveling with an open mind and heart is more important than where one ultimately arrives. With this attitude, how quickly contemporaries travel becomes less important and the risk of pointless jealousy subsides. If life is a race—something I doubt—at least think of it as a marathon rather than a sprint.

✦ **Embrace death as a constant traveling companion.** After suffering a major bereavement in my thirties, I learned that death could be a friend rather than the enemy. With every major decision or fork on the journey, I am always aware of the time limit on life and love, and I am guided to make the fullest use of my share. Richard Holloway, formerly Bishop of Edinburgh, puts this more poetically in his book *Looking in the Distance: The Human Search for Meaning* (Canongate, 2004). He concludes: "Our brief finitude is but a beautiful spark in the vast darkness of space. So we should live the fleeting day with passion and, when the night comes, depart from it with grace."

These are only a few first thoughts, as probably we spend our whole lives redefining our personal big questions, testing our answers, and, in the light of fresh experience, starting all over again. If you are unsure where to start your search for meaning, try rebalancing your life. Career-oriented people might need to spend more time with the family; someone who has focused on child rearing and the home might need interests away from their own four walls. Like with a mid-life readjustment, it is helpful to look back over the first half of your life, decide what is lacking, and think about what could complete the picture for the second half.

The "I Love You, but" Crisis and the Link to Our Childhood

At first sight, it seems tough on our relationships that they act like a magnet for a whole range of other problems. But twenty years of couples' counseling has shown me that a good relationship is very effective in healing deep-seated personal problems. Maybe some hidden part of our brain, which is more intuitive, understands this power and is, therefore, determined to lay a range of disparate personal problems at the relationship's door—even if they do not really belong there.

To explain this idea, I need to explain the basic tenet of psychoanalysis: Your first relationship, with your mother or primary caregiver, will shape all your subsequent relationships. The "good parent" will provide a baby with food and comfort when he or she cries; psychoanalysts believe these children will grow up into trusting and open adults who make good relationships. An inadequate caregiver, who is wrapped up in her or his own problems, might leave a crying baby unattended or be erratic in feeding her or him; psychoanalysts believe these children will be untrusting, find it hard to make relationships, and may even suffer severe mental illness. Obviously, most people's experience will fall somewhere between these two extremes and indeed psychologists use the term "good enough" to describe the parenting received by the majority of us.

The most famous piece of research into the influence of upbringing on personality was conducted in the 1950s on monkeys and subsequently became the foundation for the theories of John Bowlby—a psychoanalyst and former head of the children's department of the Tavistock

Clinic in Bloomsbury, England. Some baby rhesus monkeys were raised normally by their mothers; some received just food and water; and a third group was also given a surrogate (a soft cloth around a wire frame). Not surprisingly, those without any nurturing turned into delinquent monkeys, and those raised with their mothers into well-adjusted ones. The baby monkeys with the surrogate did worse than the monkeys with mothers but significantly better than those with only food and water. Bowlby argued that both our sense of security and our anxieties have their roots in our relationship with our primary caregiver. His work has led to theory called *separation anxiety.* A study by Ainsworth, Blehar, Waters, and Wall—*Patterns of Attachment* (Erlbaum, 1978)—found that people fall into three categories: those who had a "good enough" childhood and find it easy to get close to someone else (secure attachment) and make up 56 percent of the population; those who had bad experiences and find it hard to trust other people (avoidant attachment) at 25 percent; and those whose unfilled childhood needs mean they can never get enough love. People who make up this third category find that others are reluctant to get as close as they would wish (anxious or ambivalent attachment) and make up 19 percent of the population.

At first sight, it is very depressing to think that our adult relationships are so strongly shaped by our experiences as babies. After all, we cannot return to being a small infant again and undo the harm—well, not without dressing up and giving the neighbors a lot to talk about. However, a loving, adult, sexual relationship does provide a second chance to learn about closeness. It is almost as intimate as the bond between mother and child; and indeed, many lovers even use baby talk as a sign of affection. So how does this work in practice? Taking my clients' childhood history, I am frequently amazed by how much abuse some have suffered and yet still grown up into balanced, normal adults. Time and again, through a good choice of partner and plenty of hard work, these damaged children have forged a relationship that had not only reduced past pain, but also provided the strength not to pass the problems onto their own children. I could give an extreme example, but I think a middling one would be more enlightening. Angela is forty-eight and has been married for twenty-seven years: "My father left and returned several times when I was growing up, so I don't really know how old I was, but probably about eight when he never came back. Although my parents' fights had been terrible and I hated listening to my father beat my mother, the worst part was that after he left not one word was said about what happened, not one. If my friends asked about my father, I was instructed to tell them he was at work. It was terrible keeping that secret, terrible. Even as an adult, when I tried to talk about him, my mother just froze me out." Angela's mother kept a stick by the door and would not just chastise her daughter but beat her in a cold fury. It comes as no surprise that Angela found it hard to form relationships. "However, I found a wonderful man and it wasn't easy to trust him, but I did. The proudest day of my life was standing hand-in-hand with my husband, watching our daughter get married. I have the sort of relationship with her where we laugh a lot and talk about anything, the polar opposite of my relationship with my mother. I really thought on that day, *The buck stopped with me.* But I couldn't have done it without my husband's support and, sometimes, his intervention." Implicit in falling in love—and sometimes actually stated—is the pledge: "I will look after you." This is the same implicit bond between the good (or, as psychoanalysts would say, the "good enough") mother and her baby. No wonder it feels like such an extraordinary betrayal when someone falls out of love with us. The reaction is beyond rational, but then we are dealing with the part of our personality formed when we were babies, and as yet incapable of logical thought.

An adult sexual relationship might provide the opportunity to go back and work through again all the most difficult issues: trust, closeness, separation, and, of course, love. However, it is not a magic bullet. I chose the word "opportunity" very carefully because a couple needs courage, determination, and persistence. Sadly, many couples give up too soon, frightened off by the arguments and the pain. Yet what is often mistaken for an impossibly damaged relationship is actually evidence of two people struggling away with difficult deep-seated childhood issues and, therefore, ultimately, a sign of hope.

We pick partners who are like us or who we feel complement our backgrounds in some way. By this, I do not mean racial, religious, or social economic influences—although these play a part—but family quirks. R. D. Laing, one of the fathers of modern psychiatry, wrote this about our families: "We are acting parts in a play that we have never read and never seen, whose plot we don't know, whose existence we can glimpse, but whose beginnings and end are beyond our present imagination and conception." Each person's family script will influence not only his or her personality, but also the choice of partner. An example of how we click with some people better than others comes from the Family Systems exercise, which is often used to train new counselors. When the course starts, the trainees are strangers. They are asked to walk around the room and, with no talking, pair off. Afterward, they compare backgrounds, and the surprise is always how well their families match. Perhaps both had trouble showing emotions, didn't like to become angry, or there was a divorce. Whatever the link, it seems we all have an internal play waiting to be cast. We search for other people to act out the issues we were unable to resolve as children. Our partners have to speak the same language and want to play the same scenes, or there is simply no connection.

Belinda and Thomas have been married for ten years but when they first met, they were surprised that, despite coming from totally different cultures, their families had been so similar. "My dad left Mom when I was eight—and he wasn't a particularly good dad. Thomas lived with his mother and grandmother. So we had both come from fatherless households," says Belinda. One of their mutual tasks was learning how to be a couple. Thomas explains: "It was really confusing. We knew about mothers—they were fantastic—but had no idea how to be a wife or a husband. What are these creatures supposed to be like? What do they do?" It would have been tougher for Belinda if she'd been drawn to a man brought up in a very traditional family whose family script would probably say that men are in charge and, therefore, less willing to negotiate than Thomas. Conversely, Thomas would have been baffled by the expectations of a woman brought up in a patriarchal family and the demands she might make of him. Finding someone with whom to work through unconscious past issues can be very healing, but it will also cause tension. This is why I find ILYB ultimately positive: one-half of the relationship is no longer prepared to hide behind being nice, and is ready to dive into the complexity of the past to discover a more fulfilling relationship.

Summary

+ Unhappiness is like a cancer, it slowly spreads through a life, infecting every corner: relationship, work, spirituality, and friendships. However, the place that the pain was first felt might not necessarily be the source of the original infection.

+ Although few couples seek counseling because of bereavement, when I ask clients to identify when they first had problems, one of the most common triggers for turning an okay relationship into a problem is the death of a friend or family member.

+ With spiritual issues—which our society is particularly uncomfortable addressing—the pain is likely to be expressed elsewhere, such as in our relationships. If this is the case, splitting up is not cutting out the cancer but merely exorcising the secondary infections. The original unhappiness is left unchecked to ravage further.

+ People expect a lot from relationships and that "love can conquer all." While love has incredible healing potential, a couple needs to invest energy and determination into their relationship, too.

+ The main message of this chapter for someone with ILYB is to look at the bigger picture and not to put all the blame on the relationship; for someone whose partner has ILYB, try not to feel completely demoralized or give up hope too soon. Instead, both partners should look afresh at the relationship, to take responsibility for their share of the problems and no more.

EXERCISES

Self-Diagnosis: What Else Could Be Lurking Behind Your ILYB?

The following questionnaire is designed to help someone with ILYB take stock. Some of the twenty-five questions will seem a little strange, but humor me and keep going. Don't overanalyze; just write down your immediate answers. There's no need for an essay, just a few notes and key words, if that's what makes you comfortable. Conversely, you may wish to write at length, especially if your thoughts seem to be going around and around in your head. The choice is up to you. In the answers section, you will find an explanation of each question, how to interpret your answers, and how to build the bigger picture.

1. How long have you been feeling unhappy?
2. Can you put a precise date on it?
3. How old were you at this time?
4. Think back to when you were eighteen; how would you have envisioned yourself at the age you are now? What would you have expected to have done or achieved?
5. What ages were your children when you first started feeling unhappy?
6. What was happening in your life in general when you first became unhappy? Try to make this answer as detailed as possible.
7. What was happening in your partner's life?
8. What was happening in your best friend's life?
9. What was happening in your children's lives?
10. What was happening at work?
11. When you have had problems at work, how have you dealt with them?
12. What would you consider your main problem at work today?
13. What was happening in your parents' lives when you first became unhappy?
14. Looking at your parents' lives, how do they cope with adversity? Have they had any mental health issues, like depression, anxiety, or excessive worrying?

15. Focusing on your unhappiness today, if you had to choose just one thing, what is troubling you most?

16. Have you ever felt like this before?

17. What impact is this problem having on your relationship?

18. When you have had difficulties in the past with your partner, how have you dealt with them?

19. Have you had similar problems with anybody else? How have you dealt with them?

20. What are the three main strengths in your relationship?

21. What would you change about your partner if you could? Try to be as specific as possible.

22. How would you describe your sexual relationship?

23. What would you like to have happen right now?

24. How would you like your life to be in the future? Make the answer as detailed as possible. Where would you be living? What would you be doing? What would the house look like? Who else is there?

25. How might you be able to make this happen?

Interpreting Your Answers:

1. This question is checking whether there is a general background of unhappiness.

2. It helps if you can pin down the start of the current problems. Obviously, it doesn't have to be to the day, but within three to six months is very helpful when making connections. For example, reaching the same age as a parent who died can trigger a depressive episode or general unhappiness.

3. Think about your life stage and the issues that people face at this age.

4. We often forget the preconceptions we carry about with us. This question is designed to help you look at yourself through your younger eyes and reassess.

5. Remember what was happening in your own life at the ages your children were when you first became unhappy. It is amazing how often the events in a son's or daughter's life can bring back issues from our own childhood. The most classic case would be that your own parent left when you were this age. We think we have dealt

with everything, yet back it comes literally to haunt us again.

6. The more detailed the picture, the easier it is to find trigger points. So try to add a little more information; maybe find some photographs from that time that will jog your memory.

7. A relationship is such an intimate affair that events in one partner's life will necessarily influence the other.

8. What friends are doing can create a mood that affects our lives, too. Often, if one couple in a circle divorces, it will have a domino effect.

9. We identify so much with our children that their setbacks will always find echoes in our own lives. For example, school ground bullying may make us acutely aware of being bullied in the office or remind us of our own childhood unhappiness.

10. We spend so much time at work, or thinking about it, and often base our identity on it. What light can it shed on your issues?

11. This question works in conjunction with question 18. Contrast the difference between problem solving at work and at home. Do they reinforce or fight against each other?

12. Are the problems at work different or similar to the problems at home? If the two sets are diametrically opposite, it is tempting to dismiss any connections, but more often, they are the flip sides of the same issue.

13. Here, we're not only looking at spillover from your parents' lives, but any echoes from how they made you feel as a child. For example, do they still seem controlling, distant, or infuriating?

14. This question aims to pick up any inherited mental health questions. The older we become, the more like our parents we become.

15. What field of your life does this come from?

16. What are the patterns?

17. Is your relationship mirroring the problem or is it the source of your problem?

18. This works in conjunction with question 11. Men often approach work and home problems very differently. If there is a difference, how do you feel about it? Which reflects more accurately the real you?

19. Is there something about your partner that makes you act differently from the other arenas in your life? Is this a good or a bad thing?

20. Sometimes we lose sight of the good things, and it is worth remembering them.

21. If you have a general answer—for instance, I wish she would be more patient—make it more specific by adding an example: "I wish she would be more patient when I'm late." This will give you a concrete goal for change.

22. If someone had a magic pill that would solve any sexual problems between you and your partner, how would you feel? What does this tell you about your relationship?

23. This is another question about setting goals.

24. I am always interested in not only the details of the imagined life, but also *when* someone pictures it happening: one year, five years, or ten years down the road. Often, the deeper in crisis a person is, the harder to put a date on the imagined future. If you've have very little to say for this question, try again. Don't censor yourself. This is just a fantasy and, in a fantasy, you can do anything.

25. Once you have a clear picture of where you are going, the secret to achieving change is to map a clear path from today to the imagined future. Often, the first step is the hardest, so make it something small and easily achievable. What comes after that?

It will probably take several days to let these questions settle. Give yourself some space, and then return to your notes. Divide a fresh piece of paper into three columns marked Personal, Relationship, and Neither. Go through your answers and place each issue in the appropriate column. Is there anything else you wish to add? Normally, the answer lies in the column with the most entries, but sometimes, just one entry can overwhelm all the others.

Is It the Past, or Is It Today?

Although the first exercise is designed for someone with ILYB, this exercise is also for partners as sometimes the partner still "in love" has issues lurking from his or her past, too.

The exercise is to spend an evening with old photograph albums and/or home movies.

- Look at the pictures of your parents and imagine that your partner has never heard any stories about them. What sort of man was your father? What three words would best describe your mother?
- Concentrate on the way your parents made you feel, and then start to make connections between yesterday and today.
- Look at photographs of you and your partner when you were the age your children are today. What was going on?
- Get out a recent picture of your children. Are there any reflections from what is happening in your children's lives today on your own past?
- Finally, assess whether any of these photos or stories connect with or throw any fresh light on your present problems. Is there anything that you did together in the past that could be revived to help your relationship today?

Step Six

 **GIVING**

"I really appreciated what you did for me yesterday."

"No problem."

"It got me thinking, and I'd like to do something in return."

"There were no strings attached."

"It will be my pleasure."

Sometimes, the smallest gestures, particularly when done with an open and generous heart, can make a big difference. This is especially true when up against overwhelming problems—like your partner falling out of love. If, however, it is you that has lost the love, the preceding six steps may have made you take stock and find enough goodwill for your partner to feel giving.

Nine

The Theory of Tipping Points

When a relationship is in crisis, most couples think they need to make a big effort to get big results. Often, they vow to try harder and be different: more thoughtful, more open, more helpful around the house—add your own shortcomings to the list. For the first few days, both partners follow model behavior but, of course, it cannot last. The result is more bitterness and even depression.

A fresh perspective on how to effect change, in a seemingly impossible situation, can be found not in psychology but in a recent business book called *The Tipping Point* (Little Brown Co., 2000), in which Malcolm Gladwell writes that, "We have an instinctive disdain for simple solutions. There is something in all of us that feels true answers have to be comprehensive and that there is virtue in dogged and indiscriminate application of effort." He goes on to praise the Band-Aid Solution—tightly focused and targeted interventions: "Critics use it as a term of disparagement. But in our history, Band-Aids have probably allowed millions to keep on working or playing when they would otherwise have had to stop."

So when relationships are not satisfactory, the answer is not to try harder but to think smarter. To this end, it is important to understand the laws of change. Gladwell examines how ideas catch on and describes the moment when something crosses over from specialist to mainstream as the Tipping Point. For example, in the second half of 1996, an e-mail address went from being a nerd accessory to something that nearly everybody possessed. As with a line of dominos, a small push will ultimately have a big impact. Gladwell claims that, "One imaginative person applying a well placed lever can change the world." I think the theory of Tipping Points can help explain how relationships can slip almost overnight from "okay" to "unhappy."

In my first interviews with clients, I have always asked when their difficulties started, mainly to find the classic life changes that put relationships at risk: having a child, grieving, moving to a new house, getting laid off, getting a new job, and so on. Although these important events make us take stock, they were seldom given as the real cause of a couple's problems. The Negative Tipping Point—where the relationship went from satisfactory to miserable—seems to come sometime later. However, few couples can pinpoint exactly when this happened. Yet if I asked for reasons why previous marriages or live-in relationships had failed, the majority gave these definite life changes. Could it be that we retrospectively attach big issues to a relationship breakdown, because it makes sense of the big changes in our lives? After all, who would admit to seeking a divorce because of damp towels left on the bed or failing to take the trash out?

The Tipping Point theory, however, would suggest that a buildup of what my clients call "stupid things" is the real cause of marital breakdown. Remember, the key idea is that little things can make a big difference. In his book, Gladwell gives the example of cleaning graffiti from subway trains in New York. More people began traveling on the subway, and with more passengers around, there were fewer muggings, so crime went down dramatically. A virtuous circle had been set up. However, my clients seemed to be trapped in a downward spiral, where forgetting to empty the dishwasher could seed a divorce. So instead of concentrating on major issues, I decided to focus on the little things.

Julia and Graham were in their thirties, and their most common argument was about cleaning their young children's shoes. She nagged, and he could not understand the fuss. Under this seemingly trivial dispute, we found two further layers. First, Julia's father had always cleaned her shoes and, therefore, she believed that good fathers did the same. Meanwhile, Graham had been brought up to be self-reliant and clean his own shoes. Second, the shoes represented their attitudes toward bringing up their children. She wanted to nurture them, while he wanted to make them self-sufficient. Once we had this insight, not only did the shoes cease to be an issue but the relationship also dramatically improved. Instead of being defensive, Julia and Graham began explaining, and this knowledge meant better communication, which in turn further increased their understanding. We had begun building a virtuous circle.

Gladwell identified the two key elements for reaching a Positive Tipping Point: the *law of the few* and the *stickiness factor*. The first undermines an old myth about relationships: that both halves of the couple have to want to change. As with my 80/20 rule about arguments (see Chapter 3), economists talk about the 80/20 principle in the market, workplace, and wider society. They believe that in any situation, roughly 80 percent of the work will be done by 20 percent of the participants. Thus, 80 percent of crime is committed by 20 percent of criminals, and 80 percent of road accidents are caused by 20 percent of motorists. In other words, a few people have a disproportionate effect on what happens. The same principle applies in relationships. We like to think of them as an equal partnership, but often, one half works harder at maintaining the partnership than the other. Many couples arrive in counseling because the partner who used to be responsible for 80 percent of the relationship glue has given up.

Pauline, a thirty-seven-year-old human resources consultant, was typical. "Why should I make all the effort? I kept all the conversation going at mealtimes; I even kept in contact with his mom. But Jake made no effort to fulfill my needs. I felt alone in the relationship, so I just withdrew." They were stuck, angry, and waiting for the other to make the first move. I sympathized with both of them for, in their different ways, they each felt underappreciated. After several weeks, I threw my hands up and asked, "Do you want to be right or happy?"

The next week, they returned with smiles. Pauline had been less critical of Jake and he, in turn, had been more willing to help around the house. They had achieved a Positive Tipping Point, but it had required Pauline (the law of the few) to take the initiative. However, she was so pleased that it ceased to matter that she had made 80 percent of the initial effort because both were now contributing more or less equally.

So why are some messages heard, while others fall on deaf ears? The second law, the stickiness factor, is the answer. Malcolm Gladwell talks about a health trial to make students have tetanus inoculations. Yale University tried various educational booklets—some only informative while others had gory pictures—but the rate of students getting the shots remained stubbornly low. However, one small change made 28 percent of students have the jab: a brochure that included a map showing the health center and the times of when shots were available. Thus, tinkering with a message can often make it stickier. If someone is not listening to us, we find more and more dramatic ways to get their attention—shouting, tantrums, threats, walking out—when a small change can often be far more effective.

Abby, fifty-three, from Milwaukee, Wisconsin, used to seethe with anger because her husband would never finish any of the home improvements that he started. "I'd tried reminding him, I'd tried getting angry, I'd tried rational discussion, and I'd even tried ignoring him, but nothing seemed to work until I did something completely different. When he actually did some work, I'd walk past and reward him by slipping a chocolate in his mouth." In the case of Pauline and Jake, she learned that by using humor, she could ask for something without coming across as critical. Since discovering *The Tipping Point,* I have spent more time getting clients to reframe their messages to each other rather than forever upping the same ineffective stakes.

When I look back with clients at the end of counseling, they are often astounded by how much was changed by so little. Jason and Tamara, two teachers in their forties, are typical. "Instead of stomping off, I learned to stand up for myself verbally," says Jason. While Tamara learned almost the opposite: "I thought I listened, but if he said something I didn't want to hear, I interrupted and effectively shut him up." These small but effective changes allowed them to deal more successfully with their major life issues—in this case, Tamara's mother's increasingly poor health—without even needing to discuss them in their weekly counseling session. They had dramatically improved their communication skills by one small, key intervention.

Tipping the relationship back into the positive is easier than couples first think, but on every occasion, either one partner or both decides to be generous and giving, and thereby kickstarts the healing process.

What Stops Couples from Finding Their Positive Tipping Point?

Our attitudes toward relationships are underpinned by a set of assumptions so fundamental that we take them completely for granted and, therefore, rarely check to see whether they are really true. Here are four that could be stopping you tipping from negative into positive.

Nothing I Say or Do Has Any Impact

When I see clients on their own, because their partners have declined an invitation to join in, they often despair about being able to influence their other halves. They feel completely powerless. Melanie, twenty-nine, was convinced of her partner's ability to spoil her day: "He'll criticize my driving ('You could have gotten a tank through that space'), or he doesn't call when he's going to be late and I'm left in the dark. It's no accident; he knows how to get me riled." With a little encouragement, Melanie admitted she knew which of his buttons to press, too. "With each meal, Michael puts a small heap of salt on the side of his plate, and then keeps dipping his food in it," she explained. "If I say anything about how damaging this is to his health, he gets really irritated—which I doubt is good for his blood pressure either." If she is aware of the negative buttons to push, surely it follows that she knew the positive buttons to get his cooperation, too? "He loves to be complimented," she admitted and agreed to try this strategy. It took a while for Michael to respond, perhaps he was angry or suspected an ulterior motive, but instead of giving up, I encouraged Melanie to keep praising. The results were impressive, and soon, her and Michael's relationship began to improve.

Although, ultimately, both parties have to be on board to improve a relationship, it only takes one person to start the journey. Pushing positive, rather than negative buttons, will ultimately create enough goodwill to recruit the second partner into joining the mission. Indeed, Michael started phoning Melanie, not just to tell her if he was going to be late home but for a general conversation.

Turnaround tip: To get into the mood for pushing the positive buttons, think back to your courting days and what your partner enjoyed. Is there something that you could repeat today?

Me, Me, Me

This block makes people concentrate on how something impacts themselves but forget to make a leap of imagination and consider the effect on their partners. For example, Melanie found it hard to accept compliments from Michael. When he said her new hairstyle suited her, she would shrug it off with a joke: "At least it looks slimming." Eventually, Michael stopped giving compliments and Melanie started complaining that he never paid her any attention. So why did Melanie find compliments hard? "I feel all self-conscious, like I'm the big I AM." But did she imagine how Michael felt? Finally, she stopped thinking and said, quietly: "When I make a joke of it, he probably feels belittled."

Turnaround tip: Next time something upsets you, acknowledge the impact on you—preferably out loud—and then ask your partner how the problem makes her or him feel.

Keep On Going to the End of the Road

This block is caused by having one fixed idea about what will save a relationship and keeping pushing in that direction—no matter what. When Gavin and Mary started counseling, I saw each of them on their own for one session. Unable to cope with conflict, they had simply stopped talking to each other, fearing it would only cause even more arguments, but instead, they had ended up with even more misunderstandings. The situation was dire, and Gavin despaired for the future: "I've done everything to build a bridge. I saved up money to buy something special for Mary's fiftieth birthday, and I threw a party with all her work colleagues invited, friends, and family, but she barely acknowledged me. When I got an inheritance and put all the money into our joint account—to pay off an overdraft—she thanked me, but it didn't make any difference. I don't know what else to do." When they started joint counseling, Gavin was determined that they should sort out their finances and brought all the bills and statements along to the session. Although they were back in the red again, Mary sidestepped the money issue and the session went around in circles. Gavin, of course, did not want to provoke an argument so he said nothing and instead kept throwing me dark looks. "You see, I've tried everything," he seemed to be saying. For many couples, this is the point that one or both parties give up and believe divorce is the only answer. Except that Gavin had not tried everything: he had just kept on going to the end of the road.

Gladwell's *The Tipping Point* is full of stories of individuals who made a big change to their community or turned small businesses into multimillion-dollar businesses—starting what he calls a "social epidemic." He writes: "The world—much as we want it to—does not accord to our intuition. Those who are successful at creating social epidemics do not just do what they think is right." He goes on to describe how these successful innovators try other avenues—even ones that everybody else would consider counterintuitive, or even stupid. Gavin's intuition had told him that money was the root of their problems. Indeed, they were seriously in debt, and he had tried everything to solve their financial problems. But he had not tried everything to save his marriage. Within a couple of sessions, it became clear that Mary wanted Gavin to talk to her—not about money, but with a normal exchange of views and news that make up day-to-day talking in a happy relationship. Once Gavin started conversing—rather than keeping on to the end of the money road—their relationship tipped into the positive.

Turnaround tip: If you feel you've tried everything, write a list of this "everything." Next, go through the list and cross off all the items that have sent you down the same old road. Finally, think counter intuitively. What haven't you tried yet?

Old Dogs Can't Learn New Tricks

This block not only assumes that your partner cannot change but that it is morally wrong to ask. However, Gladwell writes: "What must underlie successful epidemics, in the end, is a bedrock belief that change is possible, that people can radically transform their behavior or beliefs in the face of the right kind of impetus." He goes on to add that, "We like to think of ourselves as autonomous and inner-directed, that who we are and how we act is something permanently set by our genes and our temperament. We are actually powerfully influenced by our surroundings, our immediate context, and the personalities of those around us."

Week after week of counseling, I meet people who are worried that their partners will not change and others who complain that "She wants me to be something I'm not" or "He knew I was like that when he married me." Yet week after week, I see that minor accommodations—rather than fundamental shifts in character—will both satisfy the other half's needs and lead to a more fulfilling relationship.

Returning to the couple with the money issues, Mary's fear was that Gavin wanted to change something core to her personality. She believed that she "worked hard and deserved to treat herself." (And it did involve a long commute and work she found pretty tedious.) Mary was convinced that Gavin wanted to turn her from a spender into a saver. In reality, Gavin was worried about how much money went toward eating out. "Restaurants are a waste of money," he complained. Mary fought back: "I deserve to be pampered and looked after."

Ultimately, a compromise was found where Gavin bought the best cuts of meat and all the other trimmings for a wonderful meal but cooked it himself. "I even put on my best suit and pretended to be the *maitre d',*" he joked. "You should have seen the look on Mary's face, when I showed her to our dinning room table, which I had laid with our best tablecloth, cutlery, and flowers from the garden." Mary felt indulged, and George was pleased about the money saved. Had they changed? Yes. They stopped going to fancy restaurants (except for birthdays and other special occasions). Were they happier? Most certainly. Had they fundamentally changed each other's personalities? No. Except this no longer mattered because they had made minor adjustments that had reaped large rewards.

Turnaround tip: Write down everything that you would like to change about your partner. Next go back and take the items that are about temperament or personality—which are hard to change—and turn them into specific patterns of behavior, as these are easier to change. For example, instead of "Be more thoughtful," put "Take me out on Valentine's Day."

Find Your Own Tipping Point

Often, a major change can come from a small internal shift in one or the other partner. Here are four small suggestions that will help achieve the sixth step to saving your relationship: giving.

+ Be aware of your own internal, self-imposed obstacles. Each partner often waits for the other to commit to improving the relationship. Normally, they have little tests in their mind: *If he loves me, he'd take more notice of me* or *If she loves me, she'd show more affection*—except that neither tells the other, so the test remains secret. Instead, be generous, throw away the tests, and make the commitment to change.
+ When you wake up think, *What is the one thing that I could do today, no matter how small, that could improve my relationship?*
+ Next time you and your partner have a fight, try agreeing with

him or her—not for a quiet life but with love and respect. By this I mean really trying to understand why he or she holds what seems like a very contrary position. Give your partner the benefit of the doubt; after all, this is someone you respect—if he or she holds a position dearly, it must have some validity.

✦ ILYB is caused because couples choose a quiet life and the easy option. Therefore, adopt a new personal motto: "I'll never make it easy for myself again." Whenever you are faced with two choices, always go for the most challenging. Ultimately, the more you put into your relationship, the more you will get out of it.

If you are looking for some bolder Tipping Point ideas, or your relationship is in crisis and needs something more intensive, look in the exercise section at the end of this chapter. In fact, I would go further—that these are two of the most useful exercises in the whole book—so read them anyway!

What if We Have Separated?
Is It Too Late to Try Tipping Points?

After a breakup, the temptation is either to withdraw into neutral mode or to become angry and push negative buttons. However, with ILYB, most people are ambivalent about ending their relationship and are, therefore, secretly looking for reasons to stay rather than leave. Obviously, it will take much positive button pushing to turn the relationship around, but stick with it and monitor yourself for negative button pushes. For every slip into the negative, I would recommend at least *five positives* to counteract the effect.

Summary

+ Small changes can start a positive cycle and ultimately have a big impact on the relationship. Instead of trying harder, try thinking smarter.

+ When deeply held assumptions are not challenged, a relationship risks not only continuing down the same old road, but also remaining oblivious to any alternative.

+ It is never too late to change.

+ Never underestimate the impact of a single generous, open-hearted gesture.

EXERCISES

Positive Reinforcement

Tipping Points are about finding new ways of looking at things. With a fresh perspective, small changes can lever large ones. Here is a personal example from dog training that might sound strange—but stay with me.

Puppies are exhausting. They have to be watched constantly or they start chewing the legs of the dinning room table that belonged to your great-great-grandmother. Although a puppy wants to please, it does not understand English and has no idea what is good or bad behavior. I spent so much time telling my puppy "no" that he probably thought it was part of his name. When I took Flash off to puppy socialization/dog training, the instructor asked us, "What do you do when your puppy is lying quietly?" I stuck my hand up and said, "Breathe a sigh of relief." Another class member added, "Get on with the housework." Neither of these was the correct answer. "It's what most people say," explained the instructor, "but that's the last thing you should do. How does a puppy know what is good behavior, if you completely ignore him when he does it? What happens when he has been naughty?" We all smiled because we didn't have to answer the question: the puppy got our full attention. "You're all reinforcing the bad behavior—with negative attention—and not rewarding the good," the instructor explained.

From then onward, if Flash was napping in the sun, I would tickle his tummy and praise him. When he got overexcited and started rushing around the house, I ignored him. At first I had to consciously think about rewarding good behavior. But after a few days, Flash began to calm down, and I soon realized the extra effort was more than worth it—in fact, I was actually saving time by not chasing him around the house.

Here are some tips for using positive reinforcement to "train" your partner:

1. Think back over the past twenty-four hours: How many times did you criticize your partner's behavior or habits? How often did you praise? Which came out on top, positives or negatives?

2. Stop giving negative attention. Instead of complaining, for example, when he watches too much football or she has too many nights out with the girls, wait for the behavior that you wish to encourage. If your goal is more time together, on your next joint outing, reinforce this positive by telling him or her, "I'm really enjoying sharing this with you."

3. Positive reinforcement is built around "thank you" and compliments. Don't overlook them, as nobody can have too many of either.

4. Don't take anything for granted. For example, Jeff had moved into Martina's house but was having trouble feeling at home. Eventually, Martina agreed to completely remodel the place so Jeff had a stake, too. When all the works were finished, Jeff told her, "I know it has been hard for you, especially as it meant borrowing a lot of money and you don't feel comfortable doing that. So I just wanted to let you know that I really appreciate it." Of course, Martina knew all that, but having it acknowledged and said out loud was really important. Think of something you appreciate about your partner—but that normally fits into the category of "goes without saying"—and this time, give the thanks out loud. Make the compliment as detailed as possible. Which sounds more heartfelt: "Thank you for all you do" or "Thanks for taking my car in to be serviced today; it really made it easier for me"?

Flop/Flip Technique

When under stress, we have a limited number of ways of responding. For example, we might shout, fly off the handle, or go silent. If this does not work, we up the ante: screaming, not speaking for days, or even trashing the house. Soon, we are trapped in the same loop, with our behavior getting more and more extreme. Does this sound familiar? Here is a simple trick to break out.

1. Next time you're about to launch into your usual response, stop and think, "What could I do differently?"

2. It doesn't matter what you do differently. Honest. Anything is better than the usual response; we know where that leads and that it doesn't work.

3. Try an alternative response and watch your partner's reaction. It will probably make him or her think, too, and may prevent your partner from slipping into his or her usual response groove.

4. Think of the opposite to your normal behavior and try that as an alternative. Instead of going quiet, start talking. Instead of throwing knickknacks, straighten them. It is amazing how often the opposite behavior is the key to better communication.

5. Remember: Stop using the flop response and, instead, flip it over!

Step Seven

 LEARNING

"Things seem to be going much better."

"I agree."

"Sometimes I worry that it's too good to last."

"That's in the past."

"What if we slip back into our old ways?"

Successful organizations have learned that staying where they are is not good enough; they have to continually improve. It is the same for relationships, and the best way to avoid stagnation is a commitment to keep on *learning*.

Ten

The Six Special Skills of
Successful Couples

Toward the end of their counseling, many couples reach a moment of bliss where all their hard work begins to pay off. Loving Attachment blossoms and a glimpse of reawakened Limerence helps them believe that, once again, the two of them can climb mountains and defeat all comers. The magic is fleeting, however. Before too long, they remember how easy it is to fall from the heights of Limerence, the pressures of everyday life, the demands of our twenty-four-hour work culture, and the paucity of support for couples. The bliss turns to fear. So how can we protect our relationships?

It is not only relationships that are under pressure—a series of bad judgments can put the future of well-respected brand names at risk, and public institutions can easily find themselves accused of being out of touch. Providing the same level of service is no longer enough. Competitors get an edge. Customers expect more and more. This is why many businesses champion an idea—first developed by companies like Toyota—called the Continuous Improvement Culture. Many schools have also adopted it. The Continuous Improvement Culture suggests that unless something is getting better, it is actually in decline.

Therefore, management or a teacher are not satisfied with "good," and certainly not "good enough," but instead strive for better. Although our relationships should be protected from these market forces, we can adapt some of the better ideas.

Learning, the seventh step, provides the edge that keeps a relationship fresh, ensures nothing is taken for granted, and provides avenues for making Loving Attachment deeper. But how do we learn what makes relationships happy and fulfilled? This is hard for ILYB couples, especially as many of them report that their friends regard them as the partnership least likely to have problems. In addition, most psychologists have concentrated on studying failing relationships. Therefore, I searched scientific journals and my own casebook to discover what makes for happy relationships. I found that successful couples tend, often unwittingly, to have cultivated six good habits.

Six Good Habits for a Happy Relationship

These can provide goals to help all relationships continuously improve. I have started with the easiest habit to adopt. Like the Seven Steps to Saving Your Relationship, incorporating one habit into your relationship will make the next habit easier.

Investing: Setting Aside Time Together

Couples today spend less time together. According to the DDB Needham Life Style Survey, the number of married Americans who say "definitely" that "the whole family usually eats dinner together" has declined by one-third over the last twenty years. It's not just separate meal times. There has been a 10 percent drop on even "just sitting and talking." In the United Kingdom, once work, commuting time, sleep, and watching TV have been deducted, the average couple spends just twenty-four *minutes* a day together. Couples who like each other have an incentive to buck this trend. Unfortunately, when things go badly, the temptation is to spend more time apart, which breeds yet more misunderstanding.

Nick and Anna tried investing as part of a wider attempt to make their relationship work. Their social life had revolved around their circle of friends. So they reserved one evening a week for each other and despite friends' tempting offers, this appointment came first. When their night coincided with tickets to a Shakespeare production in the local park, to which their closest friends had already booked them tickets, they came up with a second way of investing. During that particular week, they set aside fifteen minutes each evening to talk over the events of the day. Through this kind of small talk, Nick and Anna were able to keep up to date with each other and let important issues emerge naturally. "This was much better than Nick announcing, 'We need to talk,'" said Anna. "That would send me into a panic and make me all defensive." Another good tip for investing comes from Jennifer in Cheyenne, Wyoming: "We have only one TV in the house and if we both want to watch it, we get to watch together (which means I watch more car shows than I would like and he watches more reality TV than he would choose), but we have lots to talk about." Professor John Gottman of the University of Washington, who studied several hundred married couples interacting and kept in touch with them for several years afterward, proposes an investment of five hours a week to make a profound difference. By prioritizing time together, successful couples demonstrate on a daily basis that they treasure their relationship above everything else.

Laughing Together: Using Shared Jokes and Running Gags

For many successful couples, laughter is a tool to knock the edges off a hard day. "Laughter really does help," says Elizabeth a fifty-four-year-old laboratory technician who has been married to Derek, a marketing executive, for twenty-one years. "We laugh at ourselves, our families, the bizarre habits of neighbors, and old movies on TV. Sometimes it's the only thing that gets us through." "We have certain sayings," explains Derek, "that would probably mean nothing to anybody else, but I'll tease her that she'll never play for the local ladies soccer team again, and she'll tell me that being drawn and quartered would be too good for me." Germany's Max Planck Institute of Human Development has noted that happily married couples are good at stepping out of an argument for a moment, so that they can make little repairs for their wrongdoings. A common way of diffusing the moment is to make a joke, and this is particularly effective when someone pokes fun at him- or herself.

Marrying Actions to Our Words

Social psychologists argue that only 10 percent of our communication is with words, but somehow we expect our partners to trust these rather than our behavior. In the rush of day-to-day living, it is easy to buy off a partner with, "Of course I love you" rather than taking the time to show it or act thoughtfully. This is why many couples arrive in couples' counseling with one half complaining of being taken for granted. Their partner is often mystified: "But you know I don't" is the most common defense. Normally, the complaining half snaps back with, "How?" The conversation grinds to a halt. By comparison, successful couples demonstrate love, show appreciation, and perform small acts of caring—the cement that holds a relationship together—rather than just paying lip service.

Many of my clients balk at this idea of consciously deciding to demonstrate their love, complaining that this would feel artificial. Some feel saying "thank you" all the time is stupid. Others go further: "Why should I thank my husband for doing the dishes? It's not as if they are just my dishes." These clients worry that being too free with compliments will devalue them. With small acts of caring—for example, he irons a blouse for her or she collects him from the station—the fear is that taking over a task, even on just one occasion, is tantamount to having responsibility forever. But does it have to be like this? Successful couples show that really powerful praise, thank yous, and small acts of caring come out of the blue. The occasional, "Have I ever told you that you've got beautiful eyes?" or "I really appreciated the way that you helped while my mother was ill" will be remembered for a long time. The power of small acts of caring is that they are one-time events. Especially with ILYB, it is more effective to show your partner your deep affection than just to *tell* him or her about it.

Mastering the Art of Compromise

Instead of having winners and losers, or unbalanced power, successful couples find a middle ground. An example would be sharing household duties according to who has the time. When chores are rigidly divided, there are often resentments. Compromise, on the other hand, is very different from compliance (just giving in) in that partners will state their viewpoints strongly and maybe even fight for them. Rather than digging in and never giving ground, though, successful couples will look for a meeting point. This is corroborated by the findings of Professor John Gottman of the Gottman Institute in Seattle, Washington. The best predictor for which couples, studied in his laboratory, stayed married was how well they argued and resolved their differences. This turned out to be more important than either the type of issue faced or the severity.

Until David and Simone, two teachers who had been together five years, learned to compromise, they were heading for a breakup. Although the couple had few fights, both partners had entrenched positions. David was an avid hang-glider, but Simone felt that it took him away too often and did not leave enough couple time. Generally, David went once a month and Simone patrolled this tradition—in case hang-gliding ate into more weekends. When David's hang-gliding club proposed a long weekend away, Simone put her foot down, and they had a series of nasty fights. "David doesn't get much vacation time, and we like to use what there is for a decent break," Simone explained. However, Simone decided to be generous: "I decided to stop squabbling about hang-gliding because it was casting such a big shadow over our lives. He knew how I felt, and it was pointless to go on about it." Ultimately, Simone got a nice surprise. "David didn't really go hang-gliding that much more; just the occasional special opportunity, and it stopped being an issue." David added, "With the atmosphere much better at home, I've been getting away from the office earlier and spending more time with Simone. It's funny, but I found that I had been defending 'me' time and, really, there was no need." Both Simone and David discovered they had been fighting over an arbitrary line in the sand. Their new compromise worked better, each of them felt more relaxed, and their relationship flourished.

Taking Risks

When we first fall in love, Limerence provides a magic cloak of omnipotence that blinds us to the risks of starting a new relationship. However, once Limerence wears off, partners may start defending themselves and putting up barriers. Successful couples continue to take small risks (like upsetting their partners) and bigger ones (like one partner going back to school and meeting a lot of new people). By contrast, ILYB couples prefer to play safe—this means that, if they decide to take a risk, it is nearly always a sign that the relationship is on the mend. Rita fell out of love with Joe after nineteen years and three children together. Since his wife came clean about her true feelings, Joe had been even less likely to rock the boat.

"My policy is to stress the positive," he told me at our first counseling session. However, as we worked through the seven steps, he became bolder. "We were out shopping and she took my hand, after months with no physical contact, and I wanted to know why," Joe explained. "Normally, I would have kept my mouth shut, in case I heard something I didn't want to hear or maybe she would take her hand away." This time, Joe took a risk and told Rita how much he enjoyed the contact. "I told him it just felt right to hold his hand," said Rita, "and later, we had a long conversation over coffee. I hadn't meant the hand holding as some grand gesture, but the more we talked, the more important this impulse seemed."

Another example of taking risks is Whitney, a twenty-seven-year-old from a small town in Pennsylvania, who was given the opportunity to work in New York City. Her initial response was to turn it down. "I was thrilled to be asked but it involved being away from Stephen for four months and I didn't think that was fair to him." The idea of being stuck at home while his partner had an adventure did not appeal much to Stephen either. "If I could be honest," he admitted, "I could picture her being swept off her feet by some big shot." However, Stephen decided it was best to give Whitney his blessing, and she took the job. Flying off peak allowed them to spend occasional weekends together, and Stephen took a vacation in New York. "I really got into the excitement of the city, the breeze of the East River, walking past places I'd seen only on TV or at the movies. We even saw a commercial shoot in Central Park. We're now talking about relocating." Ultimately, New York became an adventure to share together, and Whitney's job was an opportunity to grow together rather than a threat. Both falling in love and maintaining love involves taking a risk, because ultimately, without risk, there is little learning or growth.

Giving Each Other Some Independence

Successful couples allow each other freedom to grow—even if this means doing things without each other. At the other end of the scale are couples who lean on each other to the extent that one, or both, fears they would collapse without an all-encompassing togetherness. Most couples sit somewhere in between these two positions, but at times of challenge, most of us are likely to veer toward controlling or clinging.

The importance of some degree of independence has been underlined in the study of lesbian couples. Women have the reputation for being good at intimacy. In theory, therefore, lesbian relationships should be extremely stable. In 1983, American sociologists Philip Blumstein and Pepper Schwartz interviewed 4,314 heterosexual couples (both married and cohabiting), 1,875 gay couples, and 1,723 lesbian couples. They returned eighteen months later and found the couples least likely to break up were the married heterosexuals (14 percent had split), followed by cohabiting heterosexuals (29 percent), and then gay couples (36 percent), but the most likely to break up were lesbians at a startling 48 percent.

So what made two women the couple least likely to stay together? This was the task that sociologist Susan E. Johnson set herself in her book *Staying Power, Long-Term Lesbian Couples* (Naiad Press, 1990). She gave questionnaires to 108 lesbian couples across twenty-one states who had been together for ten years or more, and then followed up many with an interview. In the beginning, she thought the high split-up rate could be caused by the pressures on lesbian couples and the lack of support from mainstream society, although gay couples face the same problems. Her second theory was that lesbian couples were too quick to consider themselves couples—hence the old joke: What does a lesbian bring on a second date? Answer: a moving van. However, having completed the research, her conclusion was that successful lesbian couples were prepared to allow each other to be different. "You may think you are living as part of the same relationship, but you're not," Johnson wrote about her own relationship. "My partner says ours is the easiest relationship she has been in; I say, no—for me, it is the hardest. For a long time, we argued about who was right. It took us several years to realize we're not in the same relationship. She is living with me; one experience, and I am living with her; a very different experience."

Why should gay men's relationships last longer than those of lesbian women? A possible answer—and one that reinforces the issue of giving each other independence—is the gay attitude to fidelity. Dr. David McWhirter and Andrew Mattison, who tracked the development of gay couples found that after five years, none of the partners was sexually exclusive. "There are rules about what is acceptable, which include no flirting with other people when we're together and a ban on bringing other men home," says Scott who has been with his partner for seven years. "We also have a pact to tell each other about any outside adventures. Our heterosexual friends find our arrangement extraordinary, but in my opinion it is better and more honest than the sneaky affairs conducted by many straight people I know." Gay men are, therefore, less likely to expect their partner to fulfill each and every one of their needs.

All couples like the idea of their partner being the same: having the same experiences, interpreting reality the same, coming to the same conclusions. Yet this is not only impossible, but also probably undesirable. Sameness is fine but equally important is an awareness of the differences, so each partner can create a clear space for themselves as individuals within a relationship, too. This is why independence—both in the physical sense of being apart from time to time, and in the intellectual sense of being allowed to have different thoughts and come to different conclusions—is so important.

The lesbian couples interviewed by Johnson sum up brilliantly one of my most important themes for ILYB and offers hope for all long-term couples. One woman said, "There is no such thing as a relationship without conflict. You have to have some kind of acceptance of that; it just ain't gonna happen. Another person is not the answer. There ain't nothin' out there that is perfect." Nearly all the couples in Johnson's book had been through some crisis that could have split them up. May, in an eighteen-year-long relationship, was typical: "I think sometimes— this sounds silly but I think it's true—people don't hang in long enough to know that you live past it (the crisis). It does not have to be this big gaping wound; it can heal. People aren't patient enough."

I started this chapter by explaining that successful long-term couples had unwittingly developed six positive habits. Here is a bonus. May's quote underlines that just by getting to this point in your relationship, you have already developed one skill that underpins everything: patience. This is a vital foundation for the Seven Steps to Saving Your Relationship; the work ahead is hard but ultimately very rewarding.

Summary

+ While unhappy relationships fail for a multitude of reasons, happy ones all succeed for the same ones: these couples have cultivated six special skills.

+ *Investing* will encourage a couple to *laugh together. Marrying actions and words* will create the goodwill for the *art of compromise,* that, in turn, makes *taking risks* easier and ultimately *giving each other some independence* becomes a possibility.

+ Learning completes the Seven Steps to Saving your Relationship. A commitment to continual learning will both renew a relationship and keep it on track.

EXERCISES

Building New Habits

Many couples start out with good intentions, but after a couple of weeks, everything starts to slide. The advantage of habits, over good intentions, is that they build in three key factors for lasting change: *simple events* that *happen regularly* and can be *easily measured.*

Take the first habit as an example: spending more time together. The temptation is to organize a grand gesture, like a cruise or an expensive night out. However, these fail to become habits because, by their very nature, they cannot happen regularly and, therefore, the benefits quickly fade. By contrast, eating together in the evening can build into a habit. It is definitely *simple,* can *happen regularly*—possibly most weekday evenings—and is *easily measured.* At the end of a month, a couple can look back and check how often they ate together. If this idea appeals, here are some practical tips to reap the benefits of this habit. Don't have the television on or allow other distractions that stop the two of you from talking. If one of you gets in much earlier, have a sandwich or something to keep you going. Alternatively, set up a meal together during the weekends—like a long breakfast on Sunday morning—and treat it as a fixed part of your routine.

- What new habits would you like to introduce to your relationship? How can you break them down into something *small, repeatable,* and *measurable?*
- Consider a new habit, like I have done with eating together, and try to spot any stumbling blocks in advance.

Laughing Together

If you and your partner have few opportunities to laugh together—and many couple's shared social activities are very serious adult activities like eating out—here are some ideas:

1. Make a visit to a comedy club.
2. See a funny movie or a farce at the theater.
3. Try something difficult like ice-skating together.
4. Do something ridiculous together for charity, like running a three-legged race.
5. Tickle each other.
6. Show each other your baby pictures.
7. Go to the beach and build a sandcastle.
8. Visit a children's petting zoo or a farm.
9. Share something that you haven't done since you were a kid.
10. Paint a picture together.

Part Two

If Your Relationship Has Reached Crisis Point

Eleven

Having the "I Love You, but" Conversation/Hearing the "I Love You, but" Confession

Up to this point, I have tried to address both someone who has fallen out of love and his or her partner at the same time. However, this is where a couple with ILYB issues can end up in two very different camps: One partner needs to talk and get feelings off his or her chest; the other is in shock. So I have divided the chapter in half, starting with making the confession, and then moving on to how best to react.

"Sunday dinner time, and I'd be sitting around the table with my family. My body is there but I wish I were somewhere else," explains Grant, a forty-five-year-old building manager. "My wife is laughing, and the kids are talking about their friends. The whole thing should be perfect. I love my kids to death, and Jill and I get along fine, but I feel so alone. Sometimes, she'd catch me thinking with what she calls my faraway face: 'What's up?' 'Nothing darling.' How could I tell her that inside I'm dying?" Many people with ILYB hold back. They instinctively know that there are few things more devastating than learning that someone has fallen out of love with you. Yet having these feelings trapped inside is also extremely painful.

So what can be done? The first instinct of most ILYB sufferers is to hope something will change. "I'll feel differently after the summer vacation, Christmas, moving to a new house." Add your own example to the list. But this kind of bargaining seldom provides more than temporary relief. In some of the cases I have counseled, as much as ten years has elapsed from the first doubts to the final confession. Fortunately, most people do not suffer for this long. In my research, 41 percent of people with ILYB had waited over two years to tell their partner, and 19 percent waited five years or more.

Knowing When It's Time to Talk

How do you know it is time to talk? A sure sign is the growing tension between negative feelings inside and the superficially pleasant behavior on the outside. Once someone reaches this stage, he or she starts snapping, and the partner feels like he or she is walking on eggshells. Grant wished that he had come clean before his marriage got bogged down in pettiness: "I hated myself because I'd pick, pick, pick all the time about how much noise she made in the bathroom in the morning, how I hated the way she'd sing in the shower, the way she'd turn her purse inside out to look for a breath mint. A thousand and one things that had never bothered me before all made me seethe. I was like a bear with a sore head, and I knew that if I didn't say something soon, we couldn't even be friends anymore." ILYB is difficult enough without loading the situation with unnecessary animosity.

For other people, a strong attraction to someone at work or a friendship that is in danger of crossing the line is the catalyst for an ILYB confession. Daniel, a forty-eight-year-old compliance manager, found himself drawn to a female colleague. "The weekends seemed gray and endless at home," he explained, "when my heart started racing on Monday morning, as I chose clothes that I hoped she would like, I knew I had to do something." Daniel had been suffering with ILYB for three years but had said nothing for fear of hurting his wife. "I knew that an affair was almost inevitable. If not then, certainly a few years down the line. What would hurt my wife more: telling her how I felt or cheating on her?" Even when nothing has happened, it is better to make a full confession and explain how serious the problem has become.

Having decided to confess, there is no right or wrong way to go about it. Some people prefer to set up a rendezvous. This has the advantage of committing a couple to talking but could worry the partner who is ignorant of the true nature of the conversation. Another option is to secretly stage-manage the confession: making certain the children are out and that there are no likely distractions, and then springing the discussion on the other half. This cuts out the chance of the partner worrying in advance—and conjuring up some life-threatening illness—but risks his or her interrupting, pleading work pressures, or asking for a rain check. The third alternative is to wait for an appropriate opening—like when the other half asks what is wrong. The topic comes up naturally, but this option can easily become an excuse for putting off the confession—indefinitely. For this reason, I recommend setting a time limit for waiting for an opening.

A few words of general caution. Don't bring up ILYB in anger, after a couple of drinks, or during an argument. Avoid Christmas, birthdays, and anniversaries (otherwise, these dates will always bring back memories of the confession). Although neutral places—like restaurants—can provide good forums to talk, avoid old favorites, as this can taint a partner's previously happy memories. Whatever the choice, set aside plenty of time to talk: your partner will want to go over everything again and again. In most cases, the confession will be the start of a series of conversations.

Being Honest

The most important element in the ensuing discussions is to be 100 percent honest. Some people with ILYB try to spare their partner's feelings by releasing the bad news bit by bit. However, this strategy will not only destroy trust, but also magnify the pain. Frank, a fifty-eight-year-old service manager, did not put all his cards on the table right away. He had met Christina relatively late and, without the distraction of children, they had been able to dedicate plenty of time to their shared interests: classical music concerts, theater, and walking. Frank knew Christina would be shattered by even the thought of divorce so he led her to hope that their marriage could be saved. She started cutting out helpful articles, but he would not read them. Eventually, she confronted Frank, and he told her the truth. "I'm not a little girl who has been promised a pony," said Christina. "It was so demeaning and, for the first time in our marriage, I found I couldn't believe what he told me."

Other people with ILYB are economical about what, in their opinion, has gone wrong with the relationship. "I thought it was kinder not to tell him just how miserable I felt. Why grind his face in it?" explains Sheila, a forty-four-year-old caretaker. "Would it really have helped if he knew I didn't think he pulled his weight—leaving me to earn most of the money; that I thought he was selfish in bed and how he sometimes bored me?" These things aren't easy to hear, but keeping them back robs a partner of the opportunity to change. As discussed before, when communicating criticism, avoid damning a partner's character and concentrate on the particular unwanted behavior and how it makes you feel. For example, Sheila could say, "I need more foreplay," rather than, "You're a lazy lover." However, even badly phrased, the truth is always preferable to kindly meant lies.

In other cases, the person with ILYB tries to be straightforward, but the partner chooses to minimize the confession, either by dismissing it outright or putting the most optimistic spin on it possible. In these circumstances, I recommend finding an alternative way of delivering a message—for example writing a letter or sending an e-mail. (For more advice on the clearest and the kindest way of communicating difficult feelings, see the Three-Part Statement section in Chapter 5.)

What if there is someone else involved? An affair makes an ILYB confession a hundred times more complicated. Has the affair undermined the primary relationship? Did problems in the primary relationship cause the affair? It is a real chicken and egg situation: very difficult to unravel even years afterward, and impossible under stress. However much ILYB is a contributing factor, the "innocent" partner will primarily be concerned with the betrayal. Therefore, it is best to confess to the affair first and leave the ILYB until the initial shock has worn off. When the other partner is ready, he or she will want to know what caused the affair, and that is the moment to talk about ILYB.

What happens after the initial confession? You will probably feel a short burst of relief: At last, your secret is out in the open, and the pretence has finally stopped. However, once your partner's shock wears off, be prepared for him or her to turn angry, feel sad, or even to take on all the blame. The next few days will be full of drama and, on many occasions, your preconceptions about each other will be challenged. This will be tough but ultimately can be an opportunity to grow together. Sheila expected her partner, Robert, to almost roll over and play dead: "It was such a shock because all his resentments came tumbling out. How I'd used my bigger salary to dictate what we could and what we couldn't afford; how demanding I'd become; how I wouldn't listen. He was a lot tougher than I thought and although what he said made me angry, you know something? I started to admire him again."

Sometimes, the ILYB confession can be a prelude to reconciliation, especially where one partner feels that previous attempts to rescue the relationship have been ignored. Jennifer had been unhappy with Bob, a construction worker, for many years and felt that she was bringing up their two sons alone. "Every time I tried to talk, he just shut off. It was like an invisible barrier dropped down in front of his eyes," she explained. "I thought I could carry on for the sake of the boys, but one morning I just snapped." Unlike most ILYB relationships, Jennifer had to put up with a lot of abusive language and, on some occasions, Bob would punch the wall. "I had to explain that I cared deeply for Bob, but I didn't love him anymore," she said. "I think he would have found it easier if I'd told him I hated him." However, the news galvanized Bob into action. Within a week, he had arranged individual counseling. "I don't like the person I've become either," he told me. Jennifer didn't know what to do. Could she trust Bob to really change? The first month was the most difficult, but once the truth was out in the open, Jennifer and Bob found they could talk honestly, and they began to negotiate.

Planning a Trial Separation?

Generally, I am not in favor of a trial separation—especially in the first few weeks after the confession, when there is a lot to discuss. However, some people find it easier to think away from the pressures of family life and in the words of many of my clients: "Maybe if I'm away, I'll find that I miss him/her." Certainly, the space allows each partner to unravel which issues belong to him or her personally and which to the relationship.

+ Your partner will probably be against the idea, fearing that it is the first step to a permanent separation. Even if you have no clear idea of how long apart you need, try to give an estimate. A tightly defined separation—with clear goals—will seem less threatening than something open-ended. At one end of the scale, a client has gone away for a long weekend and, at the other, for six months. Most couples settle somewhere between one and three months.

✦ What about the children? Obviously, it depends a lot on their age and for how long the parent is going away. On the one hand, if reconciliation is possible, it seems like a bad idea to worry them unnecessarily. But on the other, studies into the long-term impact of divorce show that children suffer most when the marital breakup comes out of the blue. Generally, children pick up on the atmosphere in the house and the worry of not knowing is worse than having all the facts.

✦ It is best to tell the children together about a trial separation. This act of physical togetherness underlines that you will continue to be cooperating parents whatever the future brings. Children often process emotional issues through very practical concerns; for example, "Will Daddy be here for my birthday?" Before talking to the children, think through the separation and how it will impact on them. In this way, you will already have an agreed plan. Most children need time to digest the information, so expect this to be the first of several conversations.

✦ When should the temporary separation start? Look at your diary and negotiate how to deal with joint social occasions in the next month. Should you cancel them? Should you still attend together, even though you are temporarily separated? Should just one partner attend? Or should you wait until a certain event has passed before starting your temporary separation?

✦ Start to discuss the practicalities of day-to-day. Where will you live? What contact should there be during the temporary separation? It is important to plan some time together to talk and take stock during your break—maybe even a date? In this way, there is the potential to court each other again.

Hearing the ILYB Confession

"It was like strolling along a quiet street on a sunny summer's afternoon; a nice neighborhood with well-tended lawns, kids playing, and men washing cars. When out of nowhere a car came hurtling around the corner, came up on the pavement, and knocked me down. As it flipped me in the air and my face hit the pavement, I noticed my husband was driving the car. Why was he doing this to me?" This is how Margaret, who had been married for seventeen years, described the impact of hearing her husband confess, "I love you, but I'm not in love with you." Just like in a car crash, she felt shocked, disoriented, confused, and very frightened. She kept thinking, *There must be some mistake* and *What do I do now?* But unlike a road traffic accident, there was no ambulance on the way and nobody to offer a sugary cup of coffee. Enrico from New Mexico was totally unprepared for his wife's confession: "I can't actually recollect anything of what she said exactly, but her desperation is still etched on my heart. I felt physically sick." He also felt very guilty. "My wife was going through this terrible time—like she'd been trapped in a domestic 'prison cell'—but I'd put it down to general tetchiness."

Although the situation may seem bleak, there is one enormous positive: all the relationship problems are now out in the open. The work of finding a way back to Loving Attachment can begin. But first you need to cope with the fallout from the ILYB confession. After a crash, the first step is to walk around the car and assess the damage. The same goes for hearing your partner does not love you. First, is he or she telling the truth? When a couple has been dating/seeing each other for only a few months, one partner can try to break off the relationship by using ILYB.

These partners hope it will soften the blow, partly because they do not want to hurt the other and partly to ease their own guilt. To be brutal, it is doubtful if these people know the true meaning of love, so all their previous declarations of love should be taken with a grain of salt. The second set of circumstances when ILYB can be a handy cover-up is when one partner is having an affair. These people think bad news is better broken in stages. "I thought that he wouldn't get so angry if I held back on the affair for a couple of days," explained Jill, a thirty-eight-year-old fitness instructor, "because my lover was not the *cause* of our problems, just a symptom." Often with celebrity breakups, the couple will deny anybody else is involved, but a few days later, one-half will be caught out by a photographer with a long lens. The partner is left doubly betrayed; first by the cheating, and then by the lying. In other cases, there is no affair, but the partner is indulging in an "inappropriate friendship"— either over the Internet or with flesh-and-blood colleagues at work. Here are a few questions to uncover an inappropriate friendship:

+ Are you talking on a personal level with someone else?
+ Are you calling or e-mailing someone just to talk?
+ Have you been out for lunch with someone or met for a quick drink after work?
+ Is anyone becoming more than a friend?
+ Have you touched anyone in an intimate way?

Having satisfied yourself about the facts behind ILYB, the next job is to do some first aid. Speak to a member of your family or a long-term friend who will listen and sympathize rather than take charge. Some partners, who have been told ILYB, feel disloyal confiding in others. However, the road back to a healthy relationship can be long and arduous, so good support is vital.

Often, in an attempt to gain control of an out-of-control situation, the dumped-on will magnify their weaknesses and promise to change overnight. When Tony told Maria ILYB, he also confessed that he was unhappy with their sex life. She jumped on this scrap of information, read a million books, and promised a better future. Maria was truly in overdrive, overwhelming Tony with love and hoping to win him back. For fear of embarrassing Tony in front of their friends, Maria also kept her problems to herself. Although thoughtful, this decision proved to be counterproductive. Her friends would have stopped her from taking all the blame and humiliating herself in the bargain. Remember the first of my three laws of relationship disputes (see Chapter 3): All arguments are "six of one and half dozen of the other." Tony needed to take blame for not speaking up sooner and some responsibility for their inadequate sex life.

After assessing the damage and getting support, the third part of recovering from hearing ILYB is to get angry. After a brief burst of fury, many people who have been dumped on either get weepy or become too nice and too forgiving, and many try to minimize the news. Although shock and denial are natural responses to a catastrophe—and that's no understatement for something that puts relationships, families, and homes at risk—these reactions stop a couple from really addressing the problem. In contrast, anger will bring issues, concerns, and desires to the surface. It also shows your partner that you care, take the problems seriously, and wish to really work on your relationship. Without anger, the gut instinct is to reassure: "It'll be all right" or "I'll try harder"; just the sort of nice but passionless response that drained all the love out of the relationship in the first place. If you are having trouble accessing your anger, either speak to your friend/family supporter or look at the Unable to Get Angry? exercise at the end of this chapter.

Next on the agenda, begin thinking about the changes that *you* would like. This surprises many clients who would rather keep the spotlight on their partners. Maria was particularly reluctant to talk about her issues: "If I tell him my problems, he'll think the situation is hopeless. No. I've got to concentrate on the positive." But this can easily be seen as dismissing the crisis or, even worse, not really listening. After some prompting, Maria began to think about her needs, too. "Tony keeps himself to himself, so I don't know what he's thinking of half the time," she explained. "When he doesn't share his feelings with me, I don't really feel like sharing my body with him." Finally, both Maria and Tony had something concrete to aim for that could improve their Loving Attachment. Their relationship began to turn around. Tony would talk about his day on his return from work, while Maria would try one of the tips from her magazine, for example: keeping good eye contact during their lovemaking (rather than closing her eyes or turning her head away). The following week, Maria and Tony came back with smiles on their faces. He had talked and she had looked, and both felt more intimate than they had in years.

The plan had worked because it had fulfilled three basic requirements:

1. **The needs had been expressed as a positive.** When you tell your partner, for example, "You don't talk to me," it doesn't matter how nicely you put it—he or she will hear this as a criticism. The natural response to criticism is to either get defensive or to attack back. However, a positive request—such as, "I'd really like to understand more about your job"—invites a positive response.

2. **They had asked for something concrete.** Some requests, even though they are positive, fail because the other partner has no real idea where to start. For example, "I'd like us to spend more time together" is fine, but how long, how often, and what will the couple do? Contrast this with, "I'd like us to walk the dog together on Saturday morning."

3. **It had been small and easy to do.** Instead of offering something

ambitious, like a new position for intercourse or sexy lingerie, Maria had agreed to something she knew would be achievable: keeping her eyes open during lovemaking. Instead of intimate chats about love and where the relationship was going, Tony had agreed to talk about something more neutral: his work.

For more about setting positive goals, see Accentuate the Positive in the exercise section.

What if My Partner Asks for a Trial Separation?

This is the greatest fear of anybody who has been told, "I love you, but I'm not in love with you." But don't panic.

+ Obviously it is easier to work on the relationship if the two of you are under the same roof, so make certain that your partner is truly determined to leave instead of just floating an idea.

+ Unfortunately, it is impossible to keep someone home who is determined to leave, and resisting the inevitable will soon become counterproductive. Instead of the focus being on your partner's ILYB, it switches to your "unreasonable behavior."

+ I know it is tough, but agreeing to a trial separation puts you in a stronger bargaining position than if your partner just walks out in exasperation. So give the break your blessing, but first ask for a month together to absorb the news and work through some of the Seven Steps to Saving Your Relationship. "When Frank first told me about the temporary separation, I was heartbroken, and I must admit I did everything to stop him, including using emotional blackmail," Christina confessed. "Ultimately, I couldn't change his mind. He stayed, but he was miserable, and it certainly wasn't going to make him better disposed toward me. If I love him—which I do with all my heart—I had to let him try." This act of generosity helped Frank and Christina find a compromise: a temporary separation but one where they saw a lot of each other.

- ✦ Look at the practicalities. Where will your partner go? What choices would be acceptable; what would be unacceptable? How often will you get together? My advice would be to ask for at least one "date" per week—by this I mean a couple of hours doing something pleasurable with just the two of you. If you have children, build in opportunities to meet as a family. How often should there be telephone contact and under what circumstances? Don't wait until the month together is up to start discussing the practicalities—particularly somewhere else to live—as this will help your partner realize your "blessing" is genuine.

- ✦ Spell out all the rules of engagement, so there is no room for misunderstanding. I have counseled cases where one partner believed that he was free to see other people while his partner thought they were still working on the relationship. If both parties have a clear understanding of the temporary separation, this kind of bitterness can be avoided.

- ✦ How long should the trial separation be? There are no hard or fast rules, but it will make the time apart easier if you know the duration. Your partner will probably be unable to give any idea how long he or she needs. If your partner is particularly hard to pin down, a tip is to suggest a possible duration—for example: three months. Most people will reply either "not that long" or "I'll need more than that." Keep going until you have found a possible duration to discuss. Your partner might still be resistant to a solid time span and, indeed, it is hard to predict how either of you will feel. So view the end of a trial separation as an appointment for an in-depth discussion rather than a definitive decision on whether to try again or split up. ILYB needs time and it is always better to rene-gotiate a longer break than force the issue too quickly.

What if My Partner Has Already Left?

+ All is not lost. The ideas in this book can still be used on the occa-sions when you have contact—in particular, see Chapter 9.
+ Keep the lines of communication open. My advice is to try the opposite of what you did before, as this will bring some fresh air to the situation. If you've always talked at home, go out to a cof-fee shop. If you've talked in restaurants, get take-out instead. In fact, try anything that will change the old dynamic.
+ It is important not to go into overdrive and push your partner far-ther away. Read the advice in Chapter 12 before attempting any of the relationship rescue strategies.

Summary

Confessing ILYB:

+ The longer you leave it, the harder it will be for your partner.

+ Make certain that you are as honest as possible. Any attempts to dissemble will just hurt your partner further.

+ Expect the unexpected, but be ready to talk—probably more than in all your conversations in the past five years added together.

+ If you need a trial separation or some space to think, make certain to give your partner a clear and detailed picture of what you need.

After hearing an ILYB confession:

+ Everybody reacts differently to bad news; there is no right or wrong way.

+ Instead of focusing on your partner's dissatisfaction and becoming trapped by his or her mood swings, start thinking about what she or he needs to do to win you back, too. This change of attitude will stop you from sliding into depression and will provide some direction for your life.

+ Although extremely hurtful, an ILYB confession can be the beginning of a more emotionally open and fulfilling relationship.

EXERCISES

Planning to Confess?

Think back to past bad news that you had to give or hear. Maybe you told an employee that he or she was being laid off, or perhaps you were on the receiving end? Perhaps when you were young your parents split up, or you can remember them telling you about a grandparent's death. If you are gay or lesbian, what about coming out to your parents? Write down all the things that made it easier to break unexpected news or to hear it; next, think of everything that made the experience more painful. This will give you a list of do's and don'ts, and, although not an accurate predictor for your confession, this process helps you prepare.

Accentuate the Positive

Generally, it is easier to say what we don't want than to ask for what we do want. That's why, when trying to make things better with our partners, we end up either complaining or simply describing the problem.

Part One: Look at these typical complaints and see whether you can turn them into a positive, and then find a request for a concrete but small goal. I have provided some possible ideas at the end of this chapter.

1. Why do I always have to clean up the dishes?

2. Will you stop groping me?

3. You never initiate sex.

4. You're always hanging out with your friends.

5. I hate it when you avoid me.

6. You are way too critical.

7. Why can't you lighten up?

8. Why didn't you call me?

9. You do nothing with the kids.

10. Isn't it about time you fixed the hall light?

Part Two: Thinking of your complaints about your partner, write down the top three and turn them into positive requests: what you *want* rather than what you *don't want*.

Part Three: Look for a concrete goal. If you cannot find one, ask yourself, "How will I know when this goal has been achieved?"

Examples:

Complaint: *You sulk to get your own way.*

Positive request: *Please tell me outright when you disagree.*

How will I know when this has been achieved? *When we can happily go shopping together.*

Concrete goal: *Let's choose the new faucet for the kitchen together.*

Complaint: *I'm always the driving force.*

Positive request: *I really appreciate your input; could you give me more?*

How will I know when this has been achieved? *When my partner arranges a night out.*

Concrete goal: *Actively planning a vacation together.*

Unable to Get Angry?

If you find yourself being too nice to someone who has told you ILYB, here is a list of my top seven anger prompts. Write the ones that apply to you on a card and keep them handy at all times. Next time you feel weepy or depressed, this card will provide a shot of anger to keep you going.

1. He/she told me that he/she doesn't love me anymore.
2. She/he has kept these feelings to herself/himself for ages.
3. He/she has put our relationship at risk.
4. What is the impact on our children/friends/families?
5. I feel I am putting more effort into saving this relationship than she/he is.
6. What gave him/her the right to reject me?
7. He/she could want to see other people. How will I cope with that?

Can you think of three more personal anger prompts? Even if it is something seemingly petty: "After I spent Mother's inheritance on buying him a new car" or "After all the girls' nights out, I picked her up at three in the morning." Don't try to rationalize the feelings. Write them down on your card.

Accentuate the Positive: Possible Answers for Part I

1. Why do I always have to clean up the dishes?
   Positive: I'm really grateful when you help me keep the house clean.
   Concrete goal: It would mean a lot to me if you emptied the trash.

2. Will you stop groping me?
   Positive: I like it when you stroke me gently.
   Concrete goal: Would you give me a soothing back massage?

3. You never initiate sex.
   Positive: I loved it that time you seduced me.
   Concrete goal: I'm going to back off asking and wait until you feel ready.

4. You're always hanging out with your friends.
   Positive: I love our time together.
   Concrete goal: Can we go to the movies on Wednesday?

5. I hate it when you avoid me.
   Positive: It's great when you get home early.
   Concrete goal: Let's meet up after work and go for a drink together.

6. You are way too critical.
   Positive: I really appreciated it when you complimented me about . . .
   Concrete goal: I think we should try to say thank you to each other more often.

7. Why can't you lighten up?
   Positive: I really enjoy our fun times together.
   Concrete goal: Let's do something great this weekend.

8. Why didn't you call me?
   Positive: It's so nice to hear your voice during the day.
   Concrete goal: Let's try to touch base with each other sometime tomorrow.

9. You do nothing with the kids.

    Positive: It means so much to the kids when you do things with them.

    Concrete goal: Could you take the kids to the park this afternoon?

10. Isn't it about time you fixed the hall light?

    Positive: Thank you so much for fixing the sticky drawer, it's made my life so much easier.

    Concrete goal: Do you have an idea of when you'll be able to fix the hall light?

Twelve

Coping Day to Day

After the initial shock of ILYB wears off, a couple will often be overwhelmed by a million questions: "What's going to happen? What if . . . ? How will we cope?" Of course, there are seldom any simple answers; discussions about the future go around in circles, and the pain never seems to lessen. At this point, getting through even the next few days seems almost impossible. Enrico from New Mexico found that his feelings were all over the place: "I swing from one emotion to another, retching my guts up from the worry and guilt. My mind's acting like a roller-coaster from one minute to the next, from fearful (buckets of tears for hours) to being incredibly positive the next." The pressure became so great that Enrico began to doubt his sanity.

So what can be done? The first part of the book provides a long-term strategy for rescuing a relationship, but what happens in the meantime? If you are the partner who has fallen out of love, this chapter has less directly relevant material for you, but it will provide insights into your partner's state of mind. Chapter 13 focuses on guilt, the issue that affects most people with ILYB in the first weeks and months after the confession. Whichever side of the ILYB split you're on, be gentle with your partner. This is a tough time for both the partner asking the questions and the other half who has no adequate answers.

Dealing with Worry and Overanalyzing

The biggest fear of someone who has been told ILYB is that the relationship might be over; in fact, that fear is so big that it pushes aside nearly every other question. That fear lurks, barely disguised, behind the others. This problem is multiplied by a hundred times if the partner has asked for a temporary separation. Gary, a school teacher, found himself cut adrift from his normal routine when his partner of five years, Nicola, went to stay with her mother. "I worried she would turn Nicola against me. I worried what friends would think; I worried whether I'd be able to afford the apartment on my own. I worried that I would never taste her baked polenta with goat's cheese salad again." To makes matters worse, Gary's brain was simultaneously churning over past memories of golden moments together, the pain of getting through that day, and the void where the future used to be. At work, Gary was good at coping with emergencies but this time, he felt completely de-skilled. In fact, he was facing the two biggest challenges for someone living through a temporary separation: worry and overanalyzing. Although they normally come as a pair and feed off each other, they are subtly different. While worry is about what will happen in the future, overanalyzing is normally about what happened in the immediate past. So what can be done to stop these twin enemies from overwhelming you?

Worry

Beginning with worry, the first secret is to cut the future down into manageable chunks. Instead of stewing, often needlessly, about a distant tomorrow, try concentrating on getting through the next few weeks.

This approach helped Gary: Instead of being immobilized by the prospect of spending months and months of empty weekends without Nicola, I asked him to focus on that coming weekend. When would be the dangerous moments? He had soccer on Saturday mornings, so no problems there. What about Saturday night? He decided to arrange a drink with an old school friend. Sunday afternoon dinner was another problem, so he would invite himself over to his parents' house. Sunday evening, he would be preparing for his next week at work, so he was happy to be home alone. Once he had broken the weekend down, everything seemed more manageable, until he let his focus drift again. "What about our summer vacation?" he groaned. Normally, I would sympathize, but in a crisis it is vital to concentrate on today. "That's not your responsibility at the moment," I told him. "Your job is to make it through the next week."

The second tip is to gather the facts, as this will prevent worrying in a vacuum. Most attorneys provide a free consultation, so that you can determine whether you feel comfortable with them and ask general questions. This will help clarify your options and tell where you stand, legally. Your county and state bar associations will have a list of members, and many have lawyer referral programs. Next, find a friend who will provide a sounding board and help sort reasonable from unreasonable fears. Ideally, this friend should be someone who will just listen and not offer to wade into the crisis—as this will only complicate matters.

Third, accept that everybody worries. It is a sensible and natural response. The goal should be to worry less about matters beyond your control, like "Will he call?" or, "Will she want to see me this weekend?" Instead, concentrate more on things that you can directly change—like your own behavior. During Gary and Nicola's trial separation, Nicola threw a Sunday afternoon barbecue to celebrate her birthday. She invited Gary, her parents, and various shared friends. Unfortunately, Nicola's father insisted on grilling the meat his way. "Nicola lost her temper and stormed back into the house. My instinct was to ignore the incident— even though the two of them were really shouting," Gary explained. "But then I realized that's what I'd always done, and what I'd always done had brought me to the point where I almost had to beg for an invitation to her birthday party! I needed to change, but how?" He decided to do the opposite from normal and follow her inside. "I listened to all her complaints about her dad, and she had a good cry. I kept thinking, *What would I have done before?* Probably offer to have a talk with him. So again, I told myself, *Try something different.* So I just heard her out, and you know what? That seemed to be enough." The birthday party became a turning point for Gary and Nicola. Although Gary's trick of finding a different approach from the past did not always work in spades, it worked often enough to get them out of their relationship rut. Perhaps more important, he stopped worrying what Nicola would do next and focused instead on how he could be different.

Overanalyzing

After worry, the second most common problem is overanalyzing. While it is hard to find any benefits in worrying, the ability to really analyze a problem is normally an asset. However, the stress of an unwanted separation, or the threat of one, can tip useful introspection into negative thoughts and instead of fresh insights, offer only a distorted lens on the world. The person trying to save the relationship starts playing relationship detective: endlessly going over a telephone conversation for clues; dissecting how well a meeting with the beloved went; putting all the facts together to try to build a bigger picture. Overanalyzing teases a million angles out of an issue until someone can no longer think straight and becomes chronically indecisive or, alternatively, gets panicked into making bad choices.

So how can you tell where healthy introspection ends and overanalyzing begins? The first will normally range over the whole of the relationship, while the second focuses on events over the past few months—often to the exclusion of everything else. While healthy introspection will throw up new strategies for healing a relationship, overanalyzing goes around in circles and, ultimately, goes nowhere. Zoë did a lot of hard thinking after Murray told her that he didn't love her anymore, and many of her conclusions helped improve the relationship. However, after he asked for some space to get his head straight, Zoë went into overdrive. "Everything became a clue to whether he was going to come back to me or not. How long did it take to return my text message? Did he want to come home for Sunday dinner? Reports from a mutual friend over his state of mind seemed to take on a huge importance. If he seemed to be missing me, I'd be up in the clouds. If he was tired and wanted to go home early, I'd be depressed for days." When Murray called during her down days, she'd be snappy and often attack, despite being pleased to hear from him. In our counseling session, Zoë learned to stop looking for a deeper meaning behind Murray's behavior, and instead to relax and enjoy her time with him. So what is the secret?

Phase One: Realize That Overanalyzing Is Not Constructive

People keep doing it because they feel they are getting great insights and stripping away the rose-colored glasses. But more often than not, people who overanalyze end up feeling badly about themselves or their partners. The next time you catch yourself overanalyzing, put up a mental stop sign and distract yourself with something pleasant—like exercising, engaging in a hobby, playing with the children, or picking up a magazine. Eight minutes of distraction have been found to be enough to lift your mood and avoid depressing thoughts.

Phase Two: Reschedule Your Thoughts

Tell yourself that you are not avoiding the problems but putting them off to a better time. When the rescheduled time comes, you will probably find that everything feels less overwhelming or that the problems have simply disappeared. This rescheduling is especially important in the evening, as it is best to avoid distressing thoughts before going to bed.

Phase Three: Commit Your Thoughts to Paper

Do not censor yourself. Instead, like taking dictation, write down everything. Then look back over those notes and underline just the concrete events, not your interpretations. Keep on going back to these facts. Discuss them with a practical friend who will look for solutions rather than be sympathetic and fan the flames of overanalysis.

Phase Four: Look for Simplicity

In most cases, the most straightforward interpretation of events is always the best. For example, Murray probably did not return Zoë's text message because he was in a meeting, not because of any sinister reason.

In my experience, people who overanalyze fall into three main patterns: the angry who end up blaming other people (like Zoë); the self-critical who blame themselves; and the swamped who become overwhelmed and are prone to becoming depressed. There is a questionnaire in this chapter's exercise section to diagnose whether you suffer from overanalyzing and, if so, into which category you fall. Each category has special tips and advice.

Coping During a Temporary Separation

My clients often ask about the likely outcome of a temporary separation. It is difficult to know how to respond—first, because there are no statistics, and second, because each case is different. For some people, a temporary separation can be very constructive. When Simon, in his fifties and a lawyer, left his wife, Margery, for "time to think," she became very brave. "We'd meet once in a while, so I could give him the mail and things like that. Once I asked him if I'd see him during the weekend and he told me, 'It depends how we get along today.' I was furious. I stood up in the restaurant and told him that I didn't want to be judged. He got all flustered, and then apologized. He didn't realize I felt that way. When I thought back, he was probably right, because I normally tell Simon what he wants to hear." Her back might have been against the wall, fighting for the relationship, but she decided her best option was honesty. Margery had gotten in touch with her anger and discovered that it kept Simon from walking all over her.

Conversely, Erin, a thirty-one-year-old homemaker whose husband of seven years left "to get his head straight," felt like a complete failure. "I had put my family at the center of my life. Everybody thought we were a great little family, but on the inside, I felt worthless." The sense of rejection can be even worse if the current loss gets mixed up with a past one. Indeed Erin's mother had died when she was a teenager, and many of the old feelings of abandonment came back when her husband left—even though it was just for a while. While Erin was stressed, it was pointless trying to deal with the past pain; the priority had to be making it through the immediate crisis. So I used a program that would distract her from the worst feelings of pain without regressing back into little-girl mode. (For more advice, see Kicking the Blues in the exercise section.) However well or badly your temporary separation is going, do not be tempted to make any long-term decisions in the first three months. During this time, you will be in shock, and this is not the best time for considered judgment. But be assured: it will get easier.

What if My Partner Is Slipping Away?

The first option is to try to communicate in a different way.

+ If you normally talk face to face, write a letter.
+ Alternatively, fewer words can be more powerful than lots, especially if you are someone who would normally write an eight-page letter. Buying a greeting card, sending a text, or scrawling a message in lipstick on the mirror could make your partner take notice.
+ If you normally do not talk intimately on the phone or seldom e-mail each other, these are other options.
+ In other words, anything that will surprise your partner, stop him or her from thinking "same old, same old" and switching off.

If the above fails, step back and stop chasing.

+ If your partner is trying to grapple with why he or she has fallen out of love, it is not helpful to be constantly asked, "How are you feeling today?"
+ Forever telling your partner that you still love him or her is counterproductive, too. He or she will probably say, "I know," which does not provide the reassurance that you are looking for *and* reinforces in your partner's mind his or her lack of feelings.
+ I have avoided gender stereotypes—of women who like to talk through a problem and men who like to watch their sports shows to think through their problems—because I have met plenty of men who want to engage and women who want to retreat. However, it is worth remembering that clichés contain some truth. Have you been asking your partner to respond in a way that makes you feel comfortable but him or her uncomfortable?

- If your partner is a talker, invite him or her to unburden any thoughts. If you have done this before and failed, try again, as he or she may have not taken your first approach seriously, or maybe you made it too tentatively to be believable.
- If your partner is a thinker, give him or her even more space. Through your eyes, it might feel like you have already done this, but from your partner's perspective, it may still have seemed like pursuing or placing demands on him or her.
- Pamper yourself. Get a new haircut or a day of beauty treatment—anything that will shift the focus away from your partner and onto you.
- Do something that you enjoy rather than something you hope will bring back your partner.
- Try to enjoy life. I know this sounds hard, especially after your life has fallen apart, but ask yourself who your partner is more likely to want to spend time with: a) Someone who is crying all the time and staying at home, or b) Someone upbeat and out doing interesting things?
- When you stop pursuing, your partner is more likely to pursue you.

What Should I Do if My Partner Shows Signs of Recommitting to the Relationship?

This might seem like news that you have been waiting for, but you still need to be cautious.

- If you have found the strength to step back and refocus your life, you will probably have piqued your partner's interest, and he or she might start asking questions.

- ✦ Don't get too excited or enthusiastic. These first days of reconnecting are like early days of courting, when it is better to be warm and encouraging than to throw yourself at someone.
- ✦ Accept some of the invitations to spend time together, but not all of them, and certainly do not cancel prior engagements.
- ✦ Keep the dates light and fun. Just like your original courtship, don't get too heavy too soon.
- ✦ Wait for your partner to bring up difficult subjects like your relationship or the future—and don't say, "I love you" first, as this invites a response that your partner might not be ready to give.
- ✦ If at anytime your partner starts to backpedal, check if you have begun pursuing again and rededicate yourself to focusing on your own life.
- ✦ Stay cool until you are 100 percent certain that your partner is equally interested.

Summary

- ✦ While this chapter has mainly been addressed to people who have been told ILYB, Chapter 13 is mainly for their partners.
- ✦ If you are prone to worrying, break the issues down into smaller chunks and concentrate on those within your control.
- ✦ Overanalyzing can be as destructive as taking a relationship for granted. It falls into three types: angry, self-critical, and swamped.
- ✦ If your partner seems to be slipping away, it is time to try another strategy.
- ✦ Embrace the advantages of living in the moment. After all, the present is the only place that we can actually change anything.

EXERCISES

Stop Worrying

The secret is to live in watertight compartments and not to stew needlessly about a distant tomorrow.

✦ Make a list of all your worries, and then cross off those that are not immediately relevant for the next month. If you are feeling very positive, try to bring your window of worry down to just the next week.

✦ With the worries that are left, write beside them three practical things you could do to solve them.

✦ If the answer is nothing, make a deal with yourself and refuse to think about the worry for half an hour. Get some fresh air—a walk can lift your spirits and help you think things through.

✦ Ask yourself, "Honestly, what is the worst that can happen?" Prepare yourself mentally to accept the likely worst case, and then expend your energy on calmly improving on it.

✦ Avoid caffeine and sugar and cut back on smoking and alcohol. All these are stimulants, which will make your mind race even more.

✦ If you can't sleep at night, picture your worries on the piece of paper. Tell yourself: "There's nothing I can do now," and then imagine bunching up the paper and throwing it out of a pretend hole in your head. Do it several times until you feel more calm.

Are You Prone to Overanalyzing?

Although this quiz is meant as a bit of fun, it has a serious side, too. It will help you discover your analyzing style and offer some specially targeted advice.

1. You have a huge argument with your partner, and you find yourself repeating all those insults you promised you'd never use. Do you think:

   a) about all the other ways you have let your partner down

b) that you should make a groveling apology (even if, deep down, you feel you were in the right)

c) that it's your partner's fault for provoking you

d) that arguments happen in even the best families.

2. You make an extra special effort to seduce your partner in the bedroom, but he or she rolls over and starts snoring. Do you think:

a) If he (she) isn't interested in me, my partner must be getting it somewhere else. I knew that new coworker was trouble.

b) Considering how much weight I've put on, it's a miracle anyone is ever interested in me.

c) My partner didn't thank me for preparing supper either; he (she) always takes me for granted. Why did I ever fall for such a selfish man (woman)?

d) My partner has probably been working too hard.

3. During a telephone conversation with your partner, there are a lot of awkward silences. Afterward, you find yourself dwelling on it. Do you think:

a) Why can't the two of us get along, and why do I keep rubbing everybody the wrong way? Do I actually get along with anybody?

b) Maybe if I could be more tolerant, we could still be friends.

c) Why do I have to do all the work?

d) I'm not going to let it spoil my day.

4. During a temporary separation between you and your partner, one of your best friends has a dinner party to celebrate her (or his) birthday but invites neither you nor your partner. What is your reaction?

a) Could everybody have been talking about me behind my back and decided to deliberately exclude me?

b) I'll call the member of the group I'm closest to and find out whether I've done anything to upset the hostess.

c) I wouldn't have wanted to go anyway.

d) My friend probably couldn't fit everybody around the table, or maybe it was embarrassing to invite just me.

5. Your partner tells you that his or her mother was remarkably quiet when told the news about your problems. Trying to keep things light, you joke, "Are you sure she hasn't been swapped with someone else's mother?" Your partner laughs. But later do you think:

   a) He (she) will be upset that I've made fun of his (her) mother and think I'm not supportive enough. Worse still, I don't understand him (her) and will never be told anything again.

   b) I'm always putting my foot in my mouth; I must engage my brain before my mouth!

   c) She deserved everything and more—the way she criticizes everybody, she had it coming to her.

   d) If my partner is upset about my comments, he (she) will say something about it.

6. Which is closest to your personal motto?

   a) There are more questions than answers.

   b) I must try harder.

   c) Why is everybody always picking on me?

   d) What you don't know can't harm you.

7. Your partner leaves a note asking to meet that evening to talk. What do you think?

   a) You wonder how you will tell the family that you're splitting up, and how you will ever find anybody who loves you again.

   b) Go over every recent conversation again in your mind and work out what you have done to upset your partner.

   c) Think that it's all his (or her) fault. How can he (she) expect loyalty when he (she) treats me like this?

   d) Figure you'll find out what it's about soon enough.

Mainly A's = Swamped Analysis

In your head, your thoughts have logical connections so you can easily jump from a potentially barbed comment about your partner to your appearance and maybe onto how one of your parents seemed to ignore you—even if, in reality, the thoughts have nothing to do with each other. The result is that you are flooded and do not know where to turn.

Tip: Next time you feel overwhelmed, stop and unpack all the different thoughts. Behind nearly every one will be someone else's voice telling you what to do—"You should make the most of yourself," "You shouldn't let someone down," "You should always be nice"— until you are overwhelmed with a tyranny of "shoulds." With each "should," stop and ask: "Who says? Is his or her advice still appropriate today or in this situation?"

Mainly B's = Self-Critical Analysis

It is easy for you to talk yourself down and despite being perfectly capable, you have a low opinion of yourself. Even when there is a positive spin on something, you take the opposite approach. You are probably a worrier, too.

Tip: First, you cannot change the past, so there is no point in putting yourself down. Second, learn to forgive yourself. With forgiveness, you do not get bogged down with guilt and can move on to solving problems. Finally, when thinking back over something, ask yourself if you are giving too much weight to negative thoughts. Be aware that there are positive and neutral possibilities, too.

Mainly C's = Angry Analysis

Although not quick to lose your temper, you often stew over things and end up feeling bitter. Sometimes, this can be a cold anger—often very deadly. On other occasions, you simply explode. Because you do not like yourself in this mood, you try to avoid the problem with a quick-fix solution, which often leads to long-term complications and is fertile ground for future dissatisfaction.

Tip: You have high expectations of yourself and everybody around you. However, life would be easier if you could sometimes accept things the way they are and move on. For example, when your practical mother is not more openly loving, embrace her good qualities rather than getting angry about the rest. Next time somebody upsets you, do not think, *How could he or she do this to me?* Instead, learn to forgive and focus only on the real slights and what to do about them.

Mainly D's = Well-Balanced Analysis

You do not spend hours thinking something over unless it is a genuine crisis. When you make a decision, you stick to it. These are qualities to applaud. But are you sometimes too busy "doing" to consider how other people might be feeling?

Tip: In times of trouble, your level head is an asset. However, next time you find yourself playing back a difficult conversation, look for what is happening under the surface. What might have been left unspoken? By becoming aware of these extra dimensions you will probably make even better choices.

Beat the Blues

The blues kick in whenever we feel overwhelmed by helplessness. This is why even something very minor, but empowering, can help us break out.

+ Set up small triumphs and easy successes. For example, tackling a nasty chore that you have put off for ages—like sorting out the cabinet under the sink. Afterward, these jobs will provide a real sense of achievement.

+ Find small boosts to your self-image. On the weekends, make sure you get dressed rather than spending the day in your pajamas. Or even splurge on some new clothes.

+ Help other people. Offering to clean the gutter of an elderly neighbor or volunteering with your local chapter of the American Red Cross will not only divert your attention from your own problems, but the praise and thanks will make you feel better about yourself.

+ Compare yourself to someone worse off. Cancer patients often reassure themselves by comparing themselves to someone sicker. Next time you find yourself wishing your life was like that of a lucky friend, try being thankful that your life is not like someone much less fortunate than you.

+ Take up yoga, swimming, walking, or some other form of exercise. The natural endorphins lift spirits, help you relax, and take your mind off worries.

+ If you are religious, try praying; if not, look for a meditation class. Even getting a few moments peace from an overactive brain can be very soothing.

Thirteen

Dealing with Guilt

"If only I didn't feel this guilty," moaned Gary, who had been with his wife since they were both teenagers but now, at thirty, had fallen out of love with her. Sara still loved Gary and desperately wanted the relationship to work—especially because they had two children together. However, after several weeks working on the relationship, the counseling reached a stalemate, and Gary asked Sara for time apart. During a trial separation, I stop couples' counseling and instead offer one or two individual sessions to support each partner through the first difficult weeks. It was during one of these appointments that Gary let out his moan of guilty despair. It is a refrain with which I am only too familiar. From Gary's point of view, the "space" he was getting had been going well—too well: "It is so nice just to please myself. I've had a chance to get into some books I've wanted to read and I'm caught up at work. I close my door and cocoon." During the previous weekend, the whole family had been on an outing. "We went to an animal farm, and the boys were running around scratching the pigs' backs and even helped feed an orphaned baby lamb," he explained, "but leaving after lunch was not so easy." I listened to the details of the day out—only too aware that he had

not mentioned his wife once. "How did Sara seem?" I finally asked. Gary moaned again and said, "If only I didn't feel so guilty."

At this point on the ILYB journey, a couple is almost overwhelmed by guilt. The person who has fallen out of love feels guilty for all the pain he or she is putting the family through; the partner feels guilty for not spotting the problems earlier or for his or her part in the crisis. No wonder it sometimes feels like there is guilt for breakfast, lunch, and dinner—with a couple of guilt snack attacks in between just to make certain the nasty taste never leaves the mouth. So what exactly is guilt? Why can it be so debilitating, and what is the best way to break out?

Guilt is a perfectly natural human emotion and, generally, a very useful one. We feel guilty when we have done something that violates our personal value system and, assuming that we buy into them, society's values, too. Therefore, guilt has its positive side: it binds people together and means that most citizens self-police, with the courts intervening only in exceptional circumstances. However, when guilt turns toxic, another closely related emotion is often mixed in: shame. While guilt is about an action—for example, leaving your car in a No Parking zone—shame is about one's personal unworthiness. In other words, with shame, we are bad people rather than a good person doing something bad. Gary felt guilty for breaking his marriage vows, and shameful because what sort of man would leave a woman who loved him? In most relationship breakups, where the couple hate each other, each party has built up a head of righteous indignation: "I'm leaving because of his unreasonable behavior" or "She was a bitch." Each party might feel guilty about what each did, but neither party feels like a bad person: "He made me do it" or "After what she did, what choice did I have?" Couples with ILYB have no such easy excuses and, therefore, are particularly prone to guilt.

Feelings of guilt can often be traced right back to childhood: "If you're a good boy and finish that, you can have dessert" or "Good girls go to the party; bad girls stay at home." Some parents unconsciously add an extra message: "If you don't behave, I will take my love away, too." This idea that "good things happen to good people and bad things happen to bad people" is further reinforced by religion, schools, and popular TV drama, in which virtuous characters are rewarded and the immoral suffer. With this in mind, it is no surprise that everybody likes to view themselves in the best possible light. Even though you learn as an adult that being a good employee does not stop employers from relocating your office to the other side of the world, or being a good father does not stop an uninsured drunk driver from smashing into the back of your car, people still like to believe that the childhood rules still apply. Of course, we cannot control these random life events, but deep down, we cling to the idea that being "good" will protect us. A relationship crisis challenges this belief and makes us doubly anxious not to be seen as a bad person.

Gary did not have the luxury of blaming Sara for his plight, and he needed to distance himself from feeling in the wrong. For Gary, and for many people suffering from ILYB, guilt was serving a second purpose. Toward the end of his first solo session, he said, "I know I'm being selfish but if it's any consolation, I feel really guilty about it." Even Gary did not believe Sara would draw much comfort from his suffering, so we looked more deeply. Finally, Gary admitted that, "I can't be a bad person because a bad person would not feel guilty about asking for a temporary separation." In effect, the guilt was allowing Gary to still view himself as a good. Guilt also protected him from looking at other difficult feelings: anger, pain, grief, regrets, if only I'd done this, if only I hadn't done that. Instead of engaging with these monsters, Gary would try to tame his guilt by phoning his kids or distract himself by going for a beer with a work colleague. These coping mechanisms were fine, up to a point, but did nothing to address the underlying causes. And while most emotions burn themselves out, toxic guilt can last forever. Gary might have hated the guilt, but he felt even more uncomfortable about the feelings hidden behind it. Plus, there was a final advantage to feeling guilty: it stopped him from deciding between returning home and getting divorced.

Break Out of the Guilt Trap

The following exercise will be painful and time consuming. You can write down your feelings or, alternatively, recruit a supportive friend. The ideal listener would be someone who knows both you and your partner and can be neutral. Avoid cheerleaders, who are 100 percent behind you, or anyone likely to feel uncomfortable with your pain and, therefore, want to ease the burden before it has been properly examined. A friend is particularly useful for question two, but if you can be honest with yourself, writing down your feelings will provide the necessary distance.

1. **Examine your regrets.** Start with everything over the past month and then move backward: the past year, the past five years, back to before meeting your partner, adolescence. What are the important turning points? What are the "if onlys"? Who have you hurt? Are the regrets just about today's relationship crisis or part of a larger pattern?

2. **Challenge toxic thoughts.** Taking the most important regrets, ask yourself the following questions: *Have I overestimated my responsibility? Have I underestimated someone else's responsibility? Is there any false blame? Have I denied my responsibility? Have I made the past seem very black and white without contradictions, paradoxes, and ambiguities? Did I assume superhero skills—like second sight or a super-smooth tongue to persuade someone to change?*

If your partner told you ILYB, skip the next two questions and go to question five. If you are no longer in love with your partner, move directly on to question three.

3. **Grieve.** Life always involves making choices. If you went to college, you will never know what would have happened if you had started your career earlier. If you chose not to accept a proposal from a suitor, you will never know what life would have been like with that alternative partner. With these long-past regrets, allow yourself to visualize how life might have been, along with the advantages. Later, add the potential disadvantages of the path(s) not taken and the important assets gained from the path you did take.

4. **For current regrets, allow yourself to feel the pain.** Choose the catharsis of tears over short-term distractions or small gestures to compensate. Don't overfill your diary, however; leave time to be quiet and still.

5. **Take stock.** When someone starts unpacking guilt, it is impossible to predict what will come up. If you have discovered regrets over missed opportunities from the past, look for ways to incorporate those goals from where you stand today.

Are you using guilt as a justification for inaction? If you are not ready to make a decision, that's fine, as many people rush blindly into the future. But be honest with yourself.

Could you give your relationship another try? Particularly if you are reading this when your ILYB has already reached crisis point, give yourself enough space and time to digest the ideas and try out the exercises at the end of this chapter.

Make amends. Accept your share of the responsibility and apologize.

You should neither grovel and beg for forgiveness nor worry about your partner's share of the responsibility. Just a simple direct apology with no explanations or mitigating circumstances. You could try this out first as a letter, which you may or may not later share with your partner.

Do not expect forgiveness—this may come later—and instead make the goal simply to apologize. Your approach might be received warmly and be the springboard for a useful discussion; alternatively, be prepared for an angry response and, under these circumstances, be ready to leave rather than get embroiled in bitter fighting.

Think about making appropriate reparation—a gesture toward repairing the damage. It might be a present, doing something that your partner would really appreciate, or splitting up a generous settlement.

When Gary started to *examine* his guilt, he found more than he expected. When he had first woken up with a sinking feeling—that he was not just unhappy but downright depressed—he had been sure it was due to his unexciting relationship. However, while examining the roads not taken, he started talking about the rock band that he started with some friends: "We weren't just popular at school but really had a following in the local pubs. I'm not saying that we were going to be the next Beatles but we had a real chance. But the music business seemed like a real gamble, and Sara and I were getting serious, so I got a normal job instead. I still wonder what my life would have been like if we'd stuck with it."

His next task was to *challenge the toxic thoughts,* and he had begun to look at his life in very black and white terms: success and failure. It soon became clear he felt angry with his parents, school, and Sara for not supporting him more. However, once he had actually voiced those long-hidden emotions, he almost immediately began to take his share of the responsibility for not pursuing his dream. In question three of Break Out of the Guilt Trap, he started to grieve for his lost career. "I could have been playing stadiums all around the world with thousands of screaming fans, but I could have also ended up in drug rehabilitation or penniless on the streets."

Finally, in *taking stock,* Gary learned one of the most important things about regrets: it is seldom too late. A successful rock career was probably unlikely at thirty but one of the advantages of being older is learning to be more flexible. There was nothing stopping Gary from playing in the local bars as an amateur and reconnecting with his music again. Once Gary had acknowledged his anger at Sara from keeping him in his hometown and she came to watch one of his impromptu gigs, his attitude to his marriage began to change. He no longer saw his wife as holding him back, and he became open to reexamining his marriage and rediscovering the passion.

Nicole had effectively fallen out of love with her husband five years before she announced that their marriage was over. Richard knew things had been tough five years ago: "She'd been on my case: a lot of nagging, I didn't pay enough attention, we didn't do enough together—but what did she expect? Life's not all wine and roses. Except one day, she just stopped arguing. I thought, *She's off my back—great. She's realized it can't always be like the movies.*" But five years previously, Nicole had stopped trying to fix the marriage, or as she put it: "I've exhausted every possibility. There was no emotional connection, and I just knew I'd be happier without Richard." However, she decided to wait until their youngest children reached high school before leaving the marriage. She had stayed married for the past five years but in her heart and mind, she had already left. Meanwhile, Richard was living in a fool's paradise.

When Nicole finally told Richard that she did not love him anymore, he was devastated. He finally understood the depth of her unhappiness, but Nicole was already halfway out the door. He tried everything: a week's vacation in Seattle, flowers, being more helpful around the house, a giant teddy bear, and couple's counseling. Nicole was feeling terrible: "I feel such a hard bitch. I tell him something that's wrong, and he immediately tries to fix it, but it's not enough. Then he looks at me and I am just overcome with guilt. Guilt with a capital G."

Nicole's guilt had become like a high wall, so that none of Richard's gestures to save the marriage could get over her defenses. So, in counseling, we started working on the Break Out of the Guilt Trap exercise. We *examined* Nicole's regrets, and she talked about the marriage that she had wanted. Richard wanted to interrupt and promise that the future could be that rosy, but I stopped him. At this stage, he needed to hear Nicole out. Next I *challenged her toxic thoughts.* Who had been responsible for all that unhappiness five years ago? "He didn't lift a finger; I was left to do everything around the house," she explained. This time, I allowed Richard to present his side of the story: the extra hours to bring in more money since Nicole had stopped full-time work, plus how he had helped with the children. In other words, it was not as black and white as everything had become in Nicole's mind. "Why didn't you tell me how you felt?" Richard asked. Nicole had tried but it had come out as nagging, which just pushed Richard farther away. Who was to blame?

In this case, it boiled down to the first law of relationship disputes: six of one and half dozen of the other. However, when relationship problems get really embedded, toxic thoughts can distort everything into right and wrong—with none of the gray areas in between. During *grieving,* the third part of Break Out of the Guilt Trap, Nicole wept for all the unhappiness during the five years she had lived on autopilot, and Richard's eyes were moist as he listened. When *taking stock,* Nicole admitted she dared not let Richard have a second chance in case everything went back to how it had been before. "How can I trust him?" she asked. Trust is difficult to gain overnight. It takes time. So Nicole agreed to put the divorce proceedings on hold. There was, in fact, no timetable, no ticking clock, except for the one in her head. "Ultimately, I owe it to the kids to give him some more time. Perhaps then, I can lower my defenses just a little," she said. When it came to the final step, *make amends,* we discovered that they had both already achieved that: Richard had truly listened to all Nicole's issues (without trying to persuade her to stay), while Nicole had given Richard a second chance. Eventually, they decided to stay together and found the relationship that Nicole had dreamed about. Unfortunately, it required Nicole to tell Richard that she no longer loved him—and the very real threat of divorce—before he truly heard her.

In the two case studies just mentioned, the couples decided to stay together. However, some clients find that they have been feeling needlessly guilty. Michelle had been married to David for eight years and felt watched every step of the way. Right from the beginning of their relationship, David had been very attentive. Michelle was an amateur ballroom dancer, and David was always ready to pick her up after practice—no matter how late. At the beginning of the relationship, David's attitude helped the relationship: "He was always willing to go out of his way, and this made me feel special. Plus, he certainly didn't have eyes for anybody else," she explained.

However, his caring soon turned into jealousy. "My regular dancing partner is gay but that didn't stop David from making nasty comments about how happy we looked on the floor together. I tried explaining that it was all for show, for the judges, but he thought there was no smoke without fire." Eventually, Michelle got fed up with the snide comments and decided to change partners. Although she never found someone as good at dancing, she loved David and decided it was worth the sacrifice. "I thought he'd be more confident about my feelings after we got married. Like changing dancing partners, it worked for a while but he'd always want to know where I'd been. I found him checking my text messages and, finally, he wanted me to give up dancing all together." Day by day, she felt her love draining away until she told David, "I love you, but I'm not in love with you."

Michelle felt guilty when she arrived in counseling, and David was quick to point out everything that he had done for her. "Remember your marriage vows. I meant every word when we stood at the altar. Didn't you?" he asked her. However, as we went through the Break Out of the Guilt Trap exercise, Michelle became angrier and angrier. "You're still trying to manipulate me," she exploded, "you can't use guilt to control me now."

Instead of suppressing or ignoring your guilty feelings, try analyzing them. On the one hand, the guilt could mean that you are doing something that violates your personal code of values and your conscience is telling you to stop; on the other hand, you could be taking more than your share of the responsibility for a relationship crisis.

Summary

+ Guilt is an inescapable human emotion.

+ When shame gets mixed in with guilt, it can often turn toxic.

+ Letting go of guilt involves examining regret, challenging toxic thoughts, grieving, taking stock, and making amends.

+ Guilt normally has a message for us. It is better to listen to it than rush headlong into an unknowable future.

EXERCISES

The Guilt Journal

Buy a spiral-bound notebook, rather than using scrap pieces of paper, because you will need to refer back. This exercise also involves a lot of writing, and buying a nice notebook will show a commitment to persevere.

1. **Confess.** Instead of the thoughts going around in your head, write down everything in your guilt journal. Some of the guilty feelings will be about past events, and some of them will be fresh today; it does not matter if the two types of guilt are mixed up. However, put the date at the top of each entry, so that you can look back and discover which guilty thought preoccupied your mind and when. Don't worry about style, spelling, or grammar—just let everything go in a stream of consciousness.

2. **Analyze.** You will find more objectivity if there is a gap of two or three days between writing and analyzing. Take a marker and go back over what you have written; start looking for black-and-white thinking. Words like "always" and "never" are good clues. Next, try to find thoughts that suggest superhero skills and second sight, and mark these, too. Sentences with words like "should" or "ought" are often indicators of this kind of thinking. Finally, look for sentences that blame and underline those, too—maybe one color for yourself and one for your partner. How do the different colors balance?

3. **Identify the main themes.** Although guilt can throw up a thousand and one variations, there are normally only a handful of main themes. Give your theme, or each of your themes, a name. For example, guilt about not supporting your partner enough while his or her father was dying could be *hospice*.

4. **Complete a questionnaire.** For each theme, jot down some thoughts under the following headings:

   Q. What could I have done differently?

   Q. Thinking of that time, what resources would I have needed?

Q. What prevented me from doing it?

Q. What do I feel angry about?

Q. Who am I angry with?

Q. What can I learn for the future?

5. **Reflect.** Put away your journal for a week and return to it with fresh eyes. Read through everything and allow yourself first to grieve for past mistakes, and then take stock about what comes next.

6. Reopen the journal and answer just one more question: How can I make amends? Write down as many solutions as possible, even if some of them seem ridiculous at the time. After you have exhausted all the possibilities—both sane and insane—go back and select the most appropriate.

Note: Some clients find that they feel guilty about something in the past, but the person is no longer alive. How do you make amends with someone who is dead? In these cases, I suggest writing an imaginary letter to the person concerned.

Part Three

After the Crisis

Fourteen

How to Truly Bond Again

I love the moment in counseling when it is clear that the two partners have found their way back to each other. It is a lot like the clouds parting on a rainy weekend day. Nobody wants to acknowledge that the sun is shining—because we do not want to tempt fate—but there is still undeniable hope that the day might be saved. About two weeks later, one or both halves will admit, "I do have feelings." There is a shy smile, you see a slight tilting of the head, and the eyes shine.

Falling in love again—achieving Loving Attachment—should be easy from here, but it rarely is. Many couples expect something dramatic rather than tentative. In the movies, the hero suddenly realizes that he loves her after all and starts a madcap rush to the airport where his beloved is about to fly off to become a nun in the Congo. Or the heroine is standing at the altar watching her husband-to-be pick his nose, and suddenly she knows her "other love interest" would never do anything so horrible—or if he did, it would actually be rather cute. Of course at the same moment, "other love interest" is fighting his way through a crowd of guests to stop her from making the biggest mistake of her life. Love always wins out. Real life, however, isn't like the movies. Thankfully, it is much more rewarding.

The first shoots of love are green and tender, except that many clients want to take them straight into the big wild world; some talk about ending counseling. "Thank goodness, we're out of the woods," sighed Nina, one-half of a lesbian couple who survived ILYB. "I feel I can breathe again." However, my advice is never to relax too soon. This couple had been extremely close, and ILYB had been particularly painful. In order to persuade her partner Sophia that there was everything to play for, Nina had had to swallow a lot of her own needs. The next week, Nina and Sophia had long faces. "We've had a terrible time," complained Sophia, "always picking at each other. The slightest thing would set us off, forgetting to call when I said I would, or not bringing my plate to the kitchen. What's happened to us?" After months of being positive, Nina's natural resentment about being put through ILYB was finally coming to the surface.

At the other extreme were Brenda and Mike, who had been living apart for two years and were so frightened of destroying their returning love that they tiptoed around each other. Mike agreed to attend Brenda's family celebration, even though he was worried that they might be hostile to him. It had taken a whole counseling session to set up, so I was eager to discover how everything went. "Fine," replied Brenda. "Not as bad as I thought," said Mike. Their answers sounded too defensive, so I dug deeper and discovered that Mike had escaped from the table between courses and played with the dogs. I asked Brenda how she felt about this. "Everything has been going so well, so I didn't like to say anything," admitted Brenda, "but it was rude."

Going back to the idea that rediscovered love is like a tender plant; before a seedling is ready to thrive in the garden it needs to be toughened up. Horticulturists know young plants need to be acclimatized gradually: first turning off the heat; then raising the covers for a few hours in the daytime; and finally putting the new plants out day and night. However, with rediscovered love, some couples throw off the protective covering too soon—like Nina and Sophia—while others are too frightened to say anything, leaving the glass on forever—like Brenda and Mike—and risk turning the love moldy. So how do you acclimatize gradually? I have called this chapter How to Truly Bond Again because there are two things that still need to happen: leveling and learning.

Leveling

This is an open and honest sharing of feelings—for example: "Okay, I will level with you; I've been unhappy, too." In fact, the recommitment to love is not an ending but a time when the really productive work can start. When Glenn, a salesman in his late forties, returned home to his wife, Caroline, a legal assistant also in her late forties, they stayed up late talking for three nights in a row. "I needed to really prove to Caroline that I was serious. Previously, I would have cut the conversation short, worried about being tired for work the next morning," said Glenn. "I think she really appreciated that." "When Glenn first opened up," said Caroline, "I was relieved, but it was like a dam breaking. I found myself talking about my dissatisfactions—in particular how Glenn did not take enough time to woo me before trying to have sex."

Leveling is very productive, but these conversations can easily stall. This is because leveling has four accompanying behaviors: blaming, placating, intellectualizing, and diverting. If you find yourself straying from leveling, do not be alarmed because, in moderation, these are part of the toughening-up process. Like the good gardener, the trick is to keep an eye open and spot potential frosty moments. The following sections show you how.

Blaming

Definition: To blame your partner for something that has gone wrong in the relationship rather than looking at your own contribution. An example of this from Caroline is, "You don't give me enough foreplay" and from Glenn is, "You don't pay me enough attention."

Tackling it: Although both Glenn and Caroline were telling the truth as each of them perceived it, this cast them both in the role of victim. What would happen if Caroline took some responsibility and rephrased her feelings as, "I don't ask for enough foreplay" and if George said, "I don't explain to Caroline what I need from her"? They would both become in charge of their own happiness again. Caroline could show Glenn how she likes to be caressed, and Glenn could ask Caroline to turn off the TV when he returned home.

Placating

Definition: To appease your partner with sweet words or by offering something to keep them quiet in the short term, rather than addressing the root problems. Glenn would often say "I won't leave you." Meanwhile, Caroline would immediately give in—"You're right, I've been far too wrapped up in my own stuff"—even if she did not necessarily agree with all of George's complaints.

Tackling it: There is nothing wrong with soothing your partner's pain. However, in the long term, constant placating leads to resentment. If Glenn tells Caroline only what she wants to hear, but without really meaning it, he will find it harder and harder to share his true feelings. So what can be done? Placating works well if it is just the first part of a discussion, rather than a stand-alone interaction. Obviously, Glenn needs to reassure Caroline he is not about to leave. However, he must then explain that, without fundamental changes, he cannot stay forever.

Intellectualizing

Definition: To place an excessive emphasis on rational thoughts, often with a complete disregard to feelings. An example from Caroline: "Historically, men have always treated women as sexual objects and ignored their needs." While Glenn would say, "It makes financial sense to rent a room up in town during the week rather than spending so much on train fares."

Tackling it: Being rational about a problem can be useful. It helps a couple step back, get a fresh perspective, and make the issues seem less personal. However, a lasting solution has to make sense to the heart as well as the head. Intellectualizing can also get a couple trapped in point-less arguments—about nineteenth-century sexual etiquette, for example—rather than addressing the real issues. So balance rational thoughts with feelings and generalizations with the personal impact.

Diverting

Definition: To deflect someone's attention in the hope that he or she will forget the original complaint. The three main techniques are deny-ing, distracting, and ignoring. For example, Glenn would change the subject from his bedroom prowess by saying: "Think yourself lucky that I'm not like my boss—he's got two women on the side." Caroline could try complete denial: "I'm always interested in what you have to say," when often, she would rather watch her soap opera.

Tackling it: Sometimes, diverting is an understandable response, especially late at night when one partner feels worn down. However, a more honest approach would be to trade. When Glenn asked, "Can we talk about this tomorrow?" Caroline was more likely to agree if a specific time and place is suggested: "Tomorrow after supper, we'll sit in the kitchen while the kids are watching *The Simpsons*." Obviously, it is important to honor this commitment. Diverting is only a short-term solution and, used indiscriminately, it will set up all the conditions for slipping back into ILYB.

With a little practice, leveling became second nature for Glenn and Caroline. Glenn told Caroline, "I feel disappointed when you watch TV because I want to share my day with you." And she told him, "I feel frustrated when you rush sex because I want our lovemaking to be special." If you would like more information on leveling, look at the exercise section in Chapter 5. The Three-Part Statement will help you be open and honest without unduly antagonizing your partner.

Learning

If leveling is the first part of truly bonding, the second part will be familiar if you have worked through the Seven Steps to Saving Your Relationship. Learning, the last step, is also important for bonding again. In the last few weeks of counseling, my ILYB clients are relieved that love has returned, but they are still wary.

Anna and Nick, the salesman and teacher we met at the beginning of the book, decided to stay together. Although the initial honeymoon period was wonderful, both Anna and Nick were worried that they would fall back into their old ways. So I helped them look at why their relationship had developed problems. "I was always wrapped up with our sons," Anna replied, "and Nick had his work." "When we could have had time together, we surrounded ourselves with friends," Nick added. "It was like we were frightened what would happen if it was just the two of us." What were you frightened of? I asked. "Arguing," they said in unison and laughed. "I didn't want to have terrible arguments like my parents," said Anna. "My parents never argued, so I suppose I didn't know how to," said Nick. They had their diagnosis: Their love had disappeared because they were never together enough to be intimate and their fear of arguments had trapped them on either side of this divide. Next, I asked how they had changed. "We're not afraid to speak our minds," again they answered in unison. So what could they do if they found themselves heading into trouble again? Nick and Anna didn't answer, they just looked at each other, and I knew the counseling was over. By learning what caused their problems—and remembering the new skills that pulled them out—they were confident they could avoid the same traps in the future.

For many couples, this is enough knowledge, but others like to look deeper and learn what attracted them to each other in the first place. As discussed earlier, it is something beneath the superficial explanations—looks, sense of humor, or being easy to get along with—that most couples give to explain their mutual attraction. Everybody's childhood leaves them with relationship dilemmas inherited from watching their parents' marriage. It might be "not showing feelings," "coping with unfaithfulness," "temper tantrums," or "attitudes toward loss"—the list is endless. We are drawn to people who have complementary problems and are wrestling with similar issues. For example, Julia, a thirty-five-year-old secretary, had listened to her mother complain that her father—a traveling salesman—was never around. So Julia, in turn, had no picture of how a husband and wife negotiated daily living together. She swore not to make the same mistakes as her mother but unwittingly found herself married to a workaholic who played little part in family life.

Repeating the same mistakes as our parents might seem depressing, but in fact, we have a chance to reenact the dilemmas and find a more comfortable compromise. When Julia understood that her anger about her husband's hours in the office was exacerbated by memories of her parents' fights, she was able to get her reaction back into proportion. She also admitted she would have hated her husband to be hanging around all the time, stopping her work on her projects. With this understanding, Julia and her husband were able to negotiate a routine where Saturdays were family time, but he was allowed to work on Sundays.

Forming relationships—and having children together—will always rub at the old fault lines from the past and make us question the present. While previous generations expected problems, we are more impatient and less willing to tolerate anything less than perfection. Yet if we all hung in longer and believed more, we would address the underlying issues and reap the rewards of a doubly intimate and doubly satisfying relationship. If all this sounds like hard work, perhaps a hit of Limerence will help. (See the Limerence Exercise: Remembering the Magic of the First Meeting exercise at the end of this chapter.)

What if the Honeymoon Has Stalled?

Often, four to six weeks after a couple has decided to try again, their confidence begins to slip away, and one partner can become quite depressed. In this circumstance, it is important to determine whether all the anger has been vented. The pain from a deep wound cannot be healed all at once, but every time it is reexamined, a little more of the hurt and anger will be eased. Both Nina and Sophia, the lesbian couple introduced earlier in the chapter, had questions to ask each other. Nina wanted to know if Sophia had been falling out of love when they booked a vacation that had especially good memories for her. Sophia wanted to know what Nina had said to some of their friends—who were like a surrogate family—about their troubles. Although, at times, raking over the past made Sophia and Nina feel trapped, ultimately, they found the process liberating. "When I kept something back," explained Nina, "which I often did, so as not to hurt Sophia (and I suppose myself, too), I would get more and more down. Yet if I did ask, I'd stop feeling so vulnerable." Finally, after about two months of talking, there were no more questions to ask. "My trust in us as a couple had returned," said Nina. If there is still some unresolved anger in your relationship, look at Five Useful Things to Argue About in the exercise section.

Ritual can be a potent tool for moving on—hence all religions and cultures hold some form of service to mark a death. Some couples use ritual to lay to rest old pain, while others choose to celebrate a new, stronger love. A good ending ritual is to find a couple of objects that represent the bad times and have a small ceremonial burning. A good beginning ritual could be a holiday away together. (See Rituals in the exercise section.)

The final step to reenergizing a relationship is to plan for the future. Sit down and discuss the next five years and listen to each other's thoughts with an open mind. Of course there could be differences, but a couple who has faced and survived ILYB has learned all the necessary skills to deal with this. If you are stuck for ideas for the future read Finding Your Dream, the Collaborating exercise in Chapter 2.

What if I Want to Fall in Love Again, But It Is Just Not Happening?

Lots of emotions—like trust, sexual desire, and, of course, love—are not rational. No amount of arguments or rationalization will open up the heart. Toward the end of counseling, some people with ILYB no longer want to leave but are not sure that the relationship can be what they need or whether they can truly open themselves up to love again.

Rod had fallen out of love with his wife, Gina, after fifteen years of marriage: "I could see how we'd let things slide, so we decided to make changes, and certainly everything feels less claustrophobic. But what if I still don't love Gina the way that I should?" Gina had fears about the future, too: "I know it is stupid to ask for a guarantee—life doesn't come with one—but that doesn't stop me from wanting one." So while Rod worried about loving again, Gina worried about trusting again. So what next? This is a hard one, because the solution is a paradox. On the one hand, a couple needs to have worked hard to remove the obstacles to love: anger, hurt, cynicism, and impossible expectations. Yet on the other hand, a couple needs to step back and let go. Just as Buddha found enlightenment only when he stopped seeking it and let it come to him, couples with ILYB reach a point where they need to stop pursuing love, trust, and reawakened desire. These are slippery emotions, and like enlightenment, are more elusive when placed center stage.

In counseling, we reviewed Rod and Gina's previous obstacles to love (not arguing, unspoken resentments, and Rod's unnecessarily long work hours) and remembered how much had been achieved. I also asked Rod and Gina to list any other possible obstacles, and we came up with just one minor issue. (Rod thought Gina resented his playing golf, but she was concerned only if it happened every weekend.) Finally, Gina turned to Rod and said, "We'll just have to believe we can do it." Two weeks later, love and trust were no longer issues. Although neither Rod nor Gina could put a finger on the reason, after they had stopped worrying, the emotions had returned. For couples who are unable to believe, I ask them to behave as if they trust, love, and expect to feel sexual desire again. "What would you do?" and "How would you act?" This "letting go" phase normally lasts between two to six weeks and at some point, the couple effortlessly crosses from acting to being. With couples who remain stuck, I encourage them to reexamine their relationship and seek out any remaining obstacles.

A Better Understanding of Love

When couples who have been through ILYB look back at their journeys and see the knowledge acquired and the new skills learned, they find a lasting belief in themselves. So what is this knowledge?

✦ **Love is effort.** In a good relationship, both partners regularly and routinely attend to each other's needs—no matter how they feel. This extra mile is often what is most appreciated.

✦ **Love is about both giving *and* receiving.** In a good relationship, both partners make certain they find the joy in both halves of the equation.

✦ **Love is courage.** In a good relationship, both partners share their vulnerabilities as well as their strengths and do not close themselves off, shut down, or take the easy option.

✦ **Love is rewarding.** In a good relationship, both partners support each other and help each other grow.

✦ **Love is most appreciated when a couple thought it was lost forever** but they have subsequently found a way back to each other again.

What about the skills learned?

✦ To be honest with yourself.
✦ To be honest with your partner.
✦ To be upfront about differences, rather than ignoring or hiding them away.
✦ To be a better negotiator.
✦ To find a genuine compromise, rather than one partner always backing down.

Summary

+ Providing ILYB is addressed early enough—and the couple has been honest about their feelings—there is no reason why they should not decide to give their relationship another try.

+ Do not expect reconciliation too soon; in the beginning, a commitment to a better relationship is enough.

+ To truly bond, a couple needs first to *level* with each other, and second to *learn* what went wrong; this will give them confidence that the problems will not reoccur.

+ When we first fall in love, we make fundamentally good choices. The secret of happiness is to understand the attraction and solve the relationship dilemma set by our childhood.

EXERCISES

Audit Your Reactions

This exercise requires nerves of steel, not because it is difficult but because it is very revealing. Next time your discussions seem to be going nowhere, switch on a tape recorder. After fifteen minutes, rewind the tape and look out for:

- **Blaming:** These sentences normally start with, "You make me . . ."
- **Placating:** Look for excessive use of "Sorry," "You're right," and "It won't happen again."
- **Intellectualizing:** Long rambling sentences that don't seem to go anywhere is a sure sign.
- **Diverting:** Are both of you truly listening, or blocking, contradicting, and belittling?
- **Dismissing:** How often do you interrupt each other?

After auditing the conversation, return to the topics discussed and try to cover the same ground again without falling into the same traps.

Five Useful Subjects to Argue About

The best way to bond is to have a good argument. It gets all the issues out in the open, provides a release of pent-up feelings, and gives a sense that the relationship can get better.

1. **Little things:** Small irritations such as loading the dishwasher "the wrong way" may not seem like serious crimes, but can cause huge resentment if not dealt with. Also if you find conflict especially difficult, these smaller issues can provide a dry run before tackling something really contentious.

   Tip: Bring up your complaint at the time it happens, rather than a couple of hours later when it's too late for your partner to do anything about it. Don't hide behind a joke, because your partner will wonder whether you really mean it. Also avoid slowly building up to the request with statements like "You're not going to like this" or

"There's something I need to bring up," which will put your partner on the defensive. Just ask directly.

2. **Amount of time spent together:** With so many demands on your time, it is easy to put your partner at the bottom of the list. But if Loving Attachment is not nurtured, it withers, so arrange time together.

   Tip: Don't fall into the trap of concentrating, for example, on the amount of time your partner spends outside the house or on hobbies—this just invites a justification of his or her behavior or a dispute about the facts. Instead, discuss how this makes you feel. For example, "I feel neglected/taken for granted/not important." As you are the expert on your feelings, this is harder for your partner to contradict.

3. **Different tastes:** Differences make things more interesting, highlighting your role as partners rather than best friends or twins. Choose something in the news or a movie you have both seen and discuss it together. Standing up for your views is not only healthy, but will also give you something new to learn about each other. These arguments can even take on a playful tone and give the opportunity for mock fighting—very useful if you find confrontation difficult.

   Tip: Always have an opinion. If you opt out—"It's okay if you choose what we will do this weekend"—your partner will feel 100 percent responsible for the success of an outing, which can become very tiring.

4. **Money:** Arguments about money are hard to negotiate but provide an express route to important, but often hidden, issues. Money can stand for power, self-respect, freedom, responsibility, security, and even love. So when you discuss money, be aware that you're not just talking about dollars and dimes, and try to delve deeper.

   Tip: Get your partner to talk about what money meant when he or she was growing up. Next, share the lessons you have learned from your childhood. This will help you see your differences through fresh eyes and find room for compromise.

5. **Sex:** This is another tough area but one that can pay real dividends. Whether the arguments start with, "You're not interested in me anymore" or "Why do you always push me away?" it will bring into the open deeper issues that many couples are too embarrassed to discuss.

Tip: Be extra considerate. Instead of blaming ("You make me feel . . ."), own the problem ("I feel . . ."). This will stop the argument from becoming unnecessarily confrontational.

Rituals

Mankind has always used rituals to mark the seasons. Similarly, we need to mark the end of one phase of our lives and the beginning of another. This exercise will allow you to give the past problems of ILYB a decent burial and look forward to a new closeness.

1. **Check that all the conflict is out in the open.** Spend an evening going back over the past months. How does each of you make sense of what happened? What has each of you learned about the other person? What have you learned about yourself? If this ends in an argument, you are probably not ready to close the book on ILYB. If this is the case, look at Audit Your Reactions above and keep talking. If the talk is productive and supportive, you are ready for a ritual.

2. **Design a ritual.** Find something that seems to sum up ILYB for you. Some clients write an account of what happened, others tear pages out of their diary or gather up the paper used for exercises and decide to burn those. Another strategy is to find something that encapsulates your arguments, like an old golfing sweater or a coaster from a nightclub and have a ceremonial trip to the local Dumpster. Alternatively, the act can be completely symbolic, like holding a helium-filled balloon on top of a hill and imagining that it holds all the pain and letting it go. Other cleansing ideas could be making paper boats and sailing them over a waterfall or casting petals into the wind. The only limit is your imagination.

3. **Honor the ritual.** If you are writing a letter or an account of your pain, make certain that you do it properly, not just scribbling on the back of an envelope. Find a location that speaks to you. I had a client who burned some old pictures on the beach— because she had happy childhood memories there—and watched the tide come in and wash away the ashes. Take time to talk, to think, and be together. Some clients have chosen poetry, and others have even brought music. This all helps to make it a solemn occasion and add significance. If, for practical reasons, the location is

rather ordinary—like the Dumpster—find somewhere nice to go for a walk or a drink afterward.

4. **Celebrate the new.** Just as marriage needs witnesses, so does a reborn relationship. I always think a celebration is a good way of marking an important date, and you could invite people who have been supportive over the difficult times. Discuss together what would be best for your relationship.

Limerence Exercise: Remembering the Magic of the First Meeting

For five years, I did a series of magazine profiles of celebrities and their partners. I would always start by asking for the story of how the couple first met. Within seconds, the atmosphere in the room would change—any nerves or apprehension would disappear—and I would feel real warmth as people remembered. The secret is in the detail I asked for: Where were you? What were you wearing? What did you eat? What did your partner look like? What did she say? What did he do? Normally, people have boiled down their "how we met" story into one or two sentences but this reflex story does not provide enough material to trigger proper memories. Over and over again, the celebrities—normally on tight time schedules—would stretch the time allocated for my interview. I was taking them back to the height of Limerence, and everybody enjoyed lingering on these passionate memories a while longer.

Either write a short story about your memories of how you met your partner or bring the topic up in general conversation—perhaps over a meal. It normally takes three or four questions to get someone in the mood. To give you an idea here is the first part of my interview with Twiggy (model and star of the film *The Boyfriend*) and her husband, Leigh Lawson (an actor best known for his role as Alec D'Uberville in Roman Polanski's film *Tess*). See how many facts I extracted.

Twiggy started: "In 1985, I went out for dinner at Caprice in London with three friends. At another table I spotted Jonathan Pryce—who I'd been working with—so I went over to say hello. Immediately, this handsome man stood up. It was Leigh, who reminded me that we'd met ten years earlier at a John Denver concert. Even back then I'd thought him really dishy, but we'd both been married then so nothing romantic crossed my mind. This time, the chemistry must have been obvious because I remember telling my friends to stop trying to pair me off. But I must have been curious because I bought a magazine with a big interview with Leigh. I learned he had been alone for two years and after the trauma of the breakup was not interested in seeing anyone seriously for the next ten years! Three days later, Robert Powell and his wife, Babs, who used to be in Pan's People, invited me to a restaurant in Chelsea. By a string of amazing coincidences, Leigh was invited, too. We talked and laughed but, on paper, he was trouble. Who in their right mind would trust a gorgeous actor? I was no longer an eighteen-year-old about to jump in headfirst. So I let him slip away again. Fate had other ideas."

At this point, Leigh takes up the story: "I thought Twiggy was absolutely gorgeous—but as one of the most beautiful women in the world, I knew everybody would be after her phone number. Despite fate throwing the two of us into the same restaurant twice in one week, I said goodnight and let her walk away. Perhaps I lacked confidence; perhaps my heart had just got out of intensive care; perhaps she wasn't giving the green light. Although these days, Twigs claims she was disappointed that I didn't ask for her number—but she's got to say that! Anyway, five days later I went to the newsagents for my morning paper and this big blue Jag—with an exquisite blond inside—pulled up by the curb. It was Twiggy. She wound down the window and said, 'Do you want a cup of tea?' Even I knew this was the green light!"

Every story of how two people met and fell in love is interesting, so give yourself permission to enjoy your own. With luck, there will be things to tease each other about (notice how Leigh does it over asking for the telephone number and Twiggy over the magazine interview), which, in turn, can be turned into general affectionate everyday banter between the two of you.

Fifteen

If Worse Comes to Worst: Making Sense of Endings

In an ideal world, this book would have finished at the previous chapter. ILYB relationships can be saved, the passion can be reignited, and both partners—not just the one who fell out of love—can find a deeper and more fulfilling intimacy. However, I am also a realist. Some people are determined to end their relationship and no matter how committed the partner might be, ultimately, it takes two to make a couple. For other readers, it may already be too late, and their relationship has already ended. So, after accepting the inevitable, what's next?

As the shock of the breakup starts to wear off and the pain really kicks in, most people try to distract themselves: some will have a makeover or buy a gym membership, others will bury themselves in work. In the first difficult weeks, there is no right or wrong approach— just something to make it through. However, after this first flush of energy, most recently separated people discover that they need to understand the past before moving forward. Slowly but surely, often over a bottle of wine, they will dissect what happened with their friends or family. It might be painful but, ultimately, it is the right thing to do.

Telling Your Story

In a paper presented to the British Psychological Society Conference, Dr. Carla Willig of London's City University identified three main stories ex-lovers commonly use to describe what went wrong: "There's such a strong need to have an explanation," she claims, "and those people who haven't got one find the breakup more difficult to accept. Of the people I studied, there was just one man with no story. He was still struggling through his pain many years later."

I wrote earlier about Michelle, a twenty-seven-year-old TV researcher, whose husband, Matt, disappeared for two months and reappeared on the other side of the world. Nearly two years later, she was still having trouble making sense of her divorce: "I don't have any answers; that's what makes it so hard. We only spoke a couple of times on the phone, but that's it. I just don't have a proper explanation. What possessed him to just disappear?" It is tempting to think an ex holds the answer—and that is certainly the motivation behind a lot of late-night, slightly drunken calls—but, ultimately, these conversations never get anywhere. Each half of a separating couple has to build up his or her own account of what happened and why. In fact, on many occasions, these stories will be radically different. Slowly, I helped Michelle piece together what had happened. Her husband, Matt, did not like conflict and never argued. "He just seemed happy to go along with what I suggested," she explained. What if Matt did not agree? "He'd just keep it to himself. I suppose the pressure of bottling it up was just too much," she answered. It seemed that Matt had taken avoiding conflict to its ultimate extreme and just disappeared. Michelle had begun to put her story together.

What types of stories has Dr. Willig found? The first story—"To the Bitter End"—is built around the idea of doomed lovers. From the first kiss, every twist in the tale is painful. Every jealous event, bad vacation, and discovered secret is used to illustrate how the relationship had problems all along. The reality of the relationship might, in fact, have been very different. But these former lovers use a cut and burn technique to obliterate all the tender memories, and then to move on. This is not normally the choice of ILYB couples, because Bitter Enders part hating rather than caring about each other. Sadly, I meet some people who think the whole relationship has been invalidated by the split. Roberta had been married for fifteen years and had a twelve-year-old daughter, but when her husband threatened divorce she said, "I'm so angry with him. I feel that he has stolen my best years and I can never get them back. Everything is ruined." The French philosopher Henri Bergson would label this thinking as "the illusions of retrospective determinism." Bergson argues that we often view historical events as inevitable and, consequently, our present social problems, too. With this false logic, even the good times at the beginning of the relationship hold the seeds for the ending and are somehow tainted. It is like looking back at a vacation while stranded at the airport waiting for the flight home and feeling the whole trip was a disaster. However, no matter how much discomfort during the hold-up, it cannot undo the pleasure experienced at the beginning of the vacation, eating calamari while overlooking the old fishing port.

The second story—"A Way Out"—builds on a similar principle. From the beginning, something has been not quite right: the lovers had incompatible habits or different interests. He might have been a neat freak, for example, while she had left her pajamas on the bathroom floor; or she might have been a computer expert while he was an artist. However, while Bitter Enders let these small painful events build until one final event breaks the camel's back, Way Outers find a dramatic exit. In Dr. Willig's study, it was nearly always an affair, with another lover providing an excuse for the ending. And indeed, some ILYB couples do find themselves enmeshed in affairs.

The third story—"Changed Circumstances"—is an entirely different narrative. This relationship starts well. After a honeymoon period, the couple settles down into a happy life together. However, the course of true love does not run smoothly and, as in all stories, there are obstacles to overcome. One partner is promoted and that job takes him away, the children leave home, or the couple simply grow apart—all these new circumstances can undermine what was once a happy relationship. This is the most likely story for ILYB couples as it acknowledges the love and affection, which survives the breakup.

Dr. Willig's research also explains why men are more likely than women to be emotionally damaged by relationship breakup. Previously, experts simply blamed men's tendency to keep problems bottled up, but it goes deeper than this. By not talking, men are failing to construct an ending for their relationship. By contrast, women, while off-loading onto friends, are forever rehearsing and finally settling on a version for their breakup. Whether these explanations are right or wrong is immaterial. "Any account is better than none," claims Dr. Willig.

However, Michelle's story does not truly fit into any of three stories identified by Dr. Willig. This is why I add a fourth narrative. I call it the "Unwanted Opportunity," and it works for both the person who is left against his or her wishes and the partner who leaves. "We had a good and fulfilling relationship that worked for a while," this story says. "We both made mistakes and, ultimately, we went in different directions. Being single is not what I wanted but I am determined to see the opportunities rather than dwelling on what I've lost." Unwanted Opportunity people use the painful experiences to hone their relationship skills, so when they meet someone in the future they will make the most of it. Many people move on to this fourth narrative after having first used one of the other stories, so arriving here is proof that you have made progress. (See the exercise section for a quiz to identify your story outline.)

When constructing the story of how a relationship ended, some people become fixated on the last painful section and feel overwhelmed. To get a better perspective, take a piece of paper and create a graph. On the horizontal axis write "time," and on the vertical axis write "pleasure." The first meeting with your partner is the zero point on the time axis. From there, plot your whole relationship on the graph, including all the peaks and troughs. Label all the good times so that you do not forget them. Next, examine the bad times. Were they inevitable? What is the balance between positive and negative?

Roberta used this idea to look back over her fifteen-year marriage. She had a high for the birth of her daughter, and after that everything was more or less a flat line. Beyond the last three-and-a-half years, Roberta's graph showed that her relationship had been better than she had painted it. "Obviously, I have regrets, but actually, it was not all bad," she concluded.

Looking back over a relationship, many people feel they are a complete failure and find only one person to blame: themselves. Weighed down with a million regrets and a thousand things they should have done better, they become depressed and start to despair. At this point, I would recommend coming from a fresh angle. Machiavelli, the founder of political thinking with his seminal work *The Prince,* advised the ruling Medici family on how to keep power and influence events in their favor. He is famously ruthless, but still wrote, "I believe that it is probably true that fortune is the arbiter of half the things that we do, leaving the other half or so to be controlled by ourselves." Yet most of us act as if the proportion we control is much larger and end up castigating ourselves.

Michelle, whose husband disappeared, took on all the blame: "I keep thinking that I drove him away; I should have asked what he wanted," she said. However, through counseling, she found a more balanced picture: "He could have said something if he was unhappy. When I spoke to his mother, she told me that he disappeared without explanation as a teenager, too." Michelle had found a more fifty-fifty share for the breakup of her relationship. (More on this in the exercise section under Even Split.)

If taking all the responsibility for a breakup is a mistake, so is going to the opposite extreme and blaming someone else. It might initially be comforting to feel "It was not my fault," and that either circumstances or the other person's wickedness were to blame, but playing victim in the long term makes it harder to find someone new. Instead of saying, "He or she took advantage of me," rephrase this as, "I should have stood up for myself more." The first explanation leaves you vulnerable to repeat performances; the second explanation leads to an assertiveness course. In all good films and books, the central character learns something about him- or herself from all the trials and tribulations. It is what makes satisfying drama; it also makes for a more satisfying life.

Although it is hurtful when one partner blames the other for the end of a relationship, or alternatively takes on all the blame, it should not be taken to heart. One of the few advantages of splitting up is that the ex's take on events no longer matters. Each half of the couple is heading for a different future, and even if one ex-partner has a different story, it will not hamper the other's progress.

Getting Closure

Several of my clients arrive seeking something called "closure." After the first time this happened, I consulted my dictionaries of psychological and psychoanalytical terms but found nothing. I was surprised. Where had this term come from? It is neither a medical nor a religious concept, which are the other main sources for psychological-sounding words that enter the general vocabulary. Closure, the idea that we can somehow deal with a past painful relationship, package it up, and move on, is such a seductive idea that we have invented our own word and now want to believe in it. But is it possible?

When someone is determined to reach closure, I am sympathetic but always probe deeper. Some clients hope to skip some of the pain by rationalizing and packing it away. Although this process can help, it is not a magic bullet. Other clients have used closure as the cover for some pretty nasty behavior. Hannah had been having an affair with a married man for three years: "I had no choice but to go around and tell his wife. She had a right to know and how else was I going to achieve closure?" This is dramatic, but never final. The confrontation just launches another round of recriminations. Indeed, Hannah's boyfriend turned up on her doorstep and started shouting at her. "It was not at all healing," she admitted.

The best way forward is to repackage the pain into something positive. I helped Hannah look back at her painful parting as the moment she started painting, and another client remembered how his former lover had introduced him to meditation. Even bad relationships teach us something. If this does not work for you, take a long hard look at the benefits of staying where you are. This seems crazy, because who would want to keep hurting? But sometimes it feels safer to cling to a failed relationship than face our fears: "I'll never find anyone else to love me," or "I can't cope with the loneliness." Be as honest with yourself as possible and keep digging deeper. Once everything is out in the open, the underlying assumptions can be properly challenged, anxieties chopped down to size, and a way forward found.

Finally, be patient with yourself. A relationship breakup is as traumatic as a bereavement, so never underestimate what you have been through. Congratulate yourself on your progress so far and be assured that the pain will lessen over time. Although we can never achieve complete closure, we can integrate the past into a better future.

Summary

✦ Having a story that makes sense of the breakup is the first step to healing.

✦ It is important to learn from the past before truly leaving it behind.

✦ Make certain not to place too much blame on your ex-partner or take too much yourself.

✦ The end of a relationship is like a bereavement.

EXERCISE

Put Your Breakup Under the Spotlight

This simple test will help you decide which story to tell:

1. Which statement best describes your arguments?

    a) He (she) never listened.

    b) We tried to resolve our problems but slipped back into old ways.

    c) We didn't argue very much.

    d) Somehow, we could never get through to each other.

2. Which statement best describes your sex life?

    a) It was fireworks more times than not.

    b) We got bored in bed.

    c) It was satisfactory but not earth moving.

    d) We had our good times and bad times.

3. Which statement best describes your breakup?

    a) I'm better off without him (her).

    b) The affair was a catalyst, not the cause.

    c) We became like brother and sister.

    d) Maybe we could become friends sometime in the future.

4. Which statement best describes how you're left feeling?

    a) I don't know how I put up with him (her) for so long.

    b) It could have dragged on for much longer.

    c) It was just one of those things.

    d) I learned a lot.

5. Which statement best describes your feelings about meeting someone else?

    a) Forget it—not with my track record.

    b) I'm frightened to let anybody get close.

    c) I'll have to wait and see.

    d) I'm generally optimistic.

Mostly A's = Bitter End

At least the sex was probably good—in fact, many people put up with poor relationships because of the magic of making up after a fight. However, try to see the relationship in less black-and-white terms; life is normally drawn from a far richer palette. The main advantage with such a final ending: you are spared the charade of pretending to stay friends.

Mostly B's = Way Out

Beware of a tendency to rewrite history to make your previous relationship seem worse than it was, and thereby reduce your guilt. The aftermath of an affair often produces increased levels of jealousy caused by a heightened awareness of how easily relationships break up. There is also a possibility that you might want to return to the original relationship after time, and distance has made you reassess what you've lost.

Mostly C's = Changed Circumstances

Remember that a relationship needs the right environment to flourish; just loving each other is not always enough. These good relationships can also peter out because each person swallows his or her differences to preserve the happy picture, and nothing gets solved. The positives are that you are unlikely to blame yourself or your lover, so there is always the possibility of salvaging a friendship.

Mostly D's = Unwanted Opportunity

You are making good progress, but do not be surprised if there are times when you feel depressed or angry: Recovery is never a straight line, and most people will fall back from time to time. If you find yourself stuck in one of these holes, it may be worth considering counseling to find a fresh perspective.

Even Split Exercise

1. Take a piece of paper and draw a line down the middle, on one side write "my responsibility" and on the other "his (or her) responsibility."

2. Starting with your partner's side—as this is normally the easiest—list all his or her contributing factors for the breakup. Leave space on the page directly opposite, so that later, you can go back and see whether you have a matching contribution.

3. Move down the page and list your contributing factors for the breakup on your side of the paper.

4. Look back and see whether there is again a matching contribution to be written in the opposite columns. For example, beside "He always pushed for more sex," someone might write, "I used sex as a weapon to get back at him."

5. If you find it very hard to think of anything for one particular column, ask a friend to help and make suggestions.

Sixteen

How to Fly High Again

$\mathcal{R}ecovering\ from$ a relationship breakdown—especially one not of your choosing—is hard. In my experience, people who swim, rather than sink, have pulled off a difficult trick. They spend enough time on understanding the relationship (the past), but concentrate on changing things for the better (the future); yet when times are tough, they focus down to the next few days (the present). Although the ability to alternate through these three time frames is always useful, it becomes crucial during a personal setback, such as a divorce. People who are stuck in the past risk depression, while those who set off with their eyes fixed only on the future are most likely to crash and burn. People with problems caused by sticking to today are rarer—most of us find it hard to live in the moment—but occasionally, I see clients who are living in the present hedonistically (focused only on feeling good today and becoming trapped in pointless pleasure-seeking) or in the present fatalistically (just swept along by events).

So how can you be flexible enough to find the right time frame at the right moment? The secret is to understand the advantages of all three. In Chapter 15, I looked at the lessons from the past; Chapter 12 covers the present; and this leaves the third time frame, the future, for this chapter.

The future offers the promise of a brighter tomorrow: no more tears, no more pain, and maybe even a new partner. Not surprisingly, most people want those goals now, and many clients ask, "Why does everything have to be so hard?" I do not answer, partly because I am not a philosopher but mainly because counseling is about helping people find their own answers. If I could fly in an emergency on-call philosopher, he or she would probably answer, "Because nobody has ever learned anything important from happiness or success; problems make us grow." Maybe it is just as well these flying philosophers do not exist because they would not be very popular. A woman I interviewed for a women's magazine best sums the typical response.

Nuala Bingham developed a complex viral illness when she was just twenty-nine, and her husband, Harry, had to give up a high-flying city career to nurse her around the clock. Three years later, when I met them, her energy levels were still so low that she considered it a good day when she could dress herself. She turned out to be one of the wisest people I had ever met and after the interview offered help with a problem I had been struggling with. "For the sake of full honesty, whatever depths and curious rewards this illness has brought," Nuala explained, "we would *never* choose it. Day-to-day life is harder and more wearing than I would wish on my worst enemies. For myself, I would choose to be shallow and well, rather than tortured and deep." I offer another extract from the interview with Nuala because it shows how adversity can strengthen love. "When I get very low, I can't go for a run or have a drink like other people. I just have to work on my inner self; there's nowhere else to go. It's a bit like being a Tibetan monk without the Himalayas in the background. I used to think I'd lost everything that makes someone feel worthwhile. Where is my dignity when Harry has to carry me to the bath? But I discovered it is beyond being able to wash yourself. I still feel like a human being because that's what I see reflected when I look into Harry's eyes. He still has the same respect and affection."

Going back to my clients—who asked why life is hard—if the evidence of my flying philosopher and Nuala Bingham did not work, I would probably call Dave Stewart from the pop group the Eurythmics. This talented and rich musician once suffered from Paradise Syndrome. He had panic attacks, which left him paralyzed on the floor, simply because he had nothing to worry about! It seems humans need problems, because pain provides the building blocks for a better tomorrow.

Focusing on ILYB again, here are two examples from my casebook of reaching for the future: one of them successful, and one less successful. Although Mark felt lonely after his fifteen-year marriage ended and despite missing his teenage daughter, he decided to concentrate on the opportunities. "There were two things I'd always wanted to do: flying and dancing. But I didn't have time for either before and, to be frank, my wife discouraged outside interests. Now I've not only enjoyed the new challenges but met some great people."

Although Phil had been married for a similar duration as Mark and had children, too, his story is quite different: "My friends told me I was better off without my wife. I didn't believe them, but they took me out drinking, and I'll bet you can guess the rest. I started dating the barmaid, and the beginning was incredible—such a high. Before long, we were talking about living together and planning a vacation in Florida. But I discovered she was seeing someone else, too." Phil took this breakup harder than his wife's leaving and sunk into depression. Unfortunately, he had tried to reach his future life too quickly. Phil thought he had found a woman ready for long-term commitment, whereas she had seen their relationship as a little fun.

So how do you avoid the temptation to rush headlong into the future, especially if today seems very bleak?

Surviving the First Three Months After a Breakup

With feelings all over the place, this can be a very difficult time.

+ Even if you want to remain friends, give yourself space to end the old-style relationship before starting on the new one.
+ Remember that you are dealing with grief, so be kind to yourself. Eat well, get plenty of sleep, and do not put too much pressure on yourself.
+ Disconnecting takes time. At the start of a relationship, a couple shares responsibilities. While ending a relationship, each partner takes back responsibilities previously given to the ex. Sometimes, this unhooking can be the source of joy—especially if your partner, for example, has done all the cooking, and you get a chance to rediscover your culinary skills. Sometimes, this is a time of growth: for example, your partner took care of all the money issues, and you decide it is time to learn for yourself.
+ For jobs that you cannot do yourself—and have no wish to learn—it is better to ask a friend or hire an expert than to phone your ex-partner. This last option will keep you bound to the old relationship, rather than striking out toward the future.

Finding a New Path

Rather than leaping in with both feet, it is better to carefully consider your next move.

✦ **Go for what you want rather than what you don't want.** Many people in crisis are very aware of what they do not want—for example, to be lonely. However, goals are much better if they are framed as a positive: "I want to make new friends."

✦ **Be as specific as possible.** The clearer the picture of your new life, the easier it is to spot the first steps on the path. You might think, *I want to make new friends to go with me to the theater.* This more specific goal would focus the mind toward finding out whether any colleagues at work are interested in theater and turning them from acquaintances into friends—or joining a relevant club.

✦ **When looking for new opportunities, bring new patterns into your life.** If you always do the same things, your life will always be the same. So start shaking up your routines—it could be something as simple as taking a new way to work and spotting something that triggers a new interest.

✦ **Open yourself up to inspiration.** Go for walks or take up any form of exercise—anything that occupies the body but allows the mind to wander will free an idea to pop from your subconscious into your conscious. Other possible sources include surrounding yourself with beauty (going to an art gallery or attending a concert), surfing the Internet, cleaning up the clutter in your home, doing something that makes you laugh, and asking a friend for advice.

✦ **Enjoy the steps on the way.** Sometimes, we can be so obsessed with achieving a goal that we forget to stop and smell the flowers on the way. Enjoying the journey also helps us avoid the trap of having too rigid goals and missing out on other options that could also bring happiness.

Dealing with Obstacles to Healing

If you feel ready to move on but seem blocked at every turn, it is probably down to one of the following reasons:

+ **Anger:** It is perfectly natural to be angry—especially if the relationship ended against your wishes. While expressed anger explodes and disappears, suppressed anger can bubble under the surface forever.

+ **Desire for revenge:** The Internet is full of sites dishing the dirt on ex-lovers, and newspapers full of stories of people who chopped up their ex's clothes, sewed shrimp or other seafood into the hem of the curtains, or dumped a precious wine collection on neighbors' doorsteps. While revenge can provide a short-term high, it will backfire in the medium to long term. First, it invites retribution, and second, the vengeful are tied by hate into the old relationship rather than thinking about moving on.

+ **Children:** When you have had children together, you are bound together forever. It is not just when they are small but at their graduations, their weddings, and their children's christenings. So accept the inevitable and make the most of it. In the first few months, it might be easier to drop the children outside than come in for a cup of coffee, but if personal animosity makes being civil impossible, seek out a mediation service. However much you might hate your ex, please do not express it to your children—remember that they will still love both parents—or put pressure on them to take sides.

+ **Hoping for reconciliation:** Some people give up too soon and a salvageable relationship ends, while other people hope for a reconciliation for too long and delay the healing process. So how do you strike a balance? This is very much a personal decision, but I would try to journey toward a better independent future—finding new interests—while keeping the door open. However, if your ex has started a new relationship or left because of an affair, it is unlikely he or she will return while Limerence is at its height.

✦ **Timing:** Sometimes, circumstances and plain bad luck can prevent someone from moving on. First, take a look at your life—ask what could be holding you back? Second, ask yourself whether there is another way around. Third, be patient. It takes time to recover, and when everything feels like pushing water uphill, this may not be the right choice for you now.

✦ **Do you have the right goal?** Most people just want to be happy. Unfortunately, happiness can be very elusive, especially for someone who has been through a relationship breakdown and feels that life has kicked him or her in the teeth. Although hedonistic pleasures (like a good night out) or sensual ones (a new gadget or new clothes) can bring happiness, they tend to offer only short-term relief. However, if the goal is to grow and become a better person, no experience is wasted. In addition, while happiness can focus attention on what is wrong (and leave someone trapped and dispirited) personal growth focuses on a positive future.

Finding a New Relationship

If you start a new relationship too quickly, you risk bringing all the old baggage with you. So, before dating again, consider the following:

✦ **Check whether you're really ready.** Divorce is never good for self-esteem, and someone, anyone, finding you attractive is bound to go to your head. The giddy excitement of new love will also blow away the blues, so lots of divorcees jump into a new relationship on the rebound. "It was just going to be a bit of fun," says

Maggie, a thirty-one-year-old personal assistant, "and we did laugh and I began to feel better and relaxed. That's when he thought I was getting too serious, too soon and took off. I came back to earth with a jolt and, in fact, felt worse than I did before."

Tip: Do not overlook the importance of time alone, as this is a chance to find your own individual identity before becoming half of a couple again. As a rule of thumb, people need one year to get through all the difficult dates alone—Christmas, birthday, anniversary—before beginning to heal. So surround yourself with friends or family on these difficult occasions.

+ **Don't get stuck on repeat.** Many second-time brides and grooms believe they have married someone different from their first partners, but actually have gone for someone exactly the opposite. This means that the same issues are still played out, except from a different position. "My first husband liked to take charge—to the point of forever telling me what to do and making me feel like a little girl," says Patsy a twenty-nine-year-old legal secretary. "So what I really liked about my second husband was that he was very mild and 'take it as you find it.' Except that nothing seemed to get done, so I found myself making all the decisions and nagging him. Anybody would have thought I was his mother!" Unfortunately, Patsy had not learned to negotiate properly and did not find a relationship where responsibility was split evenly.

Tip: The type of woman or man that you are attracted to stretches back to your childhood and how you first learned about relationships: watching your mother and father. The issues they struggled with will be the ones that you are trying to solve, too.

+ **Don't look too far down the line.** So a year has passed, you are over the worst, and you're dating again. The temptation is to think every new man or new woman is your happy ending.

Although this is natural—because it gives us hope that we are not completely hopeless at relationships—it does not help to fantasize about what breed of dog you will buy together on the second date. "I always kept the conversation light," says Jo, thirty-two, and divorced for eighteen months, "but either the men drifted away or became so clinging that it was claustrophobic." Although Jo was not aware of it, she was giving off signals that were putting the right men off.

Tip: Remember there are three types of dates: getting to know you (first three to five); fun dates (enjoying each other's company); and courting dates. You cannot get to the third type without moving through the first two. Sometimes, a fun relationship, where you can relax and enjoy each other's company, can be very healing and positive—even if it does not lead to a serious long-term relationship. So enjoy the moment.

+ **Work out what belongs to the past and what to the present.** When you start a new relationship, be certain that you do not get angry with your new partner about something that your ex made you angry about. It is easy to read off an old script, particularly when tired or under stress. "I felt myself freeze when John, my new husband, came into the kitchen and announced that he was stopping the painting project because he needed to go off into town to get a few things," says Suzanne, thirty-five and a mother of two. "I snapped at him, he got huffy, and we had a terrible argument about my attitude. It was only later when I'd calmed down that I told him how my first husband would use a million excuses—like not having stuff—to slip out of home-improvement jobs. But John actually did need more paint."

Tip: Become aware of the sensations in your body—heart beating faster or flushed in the face—so you are aware of the warning signs of anger. Next, remember to check it out before getting into a fight from the past relationship. For example, "I'm sensing that you're using this trip as an excuse—is that right or wrong?"

✦ **Don't compare—even in your own head.** However much you dislike your ex, there will still be things that you particularly liked: his handiness fixing the dripping tap, her green finger. Harping on the past can blind you to your new partner's virtues. Also, do not compare yourself to your partner's ex. "My second husband has a house on the beach—of course he'd bought it with his ex—but had kept joint custody," says Gillian, a forty-three-year-old saleswoman. "It's great for our combined troop of children, but the vacation was spoiled because he kept mentioning his ex-wife, how she'd liked this restaurant, about the time they bought that or did this. All the time, I kept thinking, *Is my cooking up to standard? Did she look better in a bikini?* Although your new partner will have a natural curiosity about the past after the first twelve months, don't mention the ex (even in a derogatory way).

Tip: Make friends with other couples who have no memory of either of your first spouses. Adopting only each other's old circle of friends can trap the relationship in the past.

✦ **Allow yourself to be vulnerable again.** After being hurt, it is natural to hold something back for fear of being devastated again. However, this can also mean that you are not 100 percent committed to the new relationship or, alternatively, that your new partner might feel that he or she does not really know you. "A month after the honeymoon, I was in a really strange mood—caged liked an animal," says Donna, a twenty-six-year-old fitness instructor. "My husband asked me what was the matter and I was about to push him away with 'Nothing.' Instead, a small voice said, 'I'm frightened.' He came over and held me, and I cried and cried. At that moment, I'd never felt closer to him."

Tip: It is impossible to avoid pain; it is part of what makes us human. It is better to accept the ups and downs than to take no risks and live life in neutral.

✦ **Believe in yourself.** If you have gained more self-knowledge, and in particular a greater understanding of your needs, there is no reason why your new relationship should be anything but a great success. "When I walked into the church, there were so many friends and family from my first grand wedding," says Lucy, thirty-one. "I was fearful they were thinking, 'Here we go again.' But deep down, I knew this time it was really different."

Tip: Surround yourself with people who believe in the power of good relationships, rather than friends who bad mouth potential partners. Ultimately, we make good choices, and with love and constructive arguing skills, any obstacle can be overcome.

Summary

+ During a major setback, like a relationship breakdown, it feels like the end of the world. However, the dark days could be the springboard for a new, exciting life. The secret is to turn today's bitter lemons into tomorrow's lemonade.

+ It takes time to recover from what, after all, has been a personal disaster. So care for yourself and do not put yourself under extra pressure.

+ Allow yourself to be angry, but do not take it out on the children or seek revenge, as this will stop them and you from recovering.

+ With time, self-knowledge, and a commitment not to take shortcuts, you will reach a better future and fly high again.

EXERCISES

However positive people choose to be, there are always times when the pain comes crowding back. Normally, these destructive thoughts come as pictures or short reels of film. For example, you imagine your ex-partner lying back in the bath with a favorite book and a drink. Meanwhile, you still have to cope with three kids. Alternatively, it might be an event that you regret, and your memory keeps playing it over and over. The natural response is to push down these pictures and distract ourselves with something else. Instead, try the following exercise. It works best when you're not likely to be interrupted.

Emotional Rescue Package

- Changing the picture is the best way of reprogramming your brain to cope with disaster. Give the picture a headline name. Speak it out loud, as this is the first step to distancing yourself from the pain. (For example—you could call the bath picture "Hippo." A bit of humor always helps diffuse pain.)

- Where is the picture in your imagination? (Is it straight in front of your eyes or to one side, or perhaps wrapped all around you?) Be specific. Where could you put it and feel better? Try turning the picture into a movie playing on the wall. This can make it seem even farther away and, therefore, less painful. So remember the importance of being specific and again try to speak the results out loud.

- What color is the picture? Sometimes, changing your picture from black and white to color, or vice versa, can help you make a memory or your idea of an old partner's new life feel less vivid. It depends how your imagination works.

- Is it a moving or still picture? What can you hear? Once again, changing the form of the picture or changing the voices (turning the volume down, changing the voice to Mickey Mouse style, and so on) can change the way the memory is stored. Is there a smell or a taste involved? Could you swap a sad sensation for a happier one?

- Try replaying the movie again. How would you like to change it? (For example, the bath water turns too hot and your ex-partner has to leap out, or the president is being shown through that bathroom and stops to peer over the tub.) By playing around with your fantasy of his or her new life, you will be reminded that it is only a fantasy. Alternatively, imagine the camera pulling back from the bath and seeing the rest of the house and his or her clothes laying all over. Now you can feel relieved that you do not have to pick up after him or her anymore.

Conclusion

"*I love you but* I'm not in love with you" is the most pressing relationship problem of today. We are no longer prepared to settle for comfortable relationships and expect completely fulfilling ones.

While love has become the glue that holds relationships together, our culture has treated it as a subject too big or too mystical to be truly pinned down, measured, and understood.

None of our society's myths is stronger than "Love conquers all." However, this is only one part of the story. Determination, courage, and investing time are equally important. But because we shy away from investigating the true nature of Loving Attachment, we are blind to the complexity.

It is impossible to have a fully satisfying relationship without conflict; avoiding arguments can be avoiding being truly loving. The alternative is the hopelessness and powerlessness of "Sorry, honey, I fell out of love."

ILYB is avoidable, and with a greater knowledge of love and how it changes over time, passion will return along with a truly satisfying relationship.

Index